Phonological Typology of Plosives

Phonological Typology of Plosives

First edition published by Seoul National University Press in 2022

Seoul National University Press
1 Gwanak-ro, Gwanak-gu, Seoul 08826, Republic of Korea
Tel: +82-2-880-5252
Fax: +82-2-889-0785
Homepage: http://www.snupress.com
Facebook: @snupress1947
Instagram: @snupress
E-mail: snubook@snu.ac.kr

ISBN 978-89-521-3137-9 93700

This work was supported by the Ministry of Education of the Republic of Korea and the National Research Foundation of Korea.
(NRF-2017S1A5A2A01025215)

PHONOLOGICAL TYPOLOGY of PLOSIVES

Jinho Lee

SNUPRESS
Seoul National University Press

| Contents |

Preface

The purpose of this book is to broaden the understanding of plosives by analyzing plosive inventories that appear in languages around the world. As the title suggests, this book is about a typological study of plosives. However, rather than approaching plosives from a theoretical point of view, I tried to describe in detail how static aspects such as the frequency and distribution of individual plosives or phonemic opposition between plosives appear in various languages.

Last year I published a book titled *Inventories of the Plosive in the World's Languages*. That book contains plosive inventories in 4,356 languages based on the previous works, and some features of plosives are also very briefly discussed. In the preface, I promised that I would do a full-scale study on the typology of plosives in another book. This book is the result of that promise.

It is difficult to find a study that discusses more than 4,300 languages on a single topic. Of course, the number of target languages is not absolutely important in linguistic typology. Plank (2018: 50) points right to the heart of the matter by saying the following: "Having many languages at one's analytic fingertips does not make one a typologist. Charting diversity is one thing, seeking order is another, and typology's remit includes both". However, if possible, typological studies based on large-scale language data are recommended, and their results are more reliable.

Of course, it cannot be guaranteed that all the phonemic analyzes referenced in this book have been made accurately. Some may require revision, which leads to fundamental skepticism about typological approaches. In fact, many researchers who are hesitant to study linguistic typology worry about how to trust the results of a typological study based on analyzes of which the accuracy of description about individual languages is unclear. However, no research is conducted on the basis of absolutely correct and perfect results. We have no choice but to study based on the best references available at a given time. Therefore, it is not appropriate to evaluate the results of this book as unreliable just because some phonemic analyses may be somewhat inaccurate.

In Korean, my native language, there is an expression "hitting a rock with an egg". Trying to break a rock with an egg means a hopeless attempt. For me, who was only interested in the study of Korean without being fluent in English, the decision to write this book is a typical example of such behavior. I have thrown many eggs into the rocks for a long time, but the rocks remain and show no signs of breaking. Still, it seems that my efforts were not in vain, given this result. I am willing to throw countless eggs at rocks for the rest of my academic journey.

My interest in phonological typology began about a decade ago. As it is now, there was hardly any typological study of Korean phonology at that time. So, I could not help starting everything by myself from data collection. Almost every day, even a little bit, I collected data and organized them. As this work accumulated over several years, I was able to obtain much more data than originally planned.

The data gathered seems to be very useful in typological studies on phonological topics other than plosives. With these, I intend to conduct a typological research of the syllable coda, the glottal consonants, the simple vowel system, and the functional load of the distinctive feature. It is hoped that, in a few years, I will be able to report much more diverse and interesting results than has been known so far.

Acknowledgements

A person cannot do everything on his own in life. Everyone lives with the help of many people. Researchers receive this help more broadly. They benefit not only from their colleagues around them, but also from people who are far away in time and space, so cannot be directly contacted. This is especially true when there is a need to rely heavily on previous works. In this regard, the people I should be most grateful for are the field workers who investigated and analyzed numerous language data in remote areas. Without their dedication to the individual languages, I would not have been able to write this book.

I am not sure how much Korea has contributed to the study of linguistics, but I can confidently say that it has carried out the highest level of research in the study of Korean. In particular, Seoul National University (SNU), where I studied and currently works, is a world-class base for Korean language research. Being able to study close to teachers and colleagues who are indescribably excellent is the greatest happiness I have ever had.

A person who deserves special thanks is my advisor, Myungok Choi. Having majored in Korean phonology and dialectology, he always emphasized the importance of dialects. I did not study the dialect and I regret that I did not follow his teachings properly. However, since dialects are related to the diversity of languages, the subject of this book on the various languages of the world is in line with his belief. His usual teaching is one of the important motivations for my research.

I also feel the need to express gratitude to my colleagues at SNU: Hyeonhie Lee, Sowon Chang, Seongkyu Kim, Youngchul Jun, Seungchul Jung, Yoonhee Jang, Jinho Park, Seonyeop Hwang, Hyun Kim, Sukyeong Mun. They are examples that I always want to emulate because they have great academic capability and character. Whenever I had any difficulties, I turned to them for help. In addition, I can't forget to express gratitude to my fellows majoring in Korean phonology: Inho Jeong, Sungwoo Han,

Seokkyu Lim, Bonggook Kim, Sangsin Lee, Sehwan Kim. Conversation with them was enough to make me know what academic pleasure is, and it has been a great stimulus for me. I hope that our bromance will last forever.

I am also grateful to the two academic institutions, SNU library and National Research Foundation of Korea. I was provided with a lot of material through the SNU library that would be hard to imagine if I had not been at SNU. The research funds supported by the National Research Foundation of Korea for a long time helped me a lot in purchasing many books abroad. Without the help of these two institutions, it would have been difficult for me to conduct this research properly.

Finally, I would like to express the deepest gratitude to my family. My deceased father, Sanggil Lee, endured all his inconveniences for me. My mother, Heesook Kim, helped me the most to have been able to study as I wanted up until now. Thanks to their sacrifice, I was able to walk the path of a scholar without any worries. No words can fully express my gratitude to my parents, and I will not be able to repay the debt I owe them in this life even if I am reborn in the next life. I also have to say thank you to my wife, Myungsook Jung. She always respected my work and encouraged me to do better. In addition, I want to appreciate my three beloved children: Myeongin, who is well on her way after going through the wanderings of adolescence, Myeongyun, who is so trustworthy that I feel like a friend rather than a son, and Myeongyeon, who brings laughter and joy with cuteness. They provide me with the most powerful driving force in my life.

It is a great joy to think of people I am grateful for. Even at this moment as I write acknowledgements, a smile overflows on my face. This gives me the energy to do something else. Once again, I would like to thank everyone who has helped me.

List of figures

List of tables

List of abbreviations

- AL: alveolar
- AP: alveopalatal
- BI: bilabial
- DE: dental
- DV: dentovelar
- EP: epiglottal
- GL: glottal
- LA: labial alveolar
- LL: linguolabial
- LP: labiopalatal
- LV: labiovelar
- PA: palatal
- PH: pharyngeal
- PL: plosive
- RE: retroflex
- UV: uvular
- VE: velar

Chapter 1

INTRODUCTION

In this chapter, I examine the basic features of the plosive. First, the definition of the plosive is provided, and the phonetic and phonological characteristics of the plosive are explained in detail. Several reasons why plosives constitute the most basic class of consonants are also suggested. Next, I review the terms referring to the plosive, and consider how each term is used and which are appropriate in what cases. When dealing with these topics, the previous discussion is sufficiently referenced and presented for the purposes of this book. Finally, I introduce the overall organization of this book and briefly explain the language data covered in it. This chapter will serve as a useful guide for readers to understand the contents of the book.

1.1. Definition of the plosive

Speech sounds are largely divided into two major categories: consonant and vowel. The main difference between them is whether there is an airflow obstruction in the articulation process. The consonant is pronounced through a variety of airflow obstruction. Where and how the airflow is disturbed are referred to as the place of articulation and manner of articulation, respectively. Consonants have long been classified by place and manner of articulation.[1] Subdivisions of consonants by the manner of articulation result in classes such as plosive, fricative, affricate,

1 As is well known, this tradition was derived from ancient India.

liquid, and nasal. The object of interest in this book is the plosive.[2]

The definition of the plosive does not initially seem complicated. Although there are some differences in the specific expression, the plosive refers to a consonant class that is articulated through complete blocking and releasing of airflow. This articulation process is often divided into three stages: closure (=contact, obstruction, occlusion, approach), hold (=closure, stop), and release (=burst, explosion, plosion). In Laver (1994: 205), the three articulation phases of the plosive were specified as the closing phase, closed phase, and release phase, respectively.[3] This terminology is a direct reflection of the fact that the process of blocking and exploding is the most important in the articulation of the plosive.

However, with this definition, the range of the plosive is significantly widened. If the consonants that go through the stage of closure-hold-release are plosive, all of the following types may be included.

(1) Candidates for the plosive
- a. /p, t, k, .../
- b. /m, n, ŋ, .../
- c. /pf, ʦ, ʧ, .../
- d. /p', t', k', .../
- e. /ɓ, ɗ, ɠ, .../
- f. /ʘ, !, ǂ, .../

The consonants presented in (1) all proceed through three articulation stages: closure, hold and release. They all qualify for the plosive. Therefore, if the range of the plosive is set to the widest, the consonants in (1) may all be plosive. However, (1a~f) demonstrate incremental differences in the air passage cavity, release type, airstream mechanism, and direction of airflow.

As shown in Table 1-1, (1a~f) differ in at least one of the four phonetic details. Consonants in (1a) are pronounced with the airflow

2 In general, the term 'stop' is used more commonly than 'plosive'. The consonants indicated by these two terms may be the same or different. The use of 'plosive' in this book is intended to limit the scope of the study. The problem of terminology related to the plosive will be discussed further in 1.2.

3 According to Laver (1994: 133), all segments are articulated in three phases: onset phase, medial phase, and offset phase.

Table 1-1. Phonetic details of the sounds in (1)

	Air passage cavity	Release type	Airstream mechanism	Direction of airflow
(1a)	oral	instantaneous	pulmonic	egressive
(1b)	nasal	instantaneous	pulmonic	egressive
(1c)	oral	delayed	pulmonic	egressive
(1d)	oral	instantaneous	glottalic	egressive
(1e)	oral	instantaneous	glottalic	ingressive
(1f)	oral	instantaneous	velaric	ingressive

starting from the lungs and passing only through the mouth, egressing immediately when released. (1a) is the most typical of the plosive in that it is included in both narrow and broad definitions of the category.

The most important feature that distinguishes (1b) from other classes is the cavity through which the airstream flows. (1a) and (1b) differ only in this respect. In the case of (1b), the airflow is closed in the oral cavity, but thereafter the airflow continues to the nasal cavity. Therefore, (1b) is referred to as a nasal. Sometimes (1a) and (1b) are grouped together as 'stop' and are subdivided into 'oral stop' and 'nasal stop', respectively.

(1c) is characterized by its release types. (1c) is similar to (1a), except that the closure of the airstream is released not instantaneously but gradually. This process is often called delayed release, and can be referred to as fricative release. A widespread phonetic description indicates that the latter part (including the release stage) of the consonant in (1c) is similar to the fricative consonant. In the past, scholarship has not always viewed (1a) and (1c) as distinct, but has instead grouped them as 'stop'. Now, however, it is more common to distinguish (1c) as an affricate.[4]

(1d) and (1e) are both initiated not in the lungs but in the vocal

4 In the description of individual languages, there are many cases where the plosive and affricate are not distinguished. Because of this lack of distinction, it is often unclear whether /c/ and /j/ indicate plosives or affricates. These two symbols may represent both a palatal plosive and a palatoalveolar affricate due to notational conventions. Moreover, in some languages, such as Meru and Taraka, both consonants are allophones of the same phoneme. Therefore, if /c/ and /j/ are used when describing a consonant system, it is necessary to clarify whether they refer to plosives or affricates.

folds. These two types of consonants are pronounced by moving the larynx upward or downward. The main difference between (1d) and (1e) lies in the direction of airflow.[5] (1d) is referred to as 'ejective' and (1e) as 'implosive'.

(1f) is similar to (1d, e) in that the initiator is not the lungs. However, in (1f), unlike in (1d, e), the velar functions as an initiator. (1f) is pronounced while inhaling air after blocking somewhere in front of the closed velar. These consonants are called a click. Compared to other consonants in (1), (1f) is highly distinguished phonetically, and its distribution is limited by region and language family.[6]

Among (1a)~(1f), the plosive consonant covered in this book corresponds to (1a), which is important for readers to bear in mind. (1b~f) share with (1a) the fact that closed airflow is released, but they are distinct from (1a) in other phonetic characteristics. Such distinction is why the term 'plosive' is used in this book instead of the more general and common term 'stop'. As will be seen later, using the term 'stop' is insufficient to limit the subject of this book to (1a).

In most textbooks on phonology or phonetics, when consonants are classified by the manner of articulation, the plosive corresponding to (1a) is always presented first. Given the nature of the consonant, in which airflow is disturbed during the articulation process, the plosive arguably has the highest phonological strength among the consonants. Blocking airflow is the most typical and strongest interruption. As such, the plosive is close to a prototypical consonant, so it is presented before any other consonant classes in the textbook.

In other respects, plosives are the most basic type of consonant. First, many languages worldwide do not include fricative, affricate, nasal, or liquid consonants.[7] For example, Ehueun and Wichita have no nasal consonant, and Desano has no liquid consonant. There are also languages without two consonant classes. For example, Chiripá has neither nasal nor fricative, Hupdë neither nasal nor affricate. In particular, many of Australia's indigenous languages do not have fricative and affricate

5 Another difference is that it is common for (1d) to be voiceless and for (1e) to be voiced. This tendency is so strong that there are only a few exceptions.

6 As a representative work of empirical research on the click, see Nakagawa (2006).

7 This is valid at the phonemic level.

Table 1-2. List of high-frequency consonants in PHOIBLE

Ranking	Consonant	Frequency	Ranking	Consonant	Frequency
1	m	96%	11	h	56%
2	k	90%	12	d	46%
3	p	86%	13	r	44%
4	n	78%	14	f	44%
5	t	68%	15	ɲ	42%
6	l	68%	16	ʧ	40%
7	s	67%	17	ʔ	37%
8	b	63%	18	ʃ	37%
9	ŋ	63%	19	z	30%
10	g	57%	20	ʤ	27%

consonants. In contrast, there is no language without any plosive.[8] The nine languages with the fewest consonants among the world's languages have fewer than six consonants. Nonetheless, even these languages have three or more plosives, which suggests that the plosive is an essential consonant regardless of the size of the consonant inventory.

Second, the plosive occupies the upper ranks among the consonants appearing in languages worldwide in terms of frequency. Other consonants except the plosive are not covered in this book, so for convenience, with reference to the PHOIBLE data (https://phoible.org/parameters), the top 20 high-frequency consonants are as presented in Table 1-2 above.[9]

Table 1-2 shows the consonants ranked in the top 1% of 2,000

8 According to Maddieson (1984: 25), this was already acknowledged by the 1950s, and in that respect, the plosive can be considered an optimal consonant. The claim made in the 1950s was the result of examining several well-known languages, although this conclusion has remained valid even for the 4,356 languages listed in Lee (2020).

9 PHOIBLE is a website providing various information about cross-linguistic phonological inventory data. In the PHOIBLE, semivowels, /j/ and /w/, rank third and fifth in frequency, respectively, but here, only the pure consonants excluding the semivowel are considered. Even below, when referring to consonants, the semivowels are excluded.

consonants covered by PHOIBLE.[10] A frequency of 96% in Table 1-2 indicates that the consonant appears in 96% of the languages discussed. Although the most frequent consonant is not a plosive, as many as five plosives are included in the top 10, and seven are included among the top 20. Additionally, many consonants in (1b, c) that are not plosives but have phonetic characteristics similar to the plosive, are included in Table 1-2.

The third reason why the plosive is the primary consonant is that the ratio of the plosive in language's consonant inventory is much higher than that of other consonants. This tendency is usually very strong, which is slightly different from the high frequency of the plosive mentioned earlier. As shown in (2) below, the plosive comprises, on average, 39.8% of a language's consonant inventory. Consonants of other types fall far short of this figure.

Fourth, the fact that the plosive ratio is higher in languages with fewer consonants suggests that the plosive is a basic consonant. The number of consonants varies from five to 90, depending on the language.[11] Language with fewer than 11 consonants are considered to have very small consonant inventories.[12] The ratio of the plosive in these languages is shown in (2b).

(2) Average ratio of the plosive in the consonant inventory[13]
 a. All languages: 39.8% (35,017/87,900)

10 If it is limited to the plosive, the frequency of the PHOIBLE is slightly different from that of Lee (2020). According to Lee (2020: 7), the frequencies of /k, p, t/ are 96.5%, 87.9%, 79.0%, respectively, which are higher than shown in Table 1-2. Refer to Table 5-1, for details.

11 According to WALS (https://wals.info/), the number of consonants is at least six and up to 122, which is distinguished from that shown here due to the different phonological analyses of individual languages.

12 In WALS, the size of the consonant inventory is divided into five classes. The small class includes languages with a number of consonants ranging between six and 14. However, as will be mentioned in 5.1, based on 4,356 languages in this book, there are 1,176 languages with between six and 14 consonants, comprising 27% of all languages. It is difficult to call a group of this size a small class. By contrast, just 441 languages have 11 or fewer consonants, which is 10.1% of the total number of languages, making the term 'small class' more suitable.

13 In (2a~c), the right side of '/' in parentheses is the denominator, i.e., the sum of consonants in languages, and the left side is the numerator, i.e., the sum of plosives.

b. Languages with no more than 11 consonants: 43.2% (1,860/ 4,305)
c. Languages with more than 12 consonants: 39.7% (33,157/ 83,595)

(2a) calculates the ratio of the plosive for all languages. The average number of consonants in all languages is approximately 20.2, and the average number of plosives is approximately eight. (2b) indicates the ratio of the plosive in languages with no more than 11 consonants, which is higher than (2a). (2c) indicates the ratio of the plosive in languages other than (2b), that is, languages with more than 12 consonants, which is similar to (2a). As shown in (2), the plosive ratio is higher in smaller consonant inventories, which suggests that a certain number of plosives is necessary regardless of the size of the consonant inventory because the plosive is an essential consonant. Thus, the smaller the consonant inventory is, the higher the ratio of the plosive within it.

So far, I have discussed the definition and scope of the plosive that will be examined in this book and revealed the basic characteristics of the plosive. In summary, a plosive is a consonant class whose initiator is pulmonic and whose airstream passes only through the oral cavity that is closed and then released instantaneously. In many respects, the plosive is the most typical class of consonants. Therefore, it is meaningful to examine the phonological typology based on large-scale data to illuminate how the plosive exists in various languages.

1.2. Terminology of the plosive

Ideally, there would be only one academic term representing the same concept, but in reality, such is not the case. In a language with diverse vocabulary stratification and complex lexeme alternation, there may be dozens of variations of a term representing one concept. An extreme example can be taken from Korean phonology. In Korean, there is a phonological rule in which obstruent consonants in coda are changed to one of three plain plosives: /p, t, k/. Surprisingly, there are more than 60 terms in Korean that refer to this rule, which is often cited as an example of neutralization. This complicated situation was caused by the coexistence of native words and Sino-Korean words, with the presence or absence of various grammatical morphemes.

The terms referring to the plosive are numerous but not complicated.[14] The difference in terms seems to be related to the range of the plosive examined in 1.1. In many reference grammars for individual languages, the following terms are used when referring to the plosive.

(3) Several terms referring to the plosive
'stop', 'plosive', 'explosive', 'occlusive', 'obstruent'

The frequency with which the terms in (3) are used is not the same. 'Stop' is used most often, followed by 'plosive'. The other terms are not often used. The terms mentioned in (3) may be divided into two groups according to their nature, as shown in (4).

(4) Two groups of terms referring to the plosive
a. 'stop', 'occlusive', 'obstruent'
b. 'plosive', 'explosive'

The difference between (4a) and (4b) is whether the emphasis occurs in the first or third of the three articulation stages of the plosive. As mentioned earlier, the plosive undergoes closure-hold-release in its articulation. (4a) focuses on 'closure', the first stage, and reflects the meaning of 'to be blocked', while (4b) focuses on 'release', the third stage, and reflects the meaning of 'to burst'. No English term reflecting the second stage, 'hold', has been found.[15]

The representative term for (4a) is, of course, 'stop'. This term directly reveals the fact that the airstream is blocked when pronouncing plosives. The same holds true for 'occlusion' and 'obstruent'. However, these three terms are not always used only to refer to (1a) but may also be used to indicate a more comprehensive class of consonants. For example, 'stop' is used as a superordinate concept that encompasses (1a, b, d, e, f) or (1a, d, e, f). The difference in usage between the former

14 The word 'plosive, stop', etc., in this section may indicate a class of consonant corresponding to (1a) or one of several terms referring to (1a), which may cause confusion. To reduce this ambiguity, when they are used as variants of the term, I will add ' ' to them.

15 Korean phonology has such a term. For details, see Lee (2017a: 520).

and the latter is only the inclusion of a nasal consonant. The latter is a more generalized usage. In any case, 'stop' has been used to refer to all consonants that are released instantaneously after closure, regardless of the type of initiator or cavity of airflow. Steever (1998) used 'occlusive' as a concept covering (1a, b), and Haspelmath (1993) used it as a concept covering (1a, c).

The representative term of (4b) is 'plosive'. The term 'explosive' is similar to 'plosive', but further emphasizes that the direction of airflow in the release phase is egressive. The morphological structure of the term suggests that 'ex-plosive' is as antonym of 'im-plosive' in (1e). However, the class opposed to (1e) in the direction of airflow is not (1a) but 'ejective' in (1d). For 'explosive' to have significance, there must be an opposing consonant of (1a) that is ingressive only in airflow direction while remaining the same in all other points. However, there is no such consonant. In this regard, 'explosive' may be considered to add an unnecessary prefix 'ex' to 'plosive'.

Considering their frequency in phonological studies and their appropriateness as terms, 'stop' in (4a) and 'plosive' in (4b) seem to be the final candidates. Which of these two to select concerns which stage of articulation is more important. If the emphasis is on the closure, i.e., the first stage of articulation, 'stop' will be the more appropriate term, and if the emphasis is on the third stage, i.e., release, 'plosive' will be the more appropriate.

Those who support the term 'stop' point out that there is an unreleased allophone in individual languages that omits the release. In many languages, including Korean, the plosive is realized as unreleased in syllable coda or word final.[16] Thus, some allophones of the plosive do not have release, but there are no allophones that do not undergo closure. Considering the characteristics shared by all allophones in the plosive, 'stop' appears to be a more appropriate term than 'plosive'.

On the other hand, those who support the term, 'plosive', emphasize that the perfect plosive must be accompanied by release. The articulation of the plosive is completed only when the release occurs, and the employment of the term 'plosive' to reflect this step is considered more

---

16 It is well known that this characteristic is closely related to the neutralization of syllable final obstruents.

appropriate than 'stop'. In particular, it is not necessary to consider all allophones of a phoneme when determining the term for a class of consonants. Otherwise, embarrassing situations may arise. For example, according to Bolaños (2016: 8~45), the nasal consonants of Kakua spoken in Colombia are not separate phonemes, but only allophones of the voiced plosives, /b, d, g/. If /b, d, g/ are classified by considering the common features of all allophones, they cannot be either plosive or nasal. This undermines the argument that the phonetic features of all allophones should be considered in choosing the appropriate term.

The reason why 'plosive' is selected in this work is that the third step, release, is more important. Therefore, 'plosive' is used herein to refer only to (1a). The term 'stop' is used as a superordinate concept encompassing (1a, d, e, f), as mentioned earlier. The use of terms in this way is familiar, but was discussed in detail here due to the potential for ambiguity and confusion without such clarification.

1.3. Language data

I will now introduce the language data referenced in this book. Although Lee (2020) has already explained this data in detail, for reader's convenience, it is also briefly mentioned here.[17]

The total number of languages targeted for analysis in this book is 4,356. All information about the language names, classifications and language families is based on GLOTTOLOG (https://glottolog.org/). GLOTTOLOG catalogs approximately 7,600 languages that are not artificial or extinct. Lee (2020) compiled inventories of the plosive in 4,356 languages by referring to previous phonemic analysis. All of the plosives are phonemes, which in structural linguistics are a phonemic level unit, i.e., the smallest phonological unit that can discriminate the meaning of words. Lee (2020) provided both an inventory of the plosive for each language and a bibliography of a book or paper in which the inventory was presented. The results of the typological analysis on plosives in this book are based on Lee (2020).

These 4,356 languages belong to approximately 230 language

17 The following is a summary of 2.2 in part II of Lee (2020).

families. Some of these families, such as the Atlantic-Congo and Austronesian, are so large that they contain more than 700 languages. In contrast, the smallest families comprise only two languages. Although the number or proportion of languages included in Lee (2020) varies depending on the language family, the number of languages covered is generally proportional to the size of the language family. Therefore, problems related to various biases that are common in typological studies based on small-scale sampling are unlikely to occur. As a reference, a list of large language families, i.e., containing more than 20 languages, is presented below.

Table 1-3. Major language families containing more than 20 languages

[A]	[B]	[C]	[D]	[E]
Atlantic-Congo	1,432	718	50.1%	16.5%
Austronesian	1,275	707	55.5%	16.2%
Indo-European	588	263	44.7%	6.0%
Sino-Tibetan	494	363	73.4%	8.3%
Afro-Asiatic	373	219	58.7%	5.0%
Nuclear Trans New Guinea	314	147	46.8%	3.4%
Pama-Nyungan	248	127	51.2%	2.90%
Otomanguean	180	110	61.1%	2.5%
Austroasiatic	159	100	62.9%	2.3%
Tai-Kadai	94	54	57.4%	1.20%
Dravidian	81	40	49.4%	0.9%
Arawakan	78	45	57.7%	1.0%
Mande	75	48	64.0%	1.1%
Tupian	71	50	70.4%	1.1%
Uto-Aztecan	69	45	65.2%	1.0%
Central Sudanic	64	29	45.3%	0.7%
Nuclear Torricelli	55	17	30.9%	0.4%
Nilotic	54	40	74.1%	0.9%
Uralic	48	32	66.7%	0.7%
Algic	45	35	77.8%	0.8%
Athabas-kan-Eyak-Tlingit	45	33	73.3%	0.8%

[A]	[B]	[C]	[D]	[E]
Quechuan	45	23	51.1%	0.5%
Pano-Tacanan	45	31	68.9%	0.7%
Turkic	44	28	63.6%	0.6%
Cariban	42	26	61.9%	0.6%
Hmong-Mien	39	21	53.8%	0.5%
Sepik	36	18	50.0%	0.4%
Nakh-Daghestanian	34	21	61.8%	0.5%
Mayan	33	32	97.0%	0.7%
Lower Sepik-Ramu	30	10	33.3%	0.2%
Nuclear-Macro-Je	30	18	60.0%	0.4%
Chibchan	27	19	70.4%	0.4%
Tucanoan	26	19	73.1%	0.4%
Salishan	25	24	96.0%	0.6%
Timor-Alor-Pantar	23	19	82.6%	0.4%

([A]: top-level language family // [B]: number of languages belonging to [A] in GLOTTOLOG // [C]: number of languages referenced in this book // [D]: ratio of [C] to [B] // [E]: proportion of [C] to 4,356 languages)

1.4. Organization of this book

In this book, I will attempt a typological analysis of the plosive, the most basic class of consonants, based on a big-data approach that uses 4,356 languages. To achieve these goals, four topics related to the plosive will be reviewed in separate chapters.

Chapter 2 deals with the place of articulation at which the plosive is pronounced. First, plosives are divided into the single- and double-articulated plosive according to the number of primary articulations. Following this, the possible subdivision for each place of articulation and which places of articulation are most frequent in the plosive inventory will be examined, which will reveal the preferred places or combinations of places for the articulation of the plosive in many languages.

Chapter 3 examines how the plosive is articulated differently, that is, the manner of articulation. Plosive consonants share a common articulation process, but many plosives are distinguished by the combination of additional articulations. Secondary articulation may be added, or a special adjustment of vocal folds may be implemented. Additionally, rhotic color may be added or lateral release may occur. Plosives will be divided into two classes: plain plosive and complex plosive. The former has only a common articulation of the plosive, whereas the latter has additional articulation. In this chapter, I will observe how the plosive is classified according to the manner of articulation and what typological features it shows.

Chapter 4 describes individual plosives. There are a total of 293 types of plosives found in 4,356 languages. The chapter first divides them by the place of articulation, after which several linguistic features of each plosive, such as frequency, distribution, contrast, and articulatory attributes, will be presented.

Chapter 5 deals with plosive inventories. In this chapter, I will examine the high-frequency inventories, the ratio of the plosive in the consonant inventory, and some implicational relationships between plosives. Another main topic in this chapter is the determination of common patterns and oppositions of the plosive inventories in many languages. In the last section, I will specifically examine the unusual plosive inventories in several languages.

Chapter 2

PLACE OF ARTICULATION IN THE PLOSIVE

In this chapter, I will examine the place of articulation in the plosive. The chapter has two main goals. The first is to arrange the places at which the plosive is articulated. The plosive is pronounced in more diverse places than any other consonant, so arranging its place of articulation is no different from arranging that of consonants. That is, the place of articulation in the plosive is the same as that of the consonant. In discussion of this topic, the two categories are distinguished according to their number of primary places of articulation. Most consonants have one primary place of articulation. These plosives will be referred to herein as 'single-articulated plosive'. However, there are also plosives with two primary places of articulation. In these, the two places of articulation function equally. They will be referred to as 'double-articulated plosive'.[1]

The other main goal is to examine how the place of articulation for the plosive appears in each language. Associated topics include the average number of places of articulation and preferred patterns according to the number of places. In many languages, all three places involving the main articulators, labial, coronal, and dorsal, appear. However, when the target language is expanded, many more diverse patterns are found.

1 The double-articulated plosive is distinct from the single-articulated plosive accompanied by secondary articulation, such as palatalization or labialization, related to the place of articulation. Secondary articulation is subsidiary; thus, its accompaniment does not indicate that the primary articulation has occurred in two places.

2.1. Single-articulated plosives

Plosives with one primary place of articulation appear at 12 places of articulation.

(1) Places of articulation in the single-articulated plosive[2]
Bilabial, linguolabial, dental, alveolar, retroflex, alveopalatal, palatal, velar, uvular, pharyngeal, epiglottal, glottal

Most of the places of articulation in (1) are widely known in general phonetics and do not require special mention. However, since the linguolabial, alveopalatal, pharyngeal, and epiglottal places of articulation are significantly less frequent than other places of articulation and often not discussed, I will briefly examine them here.

First, let us consider the linguolabial. The descriptions of this consonant given in previous works are provided as follows.

(2) Previous descriptions of the linguolabial

a. Maddieson (1987: 214) – Their articulation is highly distinctive, with the tongue tip frequently protruding forward of the upper lip.

b. Laver (1994: 214) – Sounds in which a stricture is created between the upper lip as the passive articulator and the tip or blade of the tongue as the active articulator

c. François (2002: 15) – They are pronounced with the tip of the tongue touching the middle of the upper lip.

d. Dodd (2014: 22) – Consonants which are articulated by allowing the tip of the tongue to come forward in the mouth to a point that it covers the bottom teeth and makes contact with the bottom lip. The top lip is then pulled tight across the top teeth while it moves down to meet the top side of the tip of the tongue.

---

2 The classification of places of articulation in single-articulated plosives differs according to the discussion. For example, Laver (1994: 242) distinguishes 11 places, whereas Ladefoged & Maddieson (1996: 15) identifies 17 places. The same is true of double-articulated plosives.

(2a~d) commonly describe linguolabials as consonants pronounced by the tip of the tongue touching the upper lip.[3] Generally, it is neutral for the tip of the tongue to be in contact with the dental or alveolar region and for the upper lip to be in contact with the lower lip. Thus, the linguolabial is unusual in that the articulator is not in the neutral position (dental or alveolar) and is in contact with another point of articulation (upper lip). Laver (1994: 214) classified this positioning as 'displaced articulation'. The only plosive that functions as a phoneme while having such characteristics is the linguolabial plosive.[4] Linguolabials have been known to appear mainly in the Malayo-Polynesian language family, which is a subfamily of Austronesian and are geographically limited to Central Vanuatu. However, Hungworo does not meet these conditions.[5]

Next, the alveopalatal is articulated between palatoalveolar and palatal regions. The place of articulation between the alveolar and hard palate can be further subdivided, and consonants closer to the hard palate are classified as alveopalatal (sometimes also called prepalatal or alveolopalatal). Depending on the analysis, this consonant may be viewed as a palatalized consonant or as a palatal. As will be revealed later, the alveopalatal is very infrequent, so it appears only in a few languages, and its proportion of the total plosive is insignificant.

Last, the pharyngeal and epiglottal share a common feature in that the articulator is the tongue root. However, they differ in the point of articulation at which the articulator touches. According to Laver (1994: 136), the pharyngeal plosive is pronounced in the middle of the pharynx, and the epiglottal plosive is pronounced in the lower part of the pharynx. The pharyngeal and epiglottal appear in very few languages. Of the 4,356 languages, the former appears in 19 languages and the latter appears in only two. In addition, the types of plosives articulated at the pharynx and epiglottis are limited to only voiceless plain plosives. This extreme constraint is not found in the plosives articulated at other places. It is thus unsurprising that no language is known to have both pharyngeal

3 The term 'apicolabial' is sometimes used instead of 'linguolabial', as it more clearly reveals the active articulator and the point of articulation.

4 These displaced articulations are also present in other manners of articulation, including nasal sounds or some allophones.

5 Hungwooro is an African language that belongs to the Atlantic-Congo language family and is spoken in Nigeria.

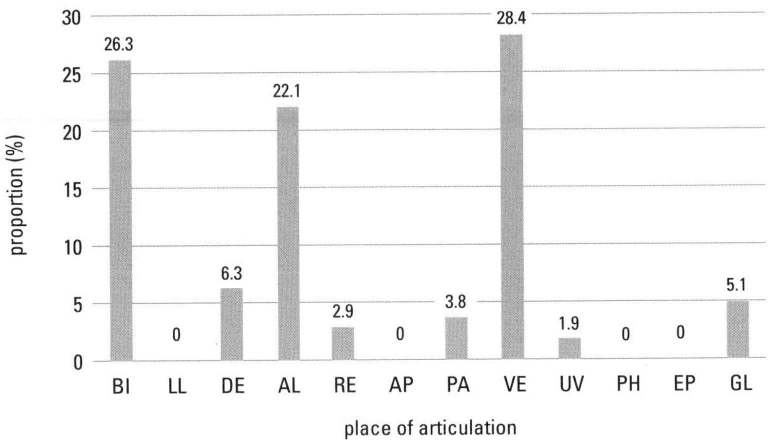

Figure 2-1. Proportion of plosives according to the place of articulation

and epiglottal plosives as separate phonemes.[6]

The plosives articulated at various places in (1) are not equal in frequency. The figure above shows the percentage of plosives at each place of articulation.[7] The percentages in Figure 2-1 are the result of calculating the sum of the number of all plosives in the denominator and the sum of the number of plosives for each place of articulation in the numerator. Figure 2-1 targets only single-articulated plosives, which comprise 97.0% of all plosives in 4,356 languages.[8]

As expected, the three main places of articulation, bilabial, alveolar, and velar, constitute very high proportions, exceeding even the combination of all the remaining places. Most languages have plosives that are articulated in these three places. The velar plosive has the highest proportion. The bilabial plosive is next, although the difference between it and the velar plosive is not considerable. The ratio of alveolar plosives is slightly lower. However, the alveolar plosive and the dental

6 Although the epiglottal is very close to the glottal, there are languages that have both plosives as separate phonemes. For example, Aghul and Dahalo, which are not related either geographically or by language family, have a phonological opposition of 'ʡ (epiglottal plosive) : ʔ (glottal plosive)'.

7 For convenience, places of articulation are indicated by abbreviations. A list of abbreviations is provided at the front of this book.

8 The double-articulated plosive, which makes up the remaining 3.0%, is covered in 2.2.

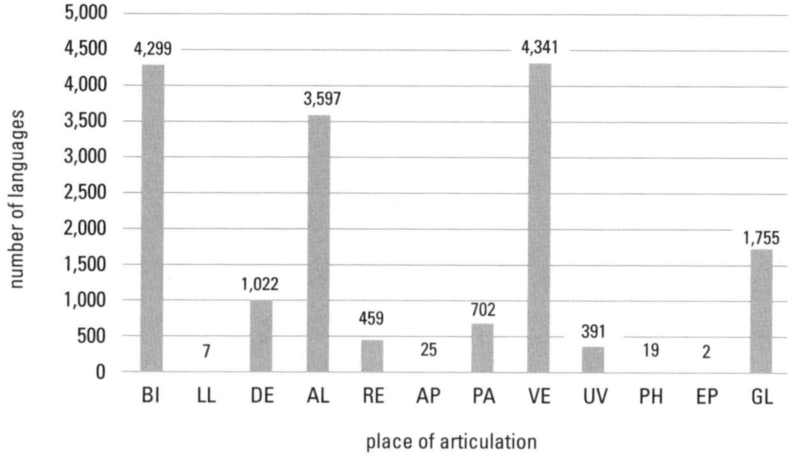

Figure 2-2. Frequency of plosives according to the place of articulation

plosive combined constitute 28.4% of the plosives in the languages under study.[9] In other words, the ratio of bilabial or velar plosives belonging to the peripheral consonant and that of alveolar (including dental) plosives belonging to the nonperipheral consonant are almost equal.

Other aspects also highlight that the plosive frequency varies significantly depending on the place of articulation. The difference is evidenced by an examination of how many languages contain plosives at each place of articulation.

Figure 2-2 shows how many of the 4,356 languages have the plosive at each place of articulation. Regardless of whether one or more than one plosive appears at one place of articulation, all are treated the same.[10] Here, too, the frequency of bilabial, alveolar and velar plosives overwhelms that of other places of articulation. The number of languages that contain the velar plosive is as high as 4,341 (99.7% of the total 4,356 languages). It is no exaggeration to say that very few languages do

9 Because few languages have both dental and alveolar plosives, it is also meaningful to combine the two into one group. Languages with both dental and alveolar plosives are examined in 2.3 and 2.4.

10 As we will see in Chapter 4, the spectrum of language offers wide plosive variety, from languages with zero plosives to languages with more than 10 plosives for each place of articulation. Figure 2-2 is the result of examining all the same values as long as the plosive exists without considering the difference in number.

not have a velar, considering that there is no language without a plosive. Moreover, there are as many languages with the bilabial plosive as with the velar. The frequency of the alveolar in Figure 2-2 is considerably lower than that of the bilabial and velar, which is the same as in Figure 2-1.

The percentage of the glottal plosive in Figure 2-1 is only 5.1%, but 1,755 (40.3%) of the 4,356 languages have at least one glottal plosive in Figure 2-2, which indicates high frequency. Compared to plosives in other places, glottal plosives are not only limited in their type but also in their frequency, except for the plain plosive 'ʔ'. Therefore, the proportion of glottal plosives is low in Figure 2-1. However, since the plain plosive 'ʔ' appears in so many languages, the glottal plosive shows a high value in Figure 2-2.[11]

The types of plosives also vary greatly depending on the place of articulation. At one place of articulation, not only plain plosives but also various complex plosives accompanied by secondary articulations or laryngeal adjustments appear. However, the diversity of the plosive is greatly influenced by the place of articulation.

There are a total of 293 types of plosives in the 4,356 languages.[12] Among them, 274 types, other than the 19 types that belong to the double-articulated plosives, are classified by the place of articulation shown in Figure 2-3. According to Figure 2-3, most types of plosives appear at three major places of articulation: bilabial (53 types), alveolar (58 types), and velar (57 types). They are fairly evenly distributed among three places of articulation.

Unlike in Figures 2-1 and 2-2, in Figure 2-3, the alveolar is on par with the bilabial or velar. Nonetheless, more subtle types of plosive are found in the alveolar group. In addition, dental plosives vary considerably in their types despite their lower proportion or frequency. Because the dental and alveolar plosives are similar in their articulator and point of articulation, it would appear phonetically advantageous to pronounce various plosives at this place.

11 The frequency of individual plosives is mentioned in Chapter 4, and the ranking and proportion of high-frequency plosives are presented in 5.1.

12 The types of plosives are much more diverse than previously known. As the number of languages to be discussed increased, the types of the plosive also increased. Each plosive is briefly described in Chapter 4.

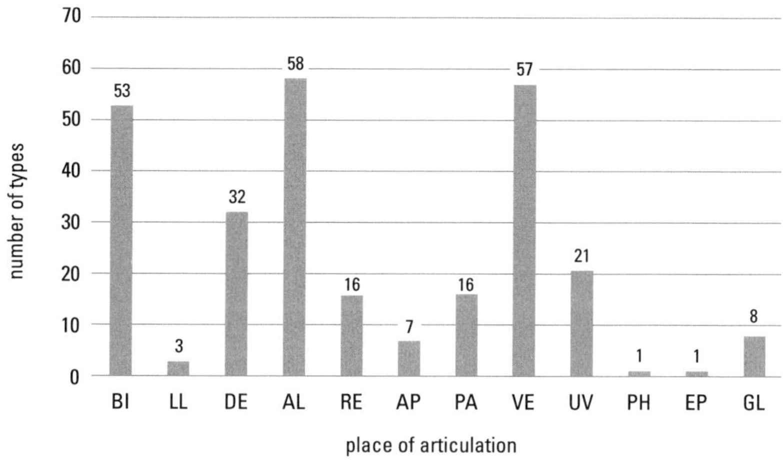

Figure 2-3. Diversity of plosives according to the place of articulation

Four plosives, the linguolabial, alveopalatal, pharyngeal, and epiglottal, have only very few types, as can be predicted from Figures 2-1 and 2-2. In particular, the types of the pharyngeal and epiglottal plosives are limited to just one: a voiceless plain plosive. Even voiced plain plosives, which are very common in other places of articulation, do not exist in the pharyngeal and epiglottal. The IPA chart also indicates that the presence of voiced pharyngeal plosives and voiced epiglottal plosives is not possible. Because the glottal plosives are all voiceless, without exception, the glottal and other plosives adjacent to it, such as pharyngeal or epiglottal plosives, have difficulty in accompanying the vibration of the vocal folds. As mentioned in Laver (1994: 206), in the case of glottal plosives, the vocal folds must be completely closed, making it impossible for them to vibrate. Although such positioning is not case for pharyngeal and epiglottal plosives, voiced plosives do not appear. Given previous discussions, which have asserted that the closer the distance from the vocal folds to the place of articulation, the more disadvantageous the vibration of the vocal folds, it is understandable that voiced plosives do not exist in the pharyngeal and epiglottal.

Comparing Figure 2-1 and 2-2 with Figure 2-3, the greater the ratio and frequency of plosives at each place of articulation, the more types of plosives there are. This result is generally to be expected. However, there are some exceptions, including the dental and alveolar plosives. These two tend to be more diverse in type compared to their ratio and frequency. As mentioned earlier, the very active articulator seems to make it advantageous for such plosives to accompany other secondary articulations or glottal adjustments.

Importantly, the type of the glottal plosive is somewhat limited compared to its frequency, which is opposite the case for the dental or alveolar plosives. The glottal plosive is highly ranked but lower than the top three (bilabial, alveolar, and velar) in Figures 2-1 and 2-2. However, it is in the bottom rank in Figure 2-3. The glottal plosive has articulatory limitations in the active movement of vocal folds, which are the main articulators. It is also difficult to add various secondary articulations within the oral cavity or adjustment of the larynx to the glottal plosive, as the primary articulation takes place in the larynx. As a result, the type of glottal plosive is highly constrained despite its high frequency.

2.2. Double-articulated plosives

Unlike the single-articulated plosive, the double-articulated plosive has two primary places articulations.[13] The two places of articulation involved in double articulation are equivalent. Laver (1994: 139) divided double articulation into three types, targeting all consonants.

(3) Three types of double articulation in Laver (1994)
a. Labial alveolar
b. Labial palatal
c. Labial velar

The three types in (3) clearly reveal the two places of articulation indicated by the term of double articulation. In (3a~c), labial appears

13 No Languages are known to have three primary articulations. If such a consonant exists, it is called a 'triple-articulated plosive'. Although the double-articulated plosive can accompany secondary articulation related to place of articulation, such as palatalization or labialization, it cannot be called a 'triple-articulated plosive'. A triple-articulated plosive requires three primary articulations in three places of articulation. Ladefoged & Maddieson (1996: 350) has argued that no triple-articulated consonant could exist given the difficulty of perceiving three places of articulation, regardless of how a consonant is articulated.

to be a shared primary place of articulation. To achieve two primary articulations, it is advantageous if the two places of articulation are farther apart. It is thus understandable that many labials, located at one end of the oral cavity, are included in double articulation.

In Ladefoged & Maddieson (1996: 344~348), the type of double-articulated plosive is more limited than that of Laver (1994). According to Ladefoged & Maddieson (1996), one of the articulators in double articulation must be labial, and except for the labial alveolar, which appears in Yeletnye, a labiovelar is the only possible double-articulated plosive.[14] That is, of the three types in (3), (3c) is the most common, whereas (3a) appears only in one language. Moreover, (3b) is not possible in Ladefoged & Maddieson (1996). However, a review of the phoneme analysis of 4,356 languages reveals some differences from the types described by Laver (1994) or Ladefoged & Maddieson (1996).[15]

Table 2-1 presents four types of double-articulated plosives. Compared with (3), the dentovelar plosive, in which the labial is not involved in articulation, is added. Table 2-1 shows that the double-articulated plosive must have two different articulators. There is no double-articulated plosive in which one articulator touches two different places of articulation. As is well known, the places of articulation can be grouped into several classes depending on the articulator. For example, the following classifications were presented in Ladefoged & Maddieson (1996: 43).[16]

Table 2-1. Types of double-articulated plosives[17]

Labiovelar (LV)	Labial alveolar (LA)	Labiopalatal (LP)	Dentovelar (DV)
kp, gb, kpʰ, ...	pt, bd[18]	bɟ	t̪k

14 Yeletnye is called Yele in GLOTTOLOG.

15 In this book, the terms referring to the double-articulated plosive are slightly different from (3).

16 (4) is the adjustment of the 12 places of articulation in this book to fit the system proposed by Ladefoged & Maddieson (1996).

17 The double-articulated plosives are indicated by a combination of two IPAs representing the primary place of articulation.

18 Depending on the discussion, 'pt, bd' are written as 'tp, db'.

(4) Articulator and place of articulation (I):
   a. Labial: bilabial
   b. Coronal: linguolabial, dental, alveolar, retroflex, alveopalatal
   c. Dorsal: palatal, velar, uvular
   d. Radical: pharyngeal, epiglottal
   e. Laryngeal: glottal

Examining (3) or Table 2-1 through (4), there is certainly no double-articulated plosive with only one articulator. It is very difficult to pronounce a plosive by closing two points almost simultaneously with the same articulator. As a result, the double-articulated plosive has the phonetic limitation that there should be two articulators.

The type and frequency of double-articulated plosives in Table 2-1 are presented in Figure 2-4. Figure 2-4 clearly shows the extent of the inequality among the double-articulated plosives. The labiovelar is the most representative of double-articulated plosives, and the labial and velar work equally as the primary articulation.[19] The labiovelar is both quantitatively and qualitatively overwhelming in the double-articulated plosive. The labiovelar comprises 2.9% of the total plosives and appears in 494 languages. It also has 15 different types. For example, 'kp, gb, kp^h, ŋmgb, ...' belong to the labiovelar plosive. The labiovelar plosive has a firm status comparable to the retroflex plosive among single-articulated plosives.

In contrast, the remaining double-articulated plosives are insignificant, appearing only in one or two languages.[20] Their frequency is too low to compare with the labiovelar. In particular, they are never accompanied by secondary articulation or glottal adjustments. Thus, their proportion of the total plosive is less than 0.1%.

If double articulation is performed through a combination of two articulators, the five articulators in (4) may be combined to produce

19 Considering its name, labiovelar should be transcribed as 'pk, bg' rather than 'kp, gb'. The order of the names and of the phonetic alphabets do not match. According to Laver (1994: 314), this conventional transcription has long been established in Africanist linguistics.

20 Catford (1977: 190) stated that the labial alveolar, along with the labiovelar, is common in West African languages but is sporadic in Casucian. However, in the data referenced in this book, the labial alveolar plosive appears only in two West African languages, Gavar and Nzima.

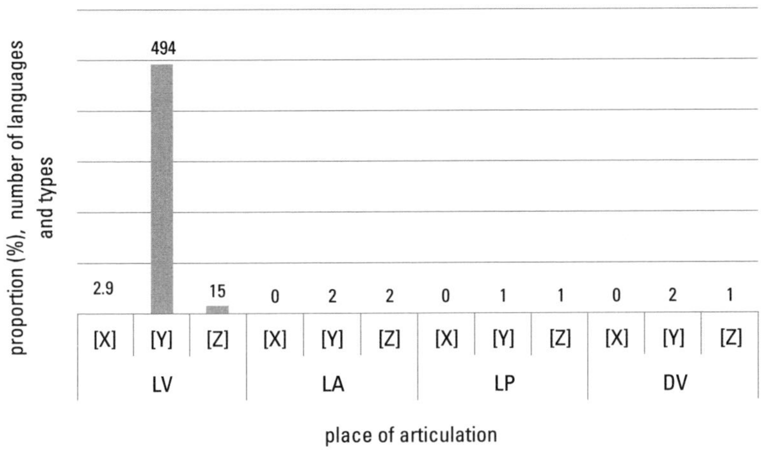

([X]: proportion, [Y]: number of languages, [Z]: type of plosives)

Figure 2-4. Types and frequency of double-articulated plosives

up to 10 double-articulated plosives. However, as we have seen before, only a few types are actually present, and even those are extremely concentrated on the labiovelar type. The fact that most of the double-articulated plosives belong to the labiovelar type is not irrelevant to the distance between two articulators involved in the double articulation. For two articulators to work equally well, increased distance between them is advantageous. The labiovelar satisfies this condition well. Labial and dorsal locations at both ends of the oral cavity are optimal for working together simultaneously. In contrast, if two articulators are closer, such shorter distances are likely to cause interference and disrupt the articulation. These phonetic constraints seem to have a decisive effect on the type and frequency of the double-articulated plosives.

2.3. Patterns in the place of articulation

So far, I have divided the plosive into single- and double-articulated plosives, and have examined the place of articulation in each category. In this section, I will examine the patterns of the place of articulation for the plosive. Each language has a combination of 12 places for the single-articulated plosive and four for the double-articulated plosive.

By determining such patterns, we can derive the typological tendency related to the place of articulation for the plosive. First, languages are classified according to the number of places of articulation for the plosive as follows.

In Table 2-2, the number of places of articulation for the plosive ranges from a minimum of two to a maximum of seven in each language.[21] Although a total of 16 places of articulation for the plosive exist, the maximum number in any language is seven, suggesting that the pattern of places of articulation in languages is quite limited. Only 0.2% of all languages have seven places of articulation for the plosive. Most languages have three (32.7%) or four (44.8%) places of articulation for the plosive.

(5) Average number of places of articulation for the plosive

$$\frac{17{,}118\ (2\times 17+3\times 1{,}426+\ldots+7\times 8)}{4{,}356\ (\text{number of languages})} \fallingdotseq 3.93$$

(5) shows the average number of places of articulation for the plosive in all languages, which is 3.93. This result is in line with the fact that, as shown in Table 2-2, languages with four places of articulation are the most common.

Now, I will examine how the number of places of articulation, as seen in Table 2-2, relates to the number of plosives. Figure 2-5 shows how the number of plosives changes according to the number of places

Table 2-2. Number of places of articulation for the plosive in each language

Number of places	Number of languages	Proportion (%)
2	17	0.4
3	1,426	32.7
4	1,951	44.8
5	778	17.8
6	176	4.0
7	8	0.2

21 This result is somewhat different from that of Nartey (1979: 27), which analyzed 317 languages in UPSID.

of articulation. Two bars are presented for each number of places of articulation on the horizontal axis. The left side shows the average number of plosives, and the right side shows the average number of plosives that appear at each place of articulation. For example, a language with three places of articulation has 6.4 plosives, and 2.13 plosives appear in each of the three places of articulation.

As shown in Figure 2-5, in general, the number of plosives increases as the number of places of articulation increases. However, when the number of places of articulation increases from five to six, the number of plosives does not change. Therefore, the number of plosives and places of articulation are not always in direct proportion. The number of plosives increases the most when the number of places of articulation changes from two to three. The number of places of articulation increases by one, but the number of plosives more than doubles. Another leap in the number of plosives is found when the number of places of articulation changes from six to seven, at which point, the number of plosives increases by approximately 50%.

It is difficult to find a certain proportional relationship by dividing the number of plosives by the number of places of articulation and considering the number of plosives per place of articulation. According to Figure 2-5, the number of plosives is between 1.53 and 2.23 per place

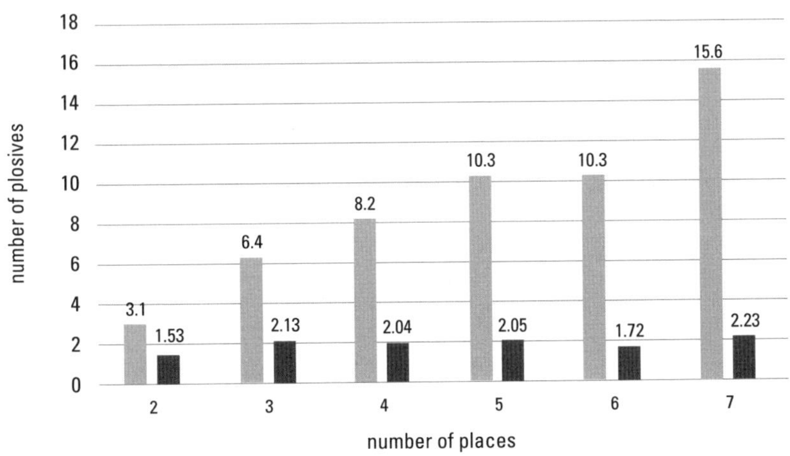

Figure 2-5. Correlation between the number of places of articulation and the number of plosives

of articulation, which seems to show no particular correlation with the number of places of articulation. On average, 1.95 plosives appear at one place of articulation. In other words, it is common for the plosive to form a two-way opposition at each place of articulation regardless of the number of places of articulation.

The next topic is the pattern of places of articulation that most commonly appear in the world's languages, which forms the core of this section. I will examine how the pattern of places of articulation varies depending on their number. The languages with the fewest places of articulation are examined first. There are 17 languages with only two places of articulation for the plosive. The patterns of two places of articulation in these languages are presented in Table 2-3.

Languages in which plosives occur only in two places of articulation are extremely rare, comprising only 0.4% of all languages. Moreover, there are only four possible places of articulation for the plosive in these languages: bilabial, dental, alveolar, and velar. When two of these four places are combined, six patterns can appear, but in reality only the four shown in Table 2-3 exist. Not all six patterns appear because the dental only combines with the velar, and this pattern is only found in Mixtepec Mixtec. Considering that the alveolar plosive does not exist in this language, if the dental plosive is reanalyzed as the alveolar, the places of articulation in Table 2-3 are reduced to three: bilabial, alveolar, and velar. Additionally, the patterns in Table 2-3 are reduced to three. These three patterns cover all types that can originate from a combination of bilabial, alveolar, and velar plosives. Thus, in languages with two places of articulation, all possible combinations from the three major places of articulation (bilabial, alveolar, and velar) have been found. That is, patterns that include places of articulation other than the major articulation, such as palatal or uvular, do not appear.

Table 2-3. Patterns of two places of articulation

	BI	DE	AL	VE	Example
a.			◎	◎	10 languages including Gusii
b.	◎			◎	3 languages including Abau
c.	◎		◎		3 languages including Omurano
d.		◎		◎	1 language (Mixtepec Mixtec)

The most common pattern in Table 2-3 is type-(a), a combination of alveolar and velar. Ten of the 17 languages have this type. Type-(d) may also be included in this group, as both types lack a bilabial. Type-(b) has no alveolar, and type-(c) has no velar. In Table 2-3, there are three languages without alveolar or velar, whereas 11 languages do not have a bilabial. This fact suggests that the alveolar or velar is the preferred place of articulation over the bilabial in languages with a small number of places of articulation for the plosive. This tendency differs from the frequency hierarchy of the plosives by place of articulation shown in Figure 2-2.

It is noteworthy that the glottal plosive does not appear in any type of Table 2-3. As shown in Figure 2-2, the glottal plosive appears frequently, in a total of 1,755 languages, but is not found in languages with only two places of articulation. It is also notable that double-articulated plosives do not appear in Table 2-3. Although the glottal plosive and double-articulated plosive are unrelated, neither are included in Table 2-3. Even where a new language other than the 4,356 languages covered here to be added, this trend is unlikely to change because, as noted earlier, if the plosive in certain language appears in only two places of articulation, the pattern is formed by combining two of the three major places of articulation, such as bilabial, alveolar, and velar.

There are 1,426 languages with three places of articulation for the plosive, and approximately one-third of all languages fall into this group. In addition to the three major places of articulation, the glottal (43), labiovelar (3), uvular (2), palatal (1), and alveopalatal (1) appear in these languages.[22] This is the greatest difference compared to the previous class. As a result, compared to Table 2-3, which shows two places of articulation, the types are more diverse. However, the three major places, bilabial, alveolar and velar, still form the central axis regarding their frequency. The frequent patterns in languages with three places of articulation are shown is Table 2-4.

Types-(a) and (b) in Table 2-4 appear in as many as 1,376 of 1,426 languages (96.5%) with three places of articulation for the plosive. Compared with Table 2-3, the patterns of the place of articulation

22 The numbers in parentheses indicate the number of languages in which the consonant appears.

Table 2-4. Patterns of three places of articulation

	BI	DE	AL	VE	Example
a.	◎		◎	◎	1,163 languages including Korean
b.	◎	◎		◎	213 languages including Kwese

in Table 2-4 are much more unified and consistent. All the places of articulation in Table 2-4 are related to major articulators, such as the labial, coronal, and dorsal. The difference between type-(a) and (b) is whether the articulatory point that the coronal touches is alveolar or dental. As expected, there are many more of type-(a) with the alveolar than of type-(b) with the dental. Given that the dental and alveolar are relatively close, and that there is no language having both dental and alveolar plosives among the languages whose plosives appear in three places of articulation, type-(a) and (b) can be regarded as virtually identical patterns.

Languages that are not included in Table 2-4 have one of the glottal, labiovelar, uvular, palatal, and alveopalatal plosives. In other words, the three places of articulations in these languages consist of one minor and two major places of articulation. There are 50 exceptional languages, whose patterns are given in Table 2-5.

In Table 2-5, the frequency of type-(a), which includes the glottal instead of the bilabial, is far higher. Moreover, type-(b) including the glottal instead of the velar appears in several languages. However, the remaining types appear only in a few languages.

All patterns in Table 2-5 contain two of the three major places of articulation: bilabial, alveolar (including dental), and velar. In these patterns, one of the three major places is replaced by others such as the glottal, labiovelar, palatal, or uvular. That is, no pattern includes two or more minor places. Thus, it is necessary to examine which of the major places is often missing. Of the 50 languages in Table 2-5, 37 have no bilabial, nine have no velar, and four have no alveolar (including dental). The frequency of patterns that do not include the bilabial is much higher than that of other patterns.[23] This result is consistent with that of Table

23 Inventories without the bilabial often appear in languages spoken in North America, such as the Otomanguean and Iroquoian language families.

Table 2-5. Exceptions to Table 2-4

	BI	AL (DE)	AP	PA	VE	UV	GL	LV	Example
a.		◎			◎		◎		31 languages including Cayuga
b.	◎	◎					◎		9 languages including Tahitian
c.	◎				◎		◎		3 languages including Hawaiian
d.		◎			◎			◎	3 languages including Fon
e.		◎			◎	◎			2 languages including Aleut
f.	◎			◎	◎				1 language (Nyawaygi)
g.		◎	◎		◎				1 language (Ngasa)

2-3.

Next, let us consider languages whose plosives are distributed in four places of articulation. As seen in Table 2-2, 1,951 languages fall within this category, making it the largest. Patterns with four places of articulation are quite complex. The retroflex and pharyngeal plosives appear in languages with four or more places of articulation. The main patterns that appear in more than 20 languages are as presented in Table 2-6.[24]

In Table 2-6, type-(a) appears in an extraordinary number of languages. Almost half of the 1,951 languages with four places of articulation belong to type-(a). Type-(d) is similar to type-(a) in that it includes a dental instead of an alveolar. These two types are patterns in which glottal plosives are added to the types in Table 2-4. Type-(b) containing a labiovelar has the second-highest frequency. The frequency of the labiovelar plosive is not high, similar to that of the retroflex. However, as a component of the four places of articulation, it is in more common operation than the retroflex.

Table 2-6 shows some characteristics of languages with four places of articulation for the plosive. First, the most striking feature is that the fourth place of articulation is created through addition to the frequent types that occur in languages with three places of articulation. Specifically, all types in Table 2-6 are forms in which another place is added to the

24 Patterns not included in Table 2-6 appear sporadically in fewer than 10 languages.

Table 2-6. Patterns of four places of articulation

	BI	DE	AL	RE	PA	VE	UV	GL	LV	Example
a.	◎		◎			◎		◎		944 languages including Yurok
b.	◎		◎			◎			◎	255 languages including Zande
c.	◎		◎		◎	◎				188 languages including Turkish
d.	◎	◎				◎		◎		144 languages including Bembe
e.	◎	◎		◎		◎				95 languages including Tamil
f.	◎		◎			◎	◎			93 languages including Lahu
g.	◎		◎	◎		◎				58 languages including Telugu
h.	◎	◎	◎			◎				54 languages including Acoli
i.	◎	◎				◎	◎			37 languages including Kazakh
j.	◎	◎			◎	◎				36 languages including Czech
k.	◎	◎				◎			◎	25 languages including Kpala

two types shown in Table 2-4.[25] The most frequently added place of articulation is the glottal (1,088 languages), followed by the labiovelar (280), palatal (224), retroflex (153), and uvular (130). In Maddieson (1984: 33), the frequency order of places added when excluding the glottal is 'palatal>uvular>retroflex', which is slightly different from the results of this book. Despite these differences, it is sufficient to know that the expansion of the places of articulation from three to four is achieved by adding another place to the three major places of articulation.

Second, the ratio of the major places of articulation, bilabial, alveolar (dental), and velar, included in the plosive inventory of languages with four places of articulation, is higher than that of languages with three places of articulation. As shown in Table 2-5, in the case of three places of articulation, there are some exceptional languages in which one of the major places is missing. However, with four places of articulation, the rate of such exceptions is much lower. Every type shown in Table 2-6 contains all major places of articulation. Among the types not included in Table 2-6, the types without a bilabial are found in nine languages, and those without a velar are found in two. Types without an

25 Strictly speaking, type-(h) is a combination of two types in Table 2-4, but it still belongs to the same category as the other types.

alveolar (or dental) plosive do not exist in any language. Approximately 3.5% of languages with three places of articulation (50/1,426) omit one of the major places of articulation, whereas the rate of exception is only 0.6% (11/1,951) in the case of languages with four places of articulation.

Third, among the languages whose plosives appear in four places of articulation, some have both dental and alveolar plosives. In languages with three or fewer places of articulation, either the dental or the alveolar appears. However, both the dental and alveolar plosives are included in the inventory of 56 languages with four places of articulation, including Acoli, Dagik, and Herero. The minimum number of places of articulation for the dental and alveolar to coexist is four. In languages with more than four places of articulation, it is often found that both dental and alveolar plosives exist as separate phonemes.

There are 778 languages with five places of articulation for the plosive. As the number of places increases, the number of possible types also increases. In addition, since there are relatively few languages with five or more places of articulation, the likelihood of their including many large-scale dominant types is lower. The most frequent types are shown in Table 2-7.

Table 2-7 shows types appearing in more than 10 languages. As expected, there is a wide variety of type, with none occupying an overwhelmingly high ratio. Essentially, there are some similarities in the case of languages with five and four places of articulation. These two cases are common, as their frequent types are formed by adding another place to the three major places of articulation, and the glottal is most frequently added.

The types shown in Table 2-7 are those in which another place of articulation is added to the types shown in Table 2-6. That is, the frequent types for languages with five places of articulation are created by adding an additional place to the frequent types in languages with four places of articulation. For example, type-(a) and (b), which have the highest frequency in Table 2-7, are those with the uvular or palatal added to type-(a) in Table 2-6. Type-(o) and (p), which are less frequent, as shown in Table 2-7, are those with the palatal or alveolar added to type-(k) in Table 2-6. This pattern of expanding the place of articulation has been also confirmed when there are three or four places of articulation. In short, languages with more places of articulation add another place to the frequent types occurring in languages with fewer places of

Table 2-7. Patterns of five places of articulation

	BI	DE	AL	RE	PA	VE	UV	GL	LV	Example
a.	◎		◎			◎	◎	◎		129 languages including Seediq
b.	◎		◎		◎	◎		◎		114 languages including Achinese
c.	◎		◎			◎		◎	◎	76 languages including Eggon
d.	◎		◎		◎	◎			◎	61 languages including Ganang
e.	◎		◎	◎	◎	◎				49 languages including Worrorra
f.	◎	◎	◎			◎		◎		45 languages including Burun
g.	◎	◎				◎	◎	◎		39 languages including Akhvakh
h.	◎	◎	◎		◎	◎				38 languages including Otoro
i.	◎	◎		◎	◎	◎				34 languages including Kharia
j.	◎		◎	◎		◎		◎		30 languages including Brahui
k.	◎	◎	◎	◎		◎				25 languages including Malayalam
l.	◎	◎			◎	◎		◎		23 languages including Pular
m.	◎	◎		◎		◎		◎		17 languages including Manange
n.	◎		◎	◎		◎			◎	14 languages including Miyobe
o.	◎	◎			◎	◎			◎	13 languages including Cerma
p.	◎	◎	◎			◎			◎	11 languages including Ewe

articulation. The frequency hierarchy of places added in Table 2-7 is 'palatal (332)>dental (259)>labiovelar (175)>retroflex (169)>uvular (168)'.[26] This order is different from the frequency hierarchy in Table 2-6.

There are two main differences between languages with five places of articulation and languages with four or less. First, in the former, all languages have the bilabial and velar plosives, whereas in the latter, some languages don't have the bilabial or velar plosives. Another major place of articulation, the alveolar (including the dental), also appears in almost all languages having five places of articulation, with one exception. According to Gerlach (2016), Amkoe, a member of the Khoisan language family which is famous for its click, contains the alveolar plosives /t, d,

26 The number in parentheses is the sum of languages that have the added plosives in Table 2-7.

t^h/, but they are all marginal phonemes.[27] Amkoe is unique in that there is no alveolar plosive in the plosive inventory, which are not restricted in distribution or use.

Second, the proportion of languages that have both dental and alveolar plosives in the former (five places) is significantly higher than the latter (four or fewer places). In the latter, both dental and alveolar plosives appear in 56 languages, but in the former, they are seen in 121 languages. Not only has the number of languages with these plosives doubled, but their ratio has dramatically increased. Of the 1,951 languages with four places of articulation, dental and alveolar plosives coexist in 56 (less than 3%). However, of the 778 languages with five places of articulation, the dental and alveolar plosives coexist in 121 (more than 15%). In 25 languages, including Alyawarr, Badimaya, Dhangu, plosives appear at three adjacent places: dental, alveolar, and retroflex. This characteristic is unimaginable in languages with four or fewer places of articulation. In languages whose plosives are pronounced at five places of articulation, phonological opposition between detailed places involving coronal is actively established.

There are 176 languages with six places of articulation for the plosive. The number of these languages is small, accounting for only 4% of the 4,356 languages. The types of places of articulation that appear repeatedly in these languages are presented in Table 2-8.[28]

In Table 2-8, the frequency of type-(a) is very high, appearing in approximately 31% of 176 languages with six places of articulation. Type-(a) is unique in that there is no glottal plosive. The glottal plosive is most common in Table 2-6 and 2-7. However, it is not included in the most frequent type in Table 2-8, and instead is included in all other types. Type-(a) actively utilizes the phonological opposition within the nonperipheral places of articulation. Of the five places of articulation between the dental and palatal region belonging to the nonperipheral, four places of articulation, excluding alveopalatal, appear in type-(a). Because the alveopalatal plosive appears only in a few languages, it is reasonable to assert that type-(a) includes all representatives of nonperipheral places

27 As mentioned in Chapter 1, the marginal phoneme is excluded from discussion in this book.

28 The types in Table 2-8 appear in more than five languages.

Table 2-8. Patterns of six places of articulation

	BI	DE	AL	RE	PA	VE	UV	PH	GL	LV	Example
a.	◎	◎	◎	◎	◎	◎					55 languages including Kayardild
b.	◎	◎	◎		◎	◎			◎		17 languages including Uduk
c.	◎	◎		◎	◎	◎			◎		15 languages including Kanga
d.	◎		◎	◎		◎	◎		◎		10 languages including Mohave
e.	◎		◎		◎	◎	◎		◎		9 languages including Sereer
f.	◎	◎	◎			◎	◎		◎		9 languages including Cocopa
g.	◎		◎	◎	◎	◎			◎		8 languages including Maleng
h.	◎		◎		◎	◎			◎	◎	7 languages including Konkomba
i.	◎	◎				◎	◎	◎	◎		7 languages including Chechen
j.	◎		◎			◎	◎	◎	◎		6 languages including Alagwa

for the plosive. Type-(a) is particularly commonly found in the Pama-Nyungan language family, which includes the Australian languages. Compared with type-(a), the other types are significantly less frequent.

Languages with six places of articulation for the plosive have the following characteristics. First, this group has a much higher proportion of languages with both dental and alveolar plosives. As shown earlier, the coexistence of the two classes begins to appear in languages with four places of articulation, although the ratio is very low. Ninety of the 176 languages with six places of articulation have both dental and alveolar plosives, so languages with phonological opposition between both classes are more common than languages without that.[29] This difference is significant when compared to languages with five or fewer places of articulation for the plosive.

Second, this group includes more plosives articulated in the back part of the oral cavity. As shown in Table 2-8, languages with six places of articulation have many uvular and pharyngeal plosives that are articulated behind the velar, which is different from languages with five or fewer places of articualtion. In type-(i) and (j), there are more places

29 It cannot be generalized that as the number of places of articulation for the plosive increases, the ratio of the coexistence of the dental and alveolar plosives increases. As will be described later, even if the number of places of articulation is expanded from six to seven, the coexistence ratio does not increase.

of articulation belonging to the back part of the oral cavity than the front.

Third, the labiovelar plosive corresponding to the double-articulated plosive appears less often in this language group. In Table 2-8, the labiovelar is only found in type-(h), and even if the group is expanded to all 176 languages with six places of articulation, the labiovelar appears only in 20 languages. As will be described later, this result remains the same among languages with seven places of articulation. Therefore, the labiovelar arguably does not play a role in the large-scale expansion toward six or more places of articulation.

Finally, I will review languages with seven places of articulation for the plosive. There are only eight such languages, so discussing the type of place of articulation itself is meaningless. Table 2-9 lists all types of places of articulation seen in these eight languages. There is no leading type, and types appearing only in one or two languages are scattered. All types shown in Table 2-9 include the bilabial, retroflex, and velar. Unexpectedly, instead of the alveolar plosive, the retroflex plosive appears in all types shown in Table 2.9.[30] It is also peculiar that the palatal plosive appears in seven of these eight languages. Retroflex and palatal plosives are largely infrequent in other cases, and only in this group are these two classes of plosives more frequent than the alveolar plosive. The coexistence of dental and alveolar plosives is seen in four

Table 2-9. Patterns of seven places of articulation

	BI	DE	AL	RE	PA	VE	UV	PH	GL	LV	Example
a.	◎	◎	◎	◎	◎	◎			◎		Anguthimri, Djambarrpuyngu
b.	◎	◎		◎	◎	◎	◎		◎		Hmong Daw, Hmong Njua
c.	◎	◎	◎	◎	◎	◎				◎	Kara (Central African Republic)
d.	◎	◎	◎	◎	◎	◎	◎				Ngadjunmaya
e.	◎		◎	◎	◎	◎	◎		◎		Paiwan
f.	◎	◎		◎		◎	◎	◎	◎		Southern Pashto

30 The alveolar plosive appears in five and the dental appears in seven of these eight languages. It is noticeable that the frequency of the alveolar is considerably lower, but it seems difficult to ascribe significance to this differentiation because the number of target languages is so small.

languages.

So far, I have examined which types appear, and in what ratios, from languages with a minimum of two places of articulation to languages with a maximum of seven for the plosive. The results are summarized as follows.

(6) Features in the place of articulation for the plosive

a. A total of 77.5% of all languages have three or four places of articulation. Languages with four places of articulation are more common than those with three, which accords with the fact that the average number of places of articulation for the plosive is 3.93.

b. The frequency of the bilabial, alveolar (including dental), and velar, which are the major places of articulation, is very high. If any of these are missing, it is likely to be the bilabial. This trend is highly evident in languages with two or three places of articulation. When the number of places of articulation is expanded to four or more, the number of languages missing one of the major places is drastically reduced.

c. Frequent types with 'N(umber)' places of articulation are those in which another place is added to a frequent type with 'N-1' places of articulation. For example, frequent types in languages with four (N) places of articulation are those in which another place is added to the frequent type in languages with three (N-1) places of articulation. This is absolute when there are five or fewer places of articulation.

d. The coexistence of the dental and alveolar plosive, where the distance between places of articulation is very close, is found only in languages with four or more places of articulation. In languages with six or more places of articulation, it is more common that both dental and alveolar plosives are present.

e. If there are six or more places of articulation for the plosive, it is unlikely that the labiovelar corresponding to the double-articulated plosive will be included among the high-frequency types. In languages with five or four places of articulation, the labiovelar often appears among the high-frequency types.

Most of the summaries in (6) were mentioned earlier, so no

additional explanation is required. However, for (6d), further discussion is necessary. It is important to remember that the fact both dental and alveolar plosives appear in a language does not guarantee that they are opposed to each other only by the place of articulation. Although both plosives can coexist, if the manner of their articulation differs, it is difficult to say that the phonological opposition between them is established only by the place of articulation. For example, some members of the Austronesian language family, including Bannoni, have /t̪/ for the dental plosive and /d/ for the alveolar plosive. In this case, the phonological opposition of the two consonants also lies in the presence or absence of vocal fold vibrations, so it cannot be said that they are opposed only by the place of articulation. Phonological opposition by the place of articulation is established only when plosives, such as /t̪ : t/ or /d̪ : d/, which have the same features except for the place of articulation, exist in the same language. Languages in which dental and alveolar plosives coexist, as discussed above, may or may not have phonological opposition established solely by place of articulation. Therefore, it is necessary to examine to what extent there are languages in which phonological opposition is formed only by the place of articulation between the dental and alveolar plosives.

In Figure 2-6, two bars are assigned to each number of places of articulation. The left bar represents the number of languages in which both dental and alveolar plosives exist, and the right bar represents the number of languages in which dental and alveolar plosives are opposed only by the place of articulation. For example, among languages with four places of articulation, there are 56 languages in which both dental and alveolar plosives appear, and both classes are opposed only by the place of articulation in 38 languages. As shown in Figure 2-6, the more places of articulation a language has, the higher the ratio of the language in which the dental and alveolar plosives are opposed only by the place of articulation.

Table 2-10 quantifies the ratio of languages in which the dental and alveolar plosives are opposed only by place of articulation. This value is calculated by using the number of languages with both dental and alveolar plosives as the denominator, and the number of languages in which these two consonants are opposed only by place of articulation as the numerator. As the number of places of articulation increases from four to seven, the ratio of languages in which these two consonants

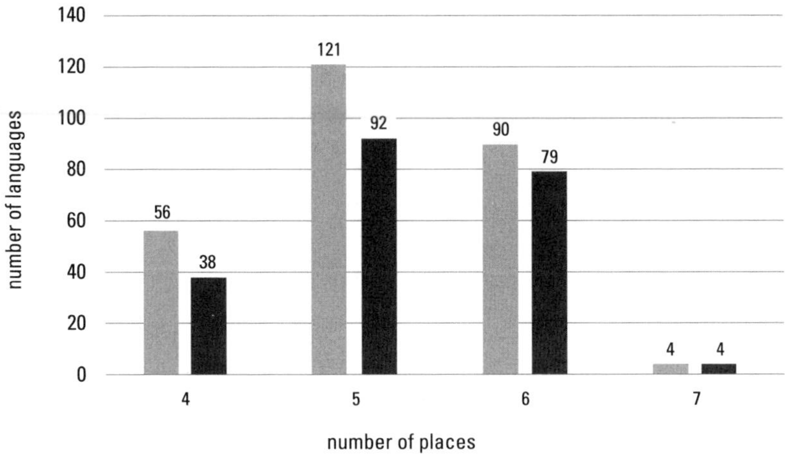

Figure 2-6. Coexistence and opposition of dental and alveolar plosives

Table 2-10. Ratio of dental and alveolar plosives opposed only by place of articulation

Number of places	4	5	6	7
Numerical value	0.68 (38/56)	0.76 (92/121)	0.87 (79/90)	1.0 (4/4)

are opposed only by place of articulation also continues to increase. For example, in the cases of four places of articulation, opposition by the place of articulation appears in 38 out of 56 languages, and the ratio is approximately 0.68. When the number of places of articulation is five, the ratio increases to 0.76, and when the number of places of articulation is six, the ratio increases to 0.87. When the number of places of articulation is expanded to the maximum of seven, all the languages in which dental and alveolar plosives coexist have minimal pairs opposed only by the place of articulation. This tells us that if a language has both dental and alveolar plosives, the more places of articulation exist, the higher the probability that the dental and alveolar plosives are opposed only by the place of articulation.

Although dental and alveolar plosives are opposed only by the place of articulation, the degree of activation of the opposition differs for each language. Some languages have only one contrastive pair, while others have multiple contrastive pairs. The language with the most contrastive pairs between dental and alveolar plosives is Soga, an African language in the Atlantic-Congo language family. According to Nabirye et al. (2016: 220), Soga has both dental and alveolar plosives, as illustrated in (7).

(7) Dental and alveolar plosives in Soga

DE	AL
t̪, d̪, (t̪^{w}), d̪^{w}, d̪^{j}, ^{n}t̪, ^{n}d̪, ^{n}d̪^{w}, ^{n}d̪^{j}	t, d, t^{w}, d^{w}, t^{j}, d^{j}, ^{n}t, ^{n}d, ^{n}t^{w}, ^{n}d^{w}, ^{n}t^{j}, ^{n}d^{j}

As shown in (7), even if the marginal phoneme in parentheses is excluded, Soga has eight contrastive pairs, 't̪ : t', 'd̪ : d', 'd̪^{w} : d^{w}', 'd̪^{j} : d^{j}', '^{n}t̪ : ^{n}t', '^{n}d̪ : ^{n}d', '^{n}d̪^{w} : ^{n}d^{w}', '^{n}d̪^{j} : ^{n}d^{j}', which are opposed only by the place of articulation. If the marginal phoneme 't̪^{w}' is included, the number of contrastive pairs increases to nine. Contrastive pairs in Soga are found in plosives accompaning various secondary articulations as well as plain plosives. Soga actively utilizes the phonological opposition between the dental and alveolar plosives.

2.4. Subdivision in the coronal and dorsal plosives

As shown above, the places of articulation can be divided into 12 places for the single-articulated plosive and four for the double-articulated plosive. In addition, these 16 places of articulation can be assigned to five main articulators. Excluding the linguolabial, alveopalatal, pharyngeal, and epiglottal plosives, which occur only rarely, results in the following list of articulators and their associated places of articulation.

(8) Articulator and place of articulation (II)
- a. Labial: bilabial
- b. Coronal: dental, alveolar, retroflex
- c. Dorsal: palatal, velar, uvular
- d. Laryngeal: glottal

In (8a) and (8d), only one place of articulation is assigned to one articulator, whereas in (8b) and (8c) three places of articulation are assigned to one articulator. As seen before, generally, the number of places of articulation for the plosive is three or four. In addition, the most frequent types contain only one place of articulation per articulator in (8). For example, in Table 2-4, the type consisting of bilabial, alveolar (including dental), and velar plosives has the highest frequency, and in Table 2-6, the type consisting of bilabial, alveolar (including dental), velar, and glottal plosives has the highest frequency.

Of course, there are languages in which two or more places of articulation are assigned to the coronal or dorsal. Here, the necessity of examining in detail how the places of articulation belonging to the coronal or dorsal appear in various languages is raised. Of the 4,356 languages, 640 languages have more than one place of articulation associated with the coronal, and 1,062 languages have more than one place of articulation associated with the dorsal. Centering on these languages, I will examine the phonological opposition between the places of articulation belonging to the coronal or dorsal.

I will begin with the coronal plosive. The number of places of articulation for the coronal plosive in each language is given in Figure 2-7. As shown in Figure 2-7, the number of places of articulation for the coronal plosive ranges from zero to three in the languages under study. Even if the alveopalatal plosive, which was excluded from (8) owing to its rarity, is included, there are just two languages that have more than three places of articulation for the coronal plosive: Narrinyeri and Wubuy.[31] In most languages, the coronal plosive appears only in one place of articulation. As expected, the number of places of articulation for the coronal plosive is closely related to the number of places of articulation for the plosive. In a given language, when there are numerous places of articulation for the plosive, the coronal plosive usually appears in many places of articulation.

Table 2-11 summarizes the number of places of articulation for the coronal plosive and all plosives. In [A], the number of places of articulation for the coronal plosive ranges from 0 to 3. [B] is the number of places of articulation for all plosives, and [C] is the frequency of [B].

The correlation between the number of places in the coronal plosive and that of all plosives can be confirmed in several ways. First, comparing

31 Although both languages are spoken in Australia, they are geographically far apart: Narrinyeri is spoken in South Australia and Wubuy in the Northern Territory.

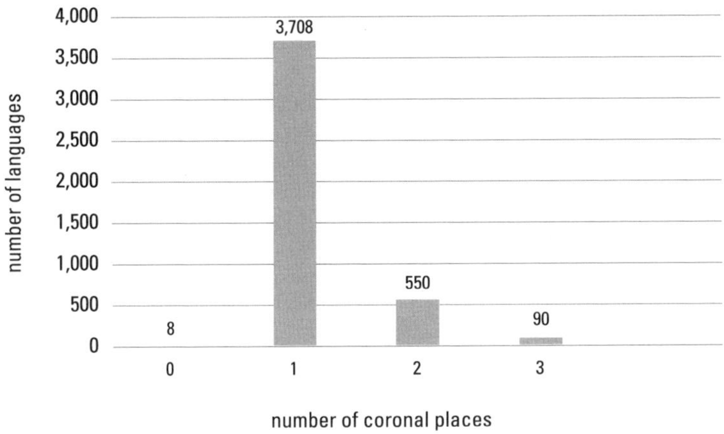

Figure 2-7. Number of places of articulation for the coronal plosive

Table 2-11. Correlation between the number of places of articulation in the coronal plosive and that of all plosives (I)

[A]	0			1					2				3		
[B]	2	3	5	2	3	4	5	6	4	5	6	7	5	6	7
[C]	3	4	1	14	1,422	1,741	490	41	210	262	74	4	25	61	4
[D]	2.9			3.8					4.8				5.8		

([A]: number of places of articulation for the coronal plosive, [B]: number of places of articulation for the plosive, [C]: number of languages, [D]: average number of places of articulation for the plosive)

[A] and [D] in Table 2-11, each time the number in [A] increases, from 0 to 1, 2, and 3, the average number in [D] also increases, to 2.9, 3.8, 4.8, and 5.8, respectively. That is, if the number in [A] increases by one, the number in [D] also increases by one.

Second, a similar tendency appears even if [A] and [D] in Table 2-11 are reversed, as shown in Table 2-12. Unlike in Table 2-11, in Table 2-12, [A] represents the number of places of articulation for all plosives, and [B] represents the average number of places of articulation for the coronal plosive. In Table 2-12, the average number in [B] increases stepwise as the number in [A] increases. In particular, when the number in [A] increases from five to six, the average number in [B] increases significantly.

Table 2-12. Correlation between the number of places of articulation in the coronal plosive and that of all plosives (II)

[A]	2	3	4	5	6	7
[B]	0.8	1.0	1.1	1.4	2.1	2.5

([A]: number of places of articulation for the plosive, [B]: average number of places of articulation for the coronal plosive)

Third, looking at [B] and [C] in Table 2-11, as the number in [A] increases, the minimum number of places of articulation for the plosive in [B] also increases. For example, languages with one place of articulation for the coronal plosive have a minimum of two places of articulation for the plosive, but languages with two places of articulation for the coronal plosive have a minimum of four, and languages with three places of articulation for the coronal plosive have a minimum of five. This relationship shows the close connection between the number of places for the coronal plosive and that for all plosives.

In row [C] of Table 2-11, the number of languages with one place of articulation for the coronal is the highest at 3,708, representing 85.1% of all languages. These languages have an average of 3.8 places of articulation for the plosive, which is approximately the same as the average of 3.93 for all languages seen in (5). This finding also suggests that the type with one place of articulation for the coronal plosive is the most common typologically. In addition, in languages with two or more places of articulation for the coronal plosive, the plosive appears in at least four places of articulation. These languages, without exception, have more places of articulation for the plosive than the average of 3.93 for all languages.

In Table 2-11, there are eight languages that have no coronal plosive. Most of them have two or three places of articulation for the plosive, which is a small number and below the average of all languages. The exception to this rule is Amkoe, in which the plosive appears in five places of articulation (bilabial, palatal, velar, uvular, and glottal), but coronal plosives such as /t, d, t^h/ only have status as marginal phonemes.[32] Excluding Amkoe, the remaining languages have fewer than

32 The exceptionality of Amkoe was mentioned in the explanation of Table 2-7.

10 consonants, and their size of consonant inventories is very small.[33] In addition, they have as few as 2.6 plosives on average. Therefore, it is difficult for the plosive to appear at various places of articulation, which result in the absence of the coronal plosive.

I will now limit myself to languages that have coronal plosives and examine several aspects related to the place of articulation. As previously discussed, languages with one place of articulation for the coronal plosive constitute an overwhelming majority. The preferred coronal place of articulation in these languages is presented in Table 2-13. As shown in Table 2-13, the preferred place of articulation is clear. Most languages have an alveolar plosive and some have a dental plosive. No language with a retroflex plosive exists.

There are 550 languages with two places of articulation for the coronal plosive. When two of the three places of articulation belonging to the coronal are combined, a total of three types emerge. The preferred types of combination are presented in Table 2-14.

Surprisingly, in Table 2-14, the frequencies of the three combination types appear almost equally without significant differences. In Table 2-13, the coronal place of articulation is concentrated on the alveolar or dental, and there is no retroflex, so the bias by place of articulation

Table 2-13. Preferred place of articulation in languages with one coronal place of articulation

Place of articulation	Dental	Alveolar	Retroflex
Number of languages	567	3,141	0

Table 2-14. Preferred combination of two coronal places of articulation

Combination type	DE+AL	DE+RE	AL+RE
Number of languages	181	184	185

33 As will be seen in Chapter 5, the average number of consonants in the 4,356 languages under study is approximately 20. Thus, languages without coronal plosives have very small consonant inventories with fewer than half of the average number of consonants. For reference, the average number of consonants in languages without coronal plosives is 7.8.

is severe. Considering this, the frequency of the combination types including the retroflex is expected to be very low in Table 2-14. However, contrary to expectations, the frequency of types including the retroflex is similar. The reason for this unexpected result is as follows. If the frequency of types including the retroflex is very low, the frequency of the type containing both dental and alveolar plosives should be very high. However, as seen in Figure 2-6, there are few languages with both dental and alveolar plosives. The results of Table 2-14 originate from this situation.

There are 90 languages with three places of articulation for the coronal plosive. These languages have a system in which the dental, alveolar, and retroflex are closely opposed in a small area within the oral cavity. These languages are expected to have many consonants and plosives. However, the average number of consonants and plosives in these 90 languages is 19.4 and 7.9, respectively, which is slightly less than the average of all 4,356 languages. Therefore, the number of places of articulation for the coronal plosive and the size of the inventory of consonants or plosives are not proportional. In terms of language family, 59 of these 90 languages belong to the Pama-Nyungan language family spoken in Australia. The remaining languages are generally spoken in Asia. As such, languages with three places of articulation for the coronal plosive are biased toward a limited language family or region.

Now I will examine the places of articulation associated with the dorsal. The dorsal plosive, like the coronal plosive, appears in three places of articulation. The following reviews how many places of articulation for the dorsal plosive appear in each language.

In Figure 2-8, most languages have one place of articulation for the dorsal plosive, which is similar to the coronal plosive. However, there are some differences between the two. Compared to the coronal plosive, there are many languages with two places of articulation for the dorsal plosive. Nonetheless, there are relatively few languages (only 28) with three places of articulation for the dorsal plosive.

As with the coronal plosive, the number of places of articulation for the dorsal plosive is directly related to the number of places of articulation for all plosives. This direct proportional relationship is well illustrated in Tables 2-15 and 2-16 below.

Table 2-15 and 2-16 are parallel to Table 2-11 and 2-12, respectively, presented above. Comparing Tables 2-15 with 2-11 and Tables 2-16 with

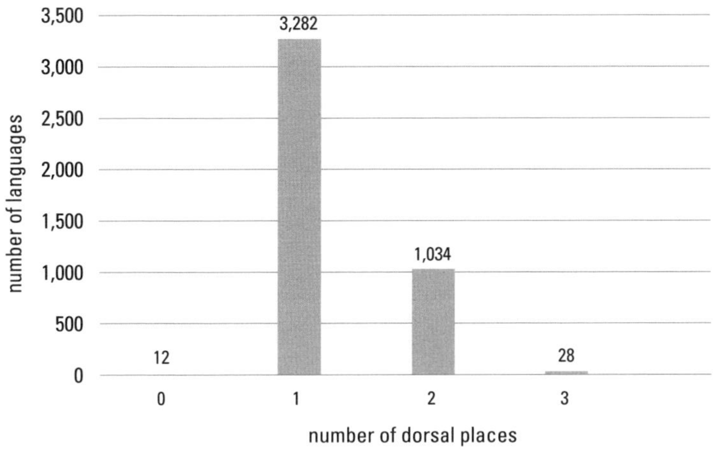

Figure 2-8. Number of places of articulation for the dorsal plosive

2-12 reveals that the number of places of articulation for the coronal and dorsal plosives are both closely related to the number of places of articulation for the plosive itself, although there are some differences in the detailed values. Additionally, in Table 2-16, the point at which the number places of articulation in [B] increases significantly is where the

Table 2-15. Correlation between the number of places of articulation in the dorsal plosive and that of all plosives (I)

[A]	0		1					2					3		
[B]	2	3	2	3	4	5	6	3	4	5	6	7	5	6	7
[C]	3	9	14	1,414	1,592	249	13	3	359	516	152	4	13	11	4
[D]	2.8		3.6					4.8					5.7		

([A]: number of places of articulation for the dorsal plosive, [B]: number of places of articulation for the plosive, [C]: number of languages, [D] average number of places of articulation for the plosive)

Table 2-16. Correlation between the number of places of articulation in the dorsal plosive and that of all plosives (II)

[A]	2	3	4	5	6	7
[B]	0.8	1.0	1.2	1.7	2.0	2.5

([A]: number of places of articulation for the plosive, [B]: average number of places of articulation for the dorsal plosive)

number of places in [A] increases from four to five, which is slightly different from the coronal plosive. However, there is no difference in overall tendency.

There are 12 languages with no dorsal plosive in Table 2-15. There are no more than three places of articulation for the plosive in these languages. In addition, the average number of consonants in these languages is 10.8, whereas the average number of plosives is only 3.9. As such, these languages lack a variety of consonants or plosives in general, and thus they have no dorsal plosive.

The number of languages with one place of articulation for the dorsal plosive is 3,282, i.e., 75.3% of all languages. The preferred place of articulation in these languages is shown in Table 2-17. The preferred place of articulation in Table 2-17 is highly one-sided. In almost all languages, with the exception of only two languages, the place of articulation is confined to the velar. In Table 2-17, there is no language with a palatal plosive as the only dorsal plosive. The two languages with a uvular plosive are Central Dusun and Obispeño.[34]

There are 1,034 languages with two places of articulation for the dorsal plosive. When two of the three places of articulation belonging to the dorsal are combined, a total of three types emerge. The preferred types of combination are given in Table 2-18.

The bias toward the velar plosive shown in Table 2-17 is also

Table 2-17. Preferred place of articulation in languages with one dorsal place of articulation

Place of articulation	Palatal	Velar	Uvular
Number of languages	0	3,280	2

Table 2-18. Preferred combination of two dorsal places of articulation

Combination type	PA+VE	PA+UV	VE+UV
Number of languages	673	1	360

34 These two languages have nothing to do with each other, either in their language family or in their regional distribution.

maintained in Table 2-18. The type without a velar plosive is found only in Ta'izzi-Adeni Arabic. According to Dawod (1952: 113), the plosive in Ta'izzi-Adeni Arabic appears at six places of articulation, but the velar plosive does not exist.[35] The combination types always include the velar plosive in languages other than Ta'izzi-Adeni Arabic. In Table 2-18, the combination type of 'PA + VE' is more frequent than 'VE + UV', which is related to the difference in frequency between the palatal and uvular plosives. According to Figure 2-1, the proportion of the palatal plosive is approximately twice that of the uvular plosive, which also seems to be reflected in Table 2-18.

There are only 28 languages with three places of articulation for the dorsal plosive. These languages have large inventories of the consonant and plosive. The average numbers of consonants and plosives are 37.4 and 13.8, respectively, which are considerably higher than those of all languages. In other words, the number of places of articulation for the dorsal plosive is proportional to the size of the inventory of the consonant and plosive. Languages with three places of articulation for the dorsal plosive are not biased by language family. Regionally, they are often seen in Africa or Asia.

35 This language has the velar fricative instead of the velar plosive.

Chapter 3

MANNER OF ARTICULATION IN THE PLOSIVE

In this chapter, I will examine the manner of articulation found in various plosives. There are 293 different plosives in the 4,356 languages included in this study.[1] The various plosives may differ in the place of articulation, but differ much more often in the manner of articulation including the phonation type. Since the previous chapter dealt with the place of articulation, this chapter will explore the manner of articulation that discriminates many plosives. The manner of articulation for the plosive is much more complex than the place of articulation, both quantitatively and qualitatively.

When examining the manner of articulation for the plosive, it is convenient to divide the plosive into two categories: plain and complex plosives. The former is the cardinal plosive in each place of articulation, and does not accompany any additional adjustment other than the basic articulatory process that the plosive undergoes. In general, the plain plosive consists of two types, a voiceless plain plosive and a voiced plain plosive, in each place of articulation. The latter (complex plosive) is a type in which a secondary articulation or other articulatory modification is added to the plain plosive. Complex plosives can be subclassified according to the types of added articulations, with secondary articulation being the most important. Complex plosives are nearly ten times more numerous than plain plosives.

1 There may be some additions or subtractions depending on the phonological interpretation.

3.1. Plain plosives

The plain plosive undergoes the typical articulatory process of the plosive, but is not accompanied by any additional articulation. Therefore, the plain plosive might also be called a primitive plosive. The type of plain plosive does not vary, but its proportion and frequency dominate those of the complex plosive. The following is an inventory of plain plosives found in the 4,356 languages.

In Table 3-1, (a) shows the single-articulated plain plosives, and (b) shows the double-articulated plain plosives. Table 3-1 presents 27 plain plosives at 16 places of articulation. As described above, since two plain plosives, voiced and voiceless, can exist in one place of articulation, the theoretically possible maximum number of plain plosives is 32 in 16 places of articulation. However, five are not found in any language. These gaps in the inventory can be categorized as systematic and accidental.

In Table 3-1, neither the epiglottal plain plosive nor the glottal plain plosive articulated deep in the back of the vocal tract, including the pharyngeal plain plosive, is accompanied by vibrations of the vocal folds. In other words, there is no voiced plain plosive in these three places of articulation.[2] As is already well known in general phonetics, if there is little distance between the larynx and the position at which the airflow is closed, it is difficult for the obstruent to be accompanied by vocal fold vibration. The absence of voiced plain plosives in the pharynx, epiglottal

Table 3-1. Inventory of the plain plosive

	BI	LL	DE	AL	RE	AP	PA	VE	UV	PH	EP	GL
a.	p, b	p̼, b̼	t̪, d̪	t, d	ʈ, ɖ	ȶ, ɖ	c, ɟ	k, g	q, ɢ	ʕ	ʡ	ʔ

	LV	LA	LP	DV
b.	kp, gb	pt, bd	bɟ	t̪k

2 According to PHOIBLE (www.https://phoible.org/), the voiced glottal plain plosive appears in Tundra Nenets, but based on the phonemic analysis referenced in this book, no voiced glottal plain plosive exists in any language. Moreover, Laver (1994: 206) suggested that the voiced epiglottal plain plosive could be sufficiently articulated, but no language with such a phoneme has been found.

and larynx is due to this articulatory constraint, which is a systematic gap.[3]

For reference, I will also examine the uvular plosive, which is located directly in front of the pharynx and is not far from the larynx. In the uvular plosive, both voiceless and voiced plain plosives exist. The voiceless plain uvular plosive appears in 373 languages, while the voiced plain uvular plosive appears in only 42. Generally, the number of voiceless plosives is greater than that of the corresponding voiced plosives. However, the difference between the two in other places of articulation is not as great as for the uvular.[4] This fact confirms that the absence or rarity of the voiced plain plosive in the place of articulation close to the larynx indicates a correlation between the distance to the vocal folds and the vibration of the vocal folds.

While the gaps in (a) of Table 3-1 are systematic, the gaps in (b) seem to be accidental. It is difficult to find an inevitable reason why there is no voiced plosive in the labiopalatal or no voiceless plosive in the dentovelar. The labiopalatal and dentovelar plosives appear in very few languages, and other double-articulated plosives, such as the labiovelar plosive, have both voiced and voiceless plosives. Moreover, it is inconsistent that the labiopalatal plosive is only voiceless, while the dentovelar plosive is only voiced.[5] These results support that the gaps in (b) are not systematic but accidental.

The 27 types of plain plosives in Table 3-1 represent less than 10% of the 293 types of total plosives, with the types of complex plosives constituting more than 90%. However, the plain plosives have a far higher frequency than that of the complex plosives. Plain plosives account for 75.3% of the total plosives, three times the rate (24.7%) of complex plosives. A more specific description of this relationship, depending on the place of articulation, is shown below.[6]

3 Particularly, in the case of the glottal plosive, it is very difficult for vocal fold vibration to accompany the plosive because the vocal folds are completely closed. Laver (1994: 206) stated that this articulatory process is logically impossible.

4 For this, see Figure 3-3.

5 It is unusual for the voiced plosive to exist instead of the voiceless plosive in the labio-palatal. However, since Birwa, an African language, is an isolated example, it is difficult for this situation to gain importance.

6 For convenience, the linguolabial, alveopalatal, pharyngeal, and epiglottal

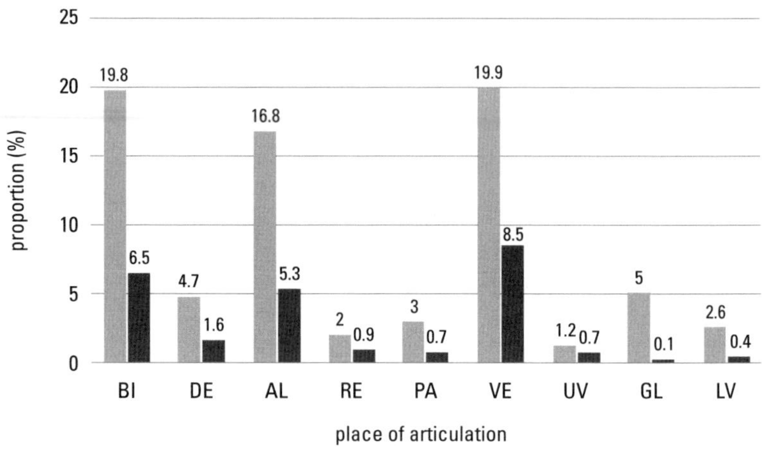

Figure 3-1. Percentage of the plain and complex plosives according to the place of articulation

Figure 3-1 is based on Figure 2-1 and shows the proportion of the plain and complex plosives separately. These percentages were calculated using the total frequency of the plosive as the denominator and the frequency of the plosive at each place of articulation as the numerator. Two bars are assigned to each place of articulation. The left bar represents the ratio of plain plosives, and the right bar represents that of complex plosives. Compared to the complex plosive, the percentage of the plain plosive is much higher.

Most languages have one or more plain plosives. Very few languages have been reported to have no plain plosive at all.

(1) Languages without a plain plosive
   a. Barai: /^{m}b, t^{h}, ^{n}d, k^{h}, ^{ŋ}g/
   b. Kombai: /^{m}b, ^{n}d, ^{ŋ}g/
   c. Zulu: /p^{h}, b̤, t^{h}, d̤, k^{h}, g̊, g̈/

The languages in (1) have complex plosives instead of plain plosives.

---

plosives, etc., with a very low frequency, are excluded. They are often excluded from other figures or tables below. The frequency of these plosives is given in Chapter 4.

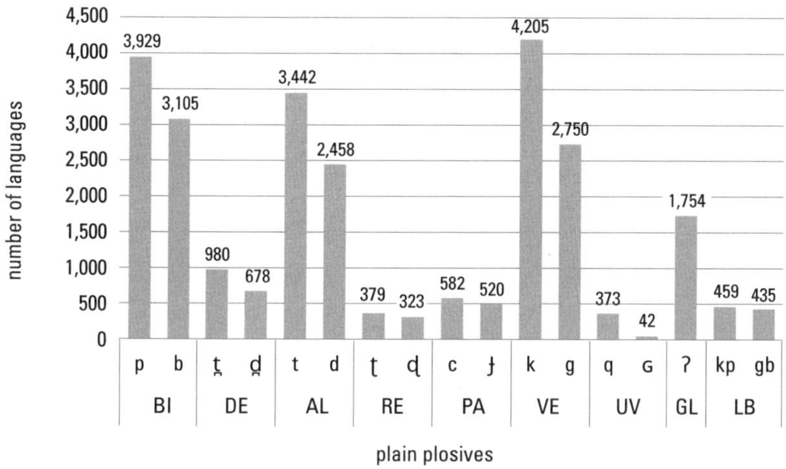

Figure 3-2. Frequency of the plain plosives

Among the complex plosives, voiceless aspirated plosives and voiced prenasalized plosives appear predominantly in these languages. However, when considering the opposition of the plosives in the languages of (1), there is ample room to reanalyze the aspirated or prenasalized plosive as the voiceless or voiced plain plosive, respectively.[7] Therefore, depending on the analysis, the languages in (1) can be considered to have a plain plosive. Even defining the plosives in (1) as complex, languages with no plain plosives are extremely rare (less than 0.1% of the 4,356 languages).

Due to the possibility of alternatives and the rarity of languages that appear to have no plain plosives, it is justifiable to say that every language has the plain plosive. However, plain plosives appear with considerable differences in frequency depending on the place of articulation and the vibration of the vocal folds.

In Figure 3-2, the frequency of the plain plosives greatly differs depending on the place of articulation. In addition, there is a significant difference in frequency between the voiced and voiceless plain plosives even at the same place of articulation. Predictably, the voiceless plosive occurs more frequently than the voiced plosive, but the addition of

7 In particular, the phonemic analysis of Zulu differs greatly depending on the discussion.

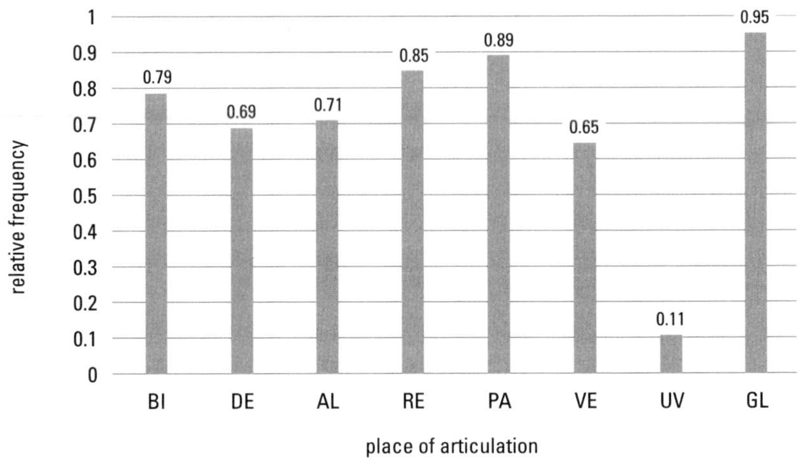

Figure 3-3. Proportions of the voiced and voiceless plain plosives

place of articulation as a variable substantially complicates the result. To elucidate Figure 3-2, I have quantified the proportion of voiced plain plosives compared to the frequency of voiceless plain plosives.

Figure 3-3 shows the value obtained by dividing the frequency of the voiced plain plosive by that of the voiceless plain plosive. This value represents the relative frequency of the voiced plain plosive, assuming that the frequency of the voiceless plain plosive is 1. In Figure 3-3, the frequency of the uvular plain plosive is the lowest (0.11), while that of the labiovelar plain plosive is the highest value (0.95). That is, the frequency of /ɢ/ is only one-ninth that of /q/, but the frequency of /gb/ is almost equal to that of /kp/. It is necessary to clarify why the frequency of /gb/ is relatively high compared to /kp/.[8]

When limited to the three major places of articulation, bilabial, alveolar, and velar, the frequency value of /b/ is the highest and the frequency value of /g/ is the lowest. This result is in line with the discussion about the absence of major plosives. In languages with phonological opposition between voiced and voiceless plosives, if a gap exists in the inventory of the plain plosive, it is likely to lack /g/

8 As mentioned earlier, the specificity of /ɢ/ is related to the place of articulation close to the larynx.

among the voiced plosives and /p/ among the voiceless plosives.[9] This is consistent with the results in Figure 3-3, in which /g/ is the least frequent among the voiced plosives at the major places of articulation, thus it is most likely to be missing from the inventory. In addition, because the rate at which /p/ is missing from the inventory is high, the relative frequency value of /b/, a voiced opposite of /p/, necessarily increases.

3.2. Complex plosives

The complex plosive refers to the plosive produced by adding certain articulatory adjustments to the plain plosive. There are several types of articulatory adjustments, the most important of which is secondary articulation. Most of the known secondary articulations are found in many complex plosives. Sometimes a plosive is accompanied by two or more secondary articulations. In addition to secondary articulation, there are also complex plosives with glottal action or liquid-colored release. Five types of articulatory modifications can be found in the complex plosive. In the following, I will examine each of them.

(2) Types of additional articulatory adjustments in the complex plosive:
- a. Single secondary articulation: aspiration, nasalization, labialization, palatalization, pharyngealization, laryngealization, velarization
- b. Multiple secondary articulations: aspiration + labialization, nasalization + palatalization, aspiration + nasalization + palatalization, ...
- c. Glottal action: breathy voice, creaky voice
- d. Liquid-colored release: lateral release, r-release
- e. Tenseness: fortis, lenis

(2a), a type in which one secondary articulation is combined with the plain plosive, constitutes the dominant majority.[10] There are seven

9 For this, see 5.4.
10 The percentages of the five types in (2) are presented in Figure 3-5.

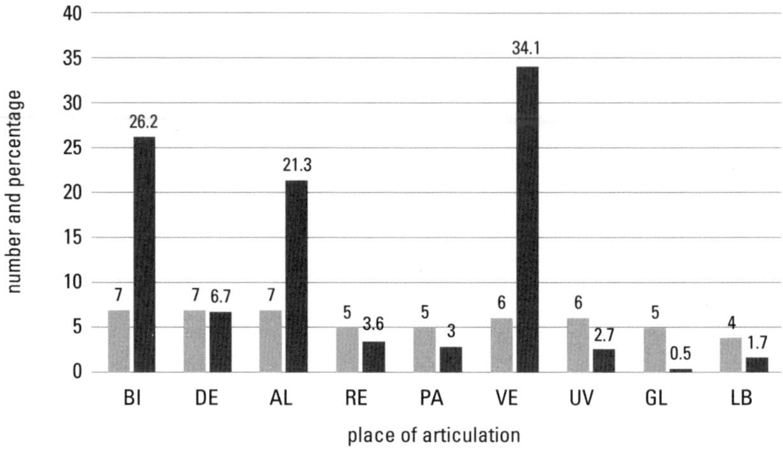

Figure 3-4. Types and proportion of secondary articulation according to the place of articulation

types of secondary articulation accompanying the plosive, as shown in (2a). Some secondary articulations require the identification of whether they are added to the front or back parts of the plosive, whereas others do not. A representative example of the former is aspiration. The complex plosive with preaspiration and the plosive with postaspiration are clearly distinguished phonetically, and there are even languages that have the two as separate phonemes.[11]

The type or frequency of the secondary articulation presented in (2a) shows a significant difference depending on the place of articulation. Figure 3-4 shows the types and frequency of secondary articulation by the place of articulation. Two bars are assigned to each place of articulation. The left bar indicates how many types among the seven secondary articulations in (2a) appear at each place of articulation. The types of secondary articulations vary from four to seven depending on the place of articulation. The right bar shows the percentage of the complex plosive at each place of articulation. This ratio was calculated with the sum of the frequency of the complex plosives in (2a) as the denominator and the frequency of the complex plosives at each place of articulation in (2a) as the numerator.

11 Each of the secondary articulations is covered in more detail in 3.5.

First, I examine which secondary articulation appears according to the place of articulation. The plosives in the bilabial, dental, and alveolar combine with all seven types of secondary articulation. Plosives articulated in the front of the oral cavity do not seem to have restrictions on combination with all secondary articulations. The velar and uvular plosive can accompany six secondary articulations but not velarization because their primary place of articulation is similar to the point at which velarization occurs. The plosives in the retroflex, palatal, and glottal can accompany five secondary articulations. The retroflex plosive and the palatal plosive cannot be combined with pharyngealization and velarization. The glottal plosive cannot be combined with the laryngealization and velarization. Velarization is accompanied by a plosive that is articulated in the front of the oral cavity, so it does not appear in the retroflex, palatal, or glottal plosives. The reason why the glottal plosive does not combine with laryngealization may be the overlap between the primary place of articulation of the glottal plosive and the point at which laryngealization occurs.

The labiovelar plosive is the most constrained in its combinations with secondary articulation and can be accompanied by only four secondary articulations. The labiovelar plosive is not combined with palatalization, pharyngealization, and velarization. The labiovelar has two primary articulations at the bilabial and velar, so it cannot accommodate velarization for the same reason as the velar plosive. However, although palatalization and pharyngealization can be combined with the bilabial or the velar plosives, they cannot be combined with labiovelar plosives: the reason for this restriction remains unclear.

Next, the percentage for the complex plosive with one secondary articulation is examined for each place of articulation. There is a high percentage of the complex plosive in the major places of articulation, such as the bilabial, alveolar, and velar, as shown in Figure 3-4. This result is similar to Figure 2-1, which shows the frequency of plosives according to the place of articulation without distinguishing between plain and complex plosives. Of course, there are differences in detail. Above all, in Figure 3-4, the percentage of the complex plosives in the glottal and labiovelar is very low. In Figures 2-1 and 2-4, the percentages of the glottal plosive and the labiovelar plosive are 5.1% and 2.9%, respectively, but in Figure 3-4, those values drop to 0.5% and 1.7%, respectively. In particular, the percentage of glottal complex plosives in

Figure 3-4 is approximately one tenth of that in Figure 2-1. The glottal plosive does not have an active articulator and the labiovelar has two primary places of articulations. These phonetic characteristics seem to prevent glottal and labiovelar plosives with one secondary articulation from appearing in many languages.

Type-(b) in (2) is closely related to type-(a) in that it includes secondary articulation. Unlike type-(a), the type-(b) complex plosives are accompanied by multiple secondary articulations. The maximum number of secondary articulations that a plosive can accommodate is three, but the distribution of plosives accompanied by three secondary articulations is very limited. Most of the complex plosives in type-(b) are combined with two secondary articulations. There are restrictions on the types of combinations, which will be covered in 3.6.

Type-(c) in (2) is related to the so-called phonation type. Various plosives, such as the voiced, voiceless, aspirated, and unaspirated, can exist through the adjustment of the vocal folds. Among them, the complex plosives that are unrelated to secondary articulation are classified as type-(c). Representative complex plosives of this type include a breathy voice and a creaky voice. These two categories are sometimes included as one of the secondary articulations. A breathy voice may be analyzed as a voiced plosive with aspiration, and a creaky voice may be analyzed as a plosive accompanied by laryngealization.[12] However, since the breathy voice and creaky voice are distinct from the plosive with aspiration or laryngealization, it would be better to divide them into a separate type. For example, plosives such as /t̤^{h}, k̤^{h}/ are breathy voices accompanied by aspirations and are opposed to /t^h, k^h/, which are not breathy voices, in Chantyal.[13] This makes it difficult to identify a breathy voice with a voiced plosive accompanied by aspiration. Additionally, as pointed out in Laver (1994: 330), the creaky voice does not completely constrict the larynx, whereas the plosive with laryngealization defined in this book has a much stronger stricture or complete stricture in the larynx, such as the unaspirated fortis of Korean. Therefore, there is a phonetic difference between the creaky voice and the laryngealized

12 According to Catford (1977: 193), a discussion relating the creaky voice to laryngealization can be found in Ladefoged (1964).

13 /t̤^{h}, k̤^{h}/ appear only in Chantyal. For the inventory of the plosive in Chantyal, see Noonan (2005: 3).

plosive.

Type-(d) in (2) refers to plosives with an unusual release. In the release stage, the plosives belonging to this type have the articulatory characteristics of lateral, trill, or flap, which are subclasses of the liquid consonant. Releases with the characteristic of trills or flaps are commonly grouped into one category. As a result, two categories of plosives with lateral release and with trill (including flap) release can be distinguished. The former is indicated by adding '^{l}', and the latter is indicated by adding '^{r}' after the plosive. Consonants of similar character to type-(d) are often analyzed as an affricate or consonant cluster. These cases are excluded from type-(d).[14] The plosives of type-(d) appear mainly in the Sino-Tibetan and Hmong-Mien language families, which are regionally distributed in Asia.

Type-(e) in (2) is related to the distinction between the fortis and lenis by the tenseness or force of articulation.[15] Sometimes the fortis is equated with the voiceless or aspirated consonant and the lenis with the voiced or unaspirated consonant. However, Northern Paiute and Wolio have voiced fortes such as 'bb, dd'. Moreover, Quapaw has the aspirated /p^{h}, t^{h}/ and fortes /pp, tt/ as separate phonemes. These languages suggest that the fortis and lenis should be set as separate classes from the voiceless and voiced plosives or the aspirated and unaspirated plosives.

In general, a fortis plosive is characterized by high air pressure inside the closure point, a stronger airflow at release, a longer closure duration, and muscle tension around the larynx. However, it is not easy to classify the fortis plosive with these various characteristics in the current consonant system. In addition, the phonetic features of consonants analyzed as the fortis plosive in different languages are not homogeneous.[16] For this reason, many scholars define the fortis differently. This embarrassing situation is also evident in the absence of an IPA for the fortis plosive. I will include in this book only those

14 Lee (2020: 62) suggested four consonants (p^{l}, p^{r}, ^{m}p^{l}, ^{m}p^{r}) as belonging to type-(d) in Central Mashan Hmong, but they are consonant clusters and should have been excluded from the plosive inventory.

15 For details on the fortis and lenis, refer to Catford (1977: 199~204) and Ladefoged & Maddieson (1996: 95~99).

16 This is related to the question of whether there are phonetic parameters that can define the fortis. For a recent discussion on this topic, refer to Butcher (2004).

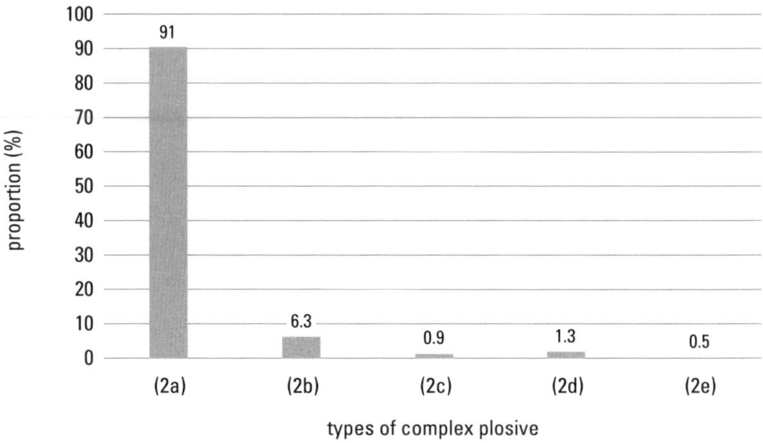

Figure 3-5. Distribution of the types of complex plosive

plosives classified as fortes in the previous descriptions and transcribed in geminate form such as 'pp, bb'.

There is a significant imbalanced distribution of complex plosives with five types of articulatory modification, shown in (2), as evidenced in Figure 3-5 above. Figure 3-5 shows the distribution of the five types in (2) by percentage. Almost all of the complex plosives are accompanied by one or more secondary articulations. The complex plosive of type-(a) combined with one secondary articulation constitutes 91% of complex plosives. Together with type-(b) with multiple secondary articulations, these types account for 97.3%. Complex plosives that are not related to secondary articulation occupy a very small proportion.[17]

3.3. Contrast by [±voiced]

When two or more plosives exist as separate phonemes in one place of articulation, the most common phonological opposition is related to

17 The values of type-(c, d, e) in Figure 3-5 were calculated to include the complex plosive with the secondary articulation. For example, a breathy voice /g̈^{w}/, a lateral-released plosive /k^{lw}/, and a fortis plosive /kk^{w}/ are accompanied by labialization, but they were considered to belong to type-(c, d, e). Strictly speaking, they belong to both type-(a) and type-(c~e).

the presence or absence of vocal fold vibrations. In other words, the phonological opposition between the voiceless and voiced plosives often appears in many languages.[18] This is the same not only for the plosives, but also for other consonant classes that belong to the obstruent, such as the fricative or affricate. Since the opposition by [±voiced] is very important in the plosive, it deserves a closer look. Among the 293 plosives, a list of contrastive pairs that are distinguished only by [±voiced] is shown in Table 3-2.

In Table 3-2, 94 contrastive pairs consisting of the voiceless and

Table 3-2. Contrastive pairs of voiced and voiceless plosives

BI	p-b (2,672), p^{h}-b^{h} (103), p^{ʔ}-b^{ʔ} (0), ^{m}p-^{m}b (83), p^{m}-b^{m} (0), p^{w}-b^{w} (55), p^{j}-b^{j} (54), p^{ʕ}-b^{ʕ} (4), ^{m}p^{h}-^{m}b^{h} (0), ^{m}p^{w}-^{m}b^{w} (2), ^{m}p^{j}-^{m}b^{j} (2), p^{wɣ}-b^{wɣ} (0), p̈-b̤ (1), p̃-b̰ (0), p^{r}-b^{r} (3), p^{l}-b^{l} (2), ^{m}p^{l}-^{m}b^{l} (0), pp-bb (0)
LL	p̼-b̼ (1)
DE	t̪-d̪ (639), t̪^{h}- d̪^{h} (67), ^{n}t̪-^{n}d̪ (7), t̪^{w}-d̪^{w} (6), t̪^{j}-d̪^{j} (22), t̪^{ʕ}-d̪^{ʕ} (12), ^{n}t̪^{h}-^{n}d̪^{h} (0), ^{n}t̪^{w}-^{n}d̪^{w} (1), ^{n}t̪^{j}-^{n}d̪^{j} (1), t̪^{r}-d̪^{r} (1), t̪^{rw}-d̪^{rw} (1)
AL	t-d (2,323), t^{h}-d^{h} (49), t^{ʔ}-t^{ʔ} (0), ^{n}t-^{n}d (84), t^{n}~d^{n} (1), t^{w}-d^{w} (14), t^{j}-d^{j} (47), t^{ʕ}-d^{ʕ} (14), t^{ɣ}-d^{ɣ} (2), ^{n}t^{h}-^{n}d^{h} (0), ^{n}t^{w}-^{n}d^{w} (2), ^{n}t^{j}-^{n}d^{j} (2), t^{wj}-d^{wj} (0), t̤-d̤ (1), t̰-d̰ (0), t^{r}-d^{r} (4), t^{l}-d^{l} (3), t^{rw}-d^{rw} (1), ^{n}t^{l}-^{n}d^{l} (1), tt-dd (0)
RE	ʈ-ɖ (245), ʈ^{h}-ɖ^{h} (75), ^{ɳ}ʈ-^{ɳ}ɖ (1), ʈ^{j}-ɖ^{j} (2), ^{ɳ}ʈ^{h}-^{ɳ}ɖ^{h} (0)
AP	ȶ-ɖ (3)
PA	c-ɟ (404), c^{h}-ɟ^{h} (18), ^{ɲ}c-^{ɲ}ɟ (11), c^{w}-ɟ^{w} (3), c^{j}-ɟ^{j} (1), ^{ɲ}c^{h}-^{ɲ}ɟ^{h} (0)
VE	k-g (2,644), k^{h}-g^{h} (104), k^{ʔ}-g^{ʔ} (0), ^{ŋ}k-^{ŋ}g (86), k^{ŋ}-g^{ŋ} (1), k^{w}-g^{w} (241), k^{j}-g^{j} (55), k^{ʕ}-g^{ʕ} (1), k̤-g̈ (1), k̰-g̃ (0), ^{ŋ}k^{h}-^{ŋ}g^{h} (0), ^{ŋʔ}k-^{ŋʔ}g (0), ^{ŋ}k^{w}-^{ŋ}g^{w} (7), ^{ŋ}k^{j}-^{ŋ}g^{j} (0), k^{wj}-g^{wj} (3), k^{r}-g^{r} (1), k^{l}-g^{l} (1), kk-gg (1), kk^{w}-gg^{w} (0)
UV	q-ɢ (31), q^{h}-ɢ^{h} (2), ^{N}q-^{N}ɢ (1), q^{w}-ɢ^{w} (4), q^{ʕ}-ɢ^{ʕ} (2), ^{N}q^{h}-^{N}ɢ^{h} (0)
PH	none
EP	none
GL	none
LV	kp-gb (404), kp^{h}-gb^{h} (6), ^{ŋm}kp-^{ŋm}gb (3), kp^{w}-gb^{w} (1), kp^{j}-gb^{j} (1), kp^{r}-gb^{r} (1)
LA	pt-bd (1)
LP	none
DV	none

18 A phonological opposition between the voiceless and voiced plosives is a contrast by the distinctive feature [±voiced].

voiced plosives are presented. Of the 293 plosives, 188 plosives have an opposite in the presence or absence of vocal fold vibration. All of the most frequent plosives, without exception, form a contrastive pair by [±voiced]. Those plosives that do not form a contrastive pair occur extremely infrequently, such as /p^{ɣ}, ^{ʔ}d, t^{hl}/.

However, the existence of a contrastive pair in Table 3-2 does not mean that the phonological opposition between the voiceless and voiced plosive actually exists in languages. Table 3-2 is nothing more than a simple arrangement of the voiceless and voiced plosives among all 293 plosives. The number in parentheses indicates how many languages have each contrastive pair. The pair /p-b/ is the most frequent, appearing in 2,672 languages. The pair /k-g/ is slightly less frequent, appearing in 2,644 languages. In contrast, the number 'zero' in parentheses indicates that no language has such a contrastive pair. For example, in the case of /p^{ʔ}-b^{ʔ}/, there are only languages with 'p^{ʔ}' or languages with 'b^{ʔ}', and no language has both of them. The same is true for the contrastive pair /p^{wɣ}-b^{wɣ}/. In the case of complex plosives accompanied by multiple secondary articulations or combined with two or more of the five types in (2), phonological opposition by vocal fold vibration is unlikely to occur. Among the fortis plosives, only /kk-gg/ appears in one language, Tyap, so the frequency of opposition by [±voiced] is also very low. In addition, a phonological opposition between the voiceless and voiced plosives is not found among the complex plosives accompanied by laryngealization or by both aspiration and nasalization. For this reason, contrastive pairs such as /^{n}t^{h}-^{n}d^{h}/, /^{m}p^{h}-^{m}b^{h}/, and /t^{ʔ}-d^{ʔ}/ do not appear in any language.

Next, I examine the typological pattern of the phonological contrast by [±voiced] as a whole. For convenience, I will consider the plain and complex plosives separately. Table 3-3 classifies each language according to the number of places of articulation in which the contrast by [±voiced] can exist, and then quantifies how many languages have the contrast by [±voiced] in the plain plosive.

When counting the number of places of articulation in column [A], some places of articulation, such as the pharyngeal, epigolttal, and glottal, in which the contrast by [±voiced] cannot appear were excluded. For example, if a language's plosives appear in the bilabial, alveolar, velar, and glottal, the glottal is ruled out, and the number of places of articulation is considered three in Table 3-3. This measure is

Table 3-3. Frequency and ratio of the contrast by [±voiced] in the plain plosive (I)

[A]	[B]	[C]	[D]
2	61	12	19.7%
3	2,485	1,735	69.8%
4	1,361	1,069	78.5%
5	379	267	70.4%
6	68	19	27.9%
7	2	1	50.0%
Total	4,356	3,103	71.2%

([A]: number of places of articulation for the plosive, [B]: number of languages, [C]: number of languages with the contrast by [±voiced], [D]: ratio of [C] to [B])

important for the accurate calculation of the value of [D].[19]

In Table 3-3, languages with three or four places of articulation in which the contrast by [±voiced] occurs constitute the majority, and the ratio of these languages in [D] is also high. Regardless of the number of places of articulation for the plosive, the percentage of languages with contrast by [±voiced] does not exceed 80%. In Table 3-3, the highest value is 78.5% and the lowest value is 19.7%. Except for the case of seven places of articulation, which has a very small number of language samples, the ratio of languages that include the contrast by [±voiced] shows a correlation with the number of places of articulation. That is, the ratio is low if there are too few or too many places of articulation, but somewhat high if there are between three and five places of articulation. The contrast by [±voiced] appears in 71.2% of languages, indicating that there are more than twice as many languages with opposition between the voiced and voiceless plosives as those without it.

The presence of contrast by [±voiced] in a language does not mean that such contrast occurs in all places of articulation. For example, in some languages, if there is a contrast by [±voiced], and the places of articulation for the plosive are bilabial, alveolar, and velar, the contrast by [±voiced] may or may not appear in all three places of articulation.

19 As a result, the value of [A] and [B] in Table 3-3 differs from that in Table 2-2.

In Table 3-3, if the languages have a contrast by [±voiced] in at least one place of articulation, they are treated equally, so there is no distinction between languages in which the contrast occurs in all places of articulation versus some places of articulation. It is necessary to compare the total number of places of articulation in each language with the number of places of articulation in which the contrast by [±voiced] appears, targeting only languages that have this contrast. Table 3-4 below summarizes this ratio.

Table 3-4. Frequency and ratio of the contrast by [±voiced] in the plain plosive (II)

[A]	[B]	[C]	[D]	[E]
2	12	1	5	41.7%
		2	7	58.3%
3	1,735	1	124	7.1%
		2	374	21.6%
		3	1,237	71.3%
4	1,069	1	33	3.1%
		2	144	13.5%
		3	262	24.5%
		4	630	58.9%
5	267	1	10	3.7%
		2	14	5.2%
		3	33	12.4%
		4	66	24.7%
		5	144	53.9%
6	19	1	2	10.5
		2	1	5.3%
		3	0	0.0%
		4	3	15.8%
		5	4	21.1%
		6	9	47.4%
7	1	5	1	100%

([A]: number of places of articulation for the plosive, [B]: number of languages, [C]: number of places with the contrast by [±voiced], [D]: number of languages, [E]: ratio of [D] to [B])

The shaded cells in Table 3-4 are cases in which the contrast by [±voiced] appears at all possible places of articulation. For example, among the languages with four places of articulation, the contrast by [±voiced] occurring in all four places of articulation is the most frequent (58.9%), but there are still many languages in which the contrast occurs only in three or fewer places of articulation.

Overall, there are more languages that have the contrast by [±voiced] in all possible places of articulation than those that do not. Moreover, this difference can be considerable, depending on the number of places of articulation. Among languages with three places of articulation, those with the contrast by [±voiced] in all three places of articulation constitute 71.3%. However, when there are six possible places of articulation, the proportion of languages with such a contrast in all possible places of articulation falls to 47.4%. As the number of places of articulation increases, the proportion of languages that have the contrast by [±voiced] in all possible places of articulation tends to decrease. On average, 61.4% of languages show contrast by [±voiced] in all possible places of articulation. In other words, in four of ten languages, the contrast by [±voiced] appears only in some places of articulation, not all. This is by no means a small percentage.

Table 3-4 shows that even though [±voiced] exists as a distinctive feature in languages, there are still differences in the degree of activeness with which this distinctive feature distinguishes plosives. In some languages, [±voiced] is highly active, so it discriminates the plosives into the voiceless and voiced at all possible places of articulation, whereas in other languages it is less active, so the contrast by [±voiced] is found in some places of articulation. For example, among the languages with five places of articulation in Table 3-4, while some languages have the contrast by [±voiced] at all five places of articulation, others have the same contrast at only one place, and the range of activeness is quite wide. In this case, there is a five-fold difference between the maximum (five places) and minimum (one place) activeness of [±voiced].[20]

A new linguistic concept is needed to explain the situation in which the activeness of the same distinctive feature is different for each language. To this end, I propose introducing the 'functional load of

20 These differences are found in the complex plosives as well as the plain plosive.

distinctive feature'. The functional load of distinctive feature is a concept that measures to what extent one distinctive feature discriminates the phonemes in a language. It can be calculated by using the total number of possible contrastive pairs that can be opposed by one distinctive feature as the denominator and the number of actual contrastive pairs as the numerator. As a simple example, consider the plosive inventories in two African languages, Bassossi and Abure.

(3) Plosive inventories in Bassossi and Abure

a.

BI	AL	VE	GL	LV
p, b	t, d	k, g	ʔ	kp, gb

b.

BI	DE	PA	VE	LV
p, b	t̪, d̪	c, ɟ	k	kp, gb

(3a) is an inventory of Bassossi and (3b) of Abure. In both languages, the plosive is articulated at five places, and [±voiced] functions as a distinctive feature. These two languages have four contrastive pairs by [±voiced] at four places of articulation, but different functional loads of distinctive feature. In Bassossi, the glottal plosive cannot have contrast by [±voiced], so the total number of possible contrastive pairs by [±voiced] is four, and the actual number of contrastive pairs is also four: 'p-b, t-d, k-g, kp-gb'. Therefore, the functional load of [±voiced] is '4/4=1.0'. By contrast, in Abure, there can be contrastive pairs by [±voiced] in all five places of articulation. However, due to the absence of a voiced velar plosive, only four contrastive pairs exist, indicating that the functional load of [±voiced] in Abure is '4/5=0.8'.

(3) is only an illustration of a relatively simple case, and additional factors need to be refined to accurately measure the functional load of a distinctive feature. However, this concept can be effectively utilized in phonological typology. Through this approach, typological tendencies can be captured and differences between languages can be classified. The functional load of a distinctive feature can enrich phonological typology alongside the 'contrast hierarchy' proposed by Dresher (2009). These two concepts help us to understand facts that can be difficult to grasp simply by collating the list of distinctive features in different languages.

Returning to the contrast by [±voiced] in the plosive, thus far, I

Table 3-5. Frequency and ratio of the contrast by [±voiced] in the plain plosive (III)

[A]	[B]	(C)	(D)	(E)
BI (p-b)	2,672	61.3%	69.8%	86.1%
DE (t̪-d̪)	639	14.7%	65.2%	94.2%
AL (t-d)	2,323	53.3%	67.5%	94.5%
RE (ʈ-ɖ)	245	5.6%	64.6%	75.9%
PA (c-ɟ)	404	9.3%	69.4%	77.7%
VE (k-g)	2,644	60.7%	62.9%	96.1%
UV (q-ɢ)	31	0.7%	8.3%	73.8%
LV (kp-gb)	404	9.3%	88.0%	92.9%

([A]: place of articulation and contrastive pair, [B]: number of languages with the contrast by [±voiced], [C]: ratio of [B] to total 4,356 languages, [D]: ratio of [B] to languages with the voiceless plain plosive, [E]: ratio of [B] to languages with the voiced plain plosive)

have examined the contrast by [±voiced] according to the number of places of articulation. Next, I will extend the discussion by considering the frequency and ratio of the contrastive pairs. There are eight places of articulation at which contrastive pairs can appear with certain frequency: bilabial, dental, alveolar, retroflex, palatal, velar, uvular, and labiovelar.

In Table 3-5, [B] indicates the number of languages with the contrast pair by [±voiced], and [C], [D], and [E] are the ratios of [B] based on different criteria. The frequency hierarchy of contrastive pairs by the place of articulation is as follows.

(4) Frequency hierarchy of contrastive pairs by the place of articulation
bilabial > velar > alveolar > dental > palatal = labiovelar > retroflex > uvular

The frequency hierarchy in (4) is almost identical to that of the voiced plain plosive shown in Figure 3-2.[21] This trend suggests that the

21 The one exception is that, as shown in Figure 3-2, the palatal voiced plain plosive is more frequent than the labiovelar voiced plain plosive, but in (4), the

higher the frequency of voiced plain plosives, the more likely there is to be a contrast between the voiceless and voiced plosives. Since the frequency of the voiced plain plosive is lower than that of the voiceless plain plosive, it is expected that the number of voiced plain plosives is more important for the existence of the contrastive pairs by [±voiced].

Column [C] in Table 3-5 is the ratio of languages in which the contrastive pairs by [±voiced] appear. The ratio of [C] differs dramatically depending on the place of articulation. In the uvular, only 0.7% of the languages have an opposition between the voiceless and voiced plosives. The ratio for the retroflex, palatal, and labiovelar plosives does not exceed 10%, whereas for the bilabial and velar plosives, the percentage jumps to approximately 60%.

The extreme difference in the ratio of [C] may be related to the high or low frequency of the plosive itself depending on the place of articulation. For example, the frequency of bilabial, alveolar, and velar plosives is much higher than that of other plosives, such as retroflex, palatal, and labiovelar plosives. Additionally, at any place of articulation, the total number of languages (4,356) is set as the denominator. As a result, the ratio of [C] is likely to be directly affected by the frequency of the plosive. The supplemental ratios calculated to avoid this risk are presented in [D] and [E]. They are the result of calculating how many of the languages with voiceless or voiced plain plosives have the contrast by [±voiced] according to the place of articulation. In [D] and [E], instead of using the total number of languages as the denominator, the number of languages with plain plosives in each place of articulation is used as the denominator. A correction such as this prevents the possibility of distortion due to the absolute frequency of the plosive.

Through [D] and [E], some interesting facts are discovered that are not illustrated in [C]. First, in [D], the ratios of languages with the contrast by [±voiced] are similar in most places of articulation. The significant difference seen in [C] is not found in [D]. At the other places of articulation, except for the uvular and labiovelar, there is a contrast by [±voiced] in 60~70% of languages with the voiceless plosive. As shown in Figure 3-3, the relative frequency ratios of the voiced plain plosive in the uvular and labiovelar are too low or too high compared to

---

numbers of contrastive pairs in these two places of articulation are same.

those at other places of articulation, resulting in a significant deviation of the ratio of languages with the contrast by [±voiced] from the average. Excluding these special cases, the ratios of the contrast by [±voiced] in [D] are highly consistent regardless of the place of articulation.

[E] differs from [D] in two respects. One is that the ratio of languages with the contrast by [±voiced] in [E] is higher than in [D] at all places of articulation. In particular, the ratio for the uvular plosive soars from 8.3% in [D] to 73.8% in [E]. This result is natural because the voiced plain plosive, which is the denominator when calculating [E], occurs much less frequently than the voiceless plain plosive, which is the denominator when calculating [D]. [E] clearly shows that the voiced plosive is more likely than the voiceless plosive to imply the presence of contrast by [±voiced].[22] Another difference is that the percentage deviation according to the place of articulation is greater in [E] than in [D]. In [D], except for some places of articulation, the percentage of contrast ranges between 60% and 70%, whereas in [E], the difference in ratio is larger depending on the place of articulation. This result reflects the difference of implicational ratios in Table 5-4.[23]

So far, I have reviewed the typological characteristics of the contrast between voiceless and voiced plain plosives. Now, let us turn to the complex plosive. Many complex plosives are very infrequent, so it does not make much sense to consider all the complex plosives. Instead, I will examine the contrast by [±voiced], targeting only those with a certain frequency among the complex plosives in Table 3-2.

Of the many contrastive pairs presented in Table 3-2, only 19 pairs that appear in more than 10 languages are included in Table 3-6 below. The number in parentheses indicates the frequency, i.e., how many languages have the contrastive pair. Compared to the frequency of the plain plosive, that of the complex plosive is very low. It is not phonetically advantageous for the complex plosive to have the contrast by [±voiced].

The contrast by [±voiced] found in Table 3-6 can be summarized

---

22 The reason why the ratio in [E] is not 100% at any place of articulation is that the voiced plosive does not imply the existence of the corresponding voiceless plosive absolutely. The implicational relationships in the plosive are discussed in 5.2.

23 For details, refer to 5.2.

Table 3-6. Contrastive pairs by [±voiced] in the complex plosive

BI	p^h-b^h (103), ^{m}p-^{m}b (83), p^w-b^w (55), p^j-b^j (54)
DE	t̪^{h}- d̪^{h} (67), t̪^{j}-d̪^{j} (22), t̪ˤ-d̪ˤ (12)
AL	t^h-d^h (49), ^{n}t-^{n}d (84), t^w-d^w (14), t^j-d^j (47), tˤ-dˤ (14)
RE	ʈ^h-ɖ^h (75)
PA	c^h-ɟ^h (18), ᶮc-ᶮɟ (11)
VE	k^h-g^h (104), ᵑk-ᵑg (86), k^w-g^w (241), k^j-g^j (55)

as follows. First, the type of complex plosives that have a contrast of [±voiced] is very simple. Among the five types classified in (2) above, only (2a), which is combined with one secondary articulation, is found. There is no other language with the contrast by [±voiced] among the other types. Second, there are restrictions on the type of secondary articulation accompanying the complex plosive. Aspiration and nasalization are frequent, whereas laryngealization and velarization do not appear at all. Labialization, palatalization, and pharyngealization are found in only some places of articulation. Third, no double-articulated plosive is found in Table 3-6. The voiced prenasalized labiovelar plosive /ᵑᵐgb/ appears in 102 languages, but the contrastive pair /ᵑᵐkp : ᵑᵐgb/ appears only in three, so it is not included in Table 3-6. Languages with the contrast by [±voiced] in a complex plosive in which the primary articulation occurs at two places of articulation are rare, the reason for which appears to be articulatory complexity.

3.4. Proportional versus nonproportional opposition

As seen in Chapter 2, the number of places of articulation for the plosive in a language ranges from two to seven. The phonological opposition of the plosive in a language may or may not be consistent at all places of articulation. In other words, some phonological oppositions may be formed in all the possible places of articulation, whereas others may be formed only in some places of articulation. The former can be classified as proportional opposition, and the latter as nonproportional opposition.[24] A simple case of the proportional and nonproportional opposition is as follows.[25]

(5) Examples of the proportional and nonproportional opposition

a.

BI	AL	VE	LV
p, b, ^{m}b	t, d, ^{n}d	k, g, ^{ŋ}g	kp, gb, ^{ŋm}gb

b.

BI	AL	VE	LV
p, b, ^{m}b	t, d, ^{n}d	k, g, ^{ŋ}g	kp, gb

(5a) is an inventory of the plosive in Kuo and (5b) in Kwakum.[26] The inventory of the plosive in the two languages is similar in both the place of articulation and the type of opposition. Kuo has a proportional opposition in which the voiceless plain plosive, the voiced plain plosive, and the voiced prenasalized plosive appear in all four places of articulation. Kwakum is similar, but its opposition is nonproportional because it does not appear in the labiovelar. The voiced prenasalized plosive is missing in the labiovelar.

As mentioned earlier in the discussion of the contrast by [±voiced], a phonological opposition does not show contrastive pairs for all possible candidates in the language. There are many cases where the phonological opposition is formed only in some phonemes and not in other phonemes. A proportional phonological opposition is formed in all candidates of a language and a nonproportional opposition in only some candidates. I will examine whether the phonological oppositions related to the manner of articulation for the plosive are proportional or nonproportional. This distinction is relevant to the functional load of distinctive feature proposed earlier. In languages with a proportional opposition, the functional load of distinctive feature is very high, whereas it is bound to be relatively low in languages with nonproportional opposition.

For the proportional opposition to be formed, there must be at least two plosives in one place of articulation. Therefore, languages in which

24 This is slightly different from the proportional opposition in the European structural phonology which divides the types of opposition into proportional and isolated oppositions.

25 An extreme examples belonging to these two types of opposition are presented in 5.5.

26 Both languages belong to the Volta-Congo, a subfamily of the Atlantic-Congo language family, and are not very distant regionally.

Table 3-7. Number of languages with proportional opposition

[B] \ [A]	2	3	4	5	6	Total
2	5	890	347	85	7	1,334
3	0	203	116	25	0	344
4	1	59	74	18	1	153
5	0	5	1	0	0	6
Total	6	1,157	538	128	8	1,837

([A]: number of places of articulation, [B]: number of opposed members)

only one plosive appears in each place of articulation should be excluded from discussion. There are approximately 560 languages among the 4,356 languages. The following results illustrate the ratios of proportional and nonproportional opposition of the plosive in the remaining languages.

Table 3-7 shows the frequency of languages according to the number of places of articulation and opposed members, targeting only the 1,837 languages with proportional opposition. Less than half of the languages in which two or more plosives appear in at least one place of articulation show proportional opposition.[27] In other languages that are not included in Table 3-7, the phonological opposition of the plosive is formed inconsistently depending on the place of articulation.

In Table 3-7, the number of places of articulation in which proportional opposition occurs ranges from two to six, and the number of opposed members ranges from two to five. These figures are lower than those of all plosives. For example, the number of places of articulation for the plosive ranges from a minimum of two to a maximum of seven, whereas Table 3-7 shows a maximum number of six. This difference is particularly noticeable in the number of opposed members. As we will see in more detail in Chapter 4, there can be up to 13 opposed members of the plosive in one place of articulation. However, in Table 3-7, the maximum number is limited to five.[28] As the number of opposed

27 Of the 3,796 languages remaining after the exclusion of 560 languages, 1,837 show proportional opposition, so the correct percentage is 48.4%.

28 Depending on how to handle the release type of the plosive, there can be one language in which the six opposed members show the proportional opposition. For details, refer to Diandongbei-Large Flowery Miao in Table 5-45.

members increases, it becomes increasingly difficult to show proportional opposition at all possible places of articulation. Therefore, it is natural that the number of opposed members of the plosive is limited in languages with proportional opposition.

In Table 3-7, the majority of languages (shaded cells) have three or four places of articulation and two or three opposed members. Outside this range, the proportion of languages that meet the conditions decreases considerably. A total of 890 languages have two opposed members appearing at three places of articulation, which is close to 50% of the 1,837 languages included in Table 3-7. In cases where the number of places of articulation is the same, types with fewer opposed members generally appear in more languages. Thus, the smaller the number of opposed members is, the more advantageous it is to have proportional opposition.

In Table 3-7, the plosive inventories are not the same simply because the languages belong to the same group. Even for languages with the same number of places of articulation and opposed members, the inventory can vary. For example, although a language may have two opposed members, the opposition between them can be formed by [±voiced] or [±aspirated]. If there are four places of articulation, the combination of the places of articulation may be different. There are various patterns of the plosive inventory for each cell in Table 3-7, although certain patterns tend to be preferred over others. This topic will be dealt with in 5.3.

3.5. Types of secondary articulation

There are 293 types of the plosives, and secondary articulation plays a large role in this diversity. Many of the complex plosives are accompanied by secondary articulation. Therefore, it is important to examine secondary articulation carefully to understand the manner of articulation for the plosive.

Several types of secondary articulations may be added to the plain plosive, and as will be seen in 3.6, a few complex plosives may be accompanied by two or three secondary articulations. This section will consider the types of secondary articulation in detail. There are seven types of secondary articulation: aspiration, nasalization, labialization,

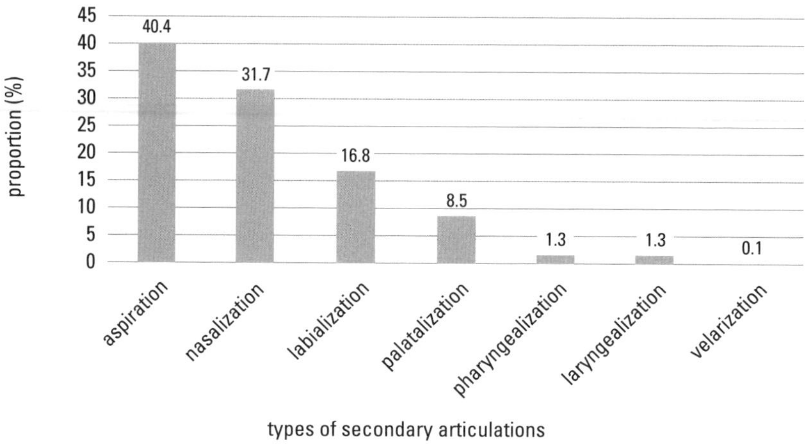

Figure 3-6. Proportion of secondary articulations

palatalization, pharyngealization, laryngealization, and velarization. The order presented here is consistent with the frequency ranking of secondary articulations.

The ratio in Figure 3-6 is calculated by using the total frequency of the complex plosives with secondary articulations as the denominator, and the frequency of the complex plosives with which each type of secondary articulation is combined as the numerator. The proportion of the seven secondary articulations shows considerable variation. Aspiration and nasalization combined exceed 70% of the total, whereas complex plosives accompanied by pharyngealization, laryngealization, and velarization are far less numerous. I will next take a closer look at each secondary articulation in order of frequency.

3.5.1. Aspiration

Aspiration is a secondary articulation in which a puff of breath is added to the edge of the primary articulation. The characteristics of aspiration are well represented in the so-called voice onset time (VOT). The voiced sound adjacent to the aspirated plosive has a lag in VOT due to the aspiration. In particular, the lag in the VOT of the voiced sound that follows the aspirated plosive is well known. Aspiration can be placed at the front or back of the primary articulation.[29] The former is called preaspiration and the latter postaspiration. Most aspirated plosives have the postaspiration, which is why aspiration mainly affects the VOT of the voiced sound that follows the aspirated consonant. However, there are also plosives in which aspiration is realized at the beginning of the primary articulation.[30]

(6) Languages with preaspirated plosives
  a. Atikamekw, Bonan, Michif, Pite Saami, Zhongu: /^{h}p, ^{h}t, ^{h}k/
  b. Osage: /^{h}p, ^{h}t̪, ^{h}k/

In (6), a list of languages with preaspirated plosives is presented with the inventory of the preaspirated plosives. Just six languages have the preaspirated plosive as a phoneme.[31] Five of these languages have the same preaspirated plosives, as shown in (6a), and the other language is represented in (6b). Ignoring the difference between the dental and alveolar, all six languages share three voiceless preaspirated plosives at the major places of articulation. There are no reports of languages in which preaspirated plosives appear in minor places of articulation, such as the retroflex, palatal, or uvular.

All of the preaspirated plosives are voiceless. The voiced plosive is not accompanied by preaspiration. Postaspiration combines with the voiced plosive to form a complex plosive such as /b^{h}, d^{h}, g^{h}/, but preaspiration cannot. In addition, postaspiration can be combined with other secondary articulations to produce a more complicated complex plosive, whereas preaspiration cannot. As such, the possible types of preaspirated plosives are very limited compared to the postaspirated plosives.

Bonan, Osage, and Zhongu in (6) deserve attention for their

29 Depending on the position of the aspiration, its diacritic '^{h}' is added in the front or back of the consonant.

30 Preaspirated plosives affect the VOT of the voiced sounds that precede them.

31 According to Chasaide (1985), Icelandic, Scottish Gaelic, and Irish have preaspirated plosives. Ladefoged & Maddieson (1996: 70) also mentions Scottish Gaelic, Icelandic, and Faroese as representative languages with preaspirated plosives based on research conducted before the 1990s. However, Stewart (2004) and Árnason (2011), which were published in the 2000s and referenced in this book, do not set the preaspirated plosives of these languages as phonemes.

preaspirated plosives. In these languages, preaspirated and postaspirated plosives exist as separate phonemes. In other words, there are two contrasting types of aspirated plosives, depending on the position of the aspiration. This unique phonemic contrast was little known before.[32] Thus, Blevins (2004: 91) argued that these two types of aspirated plosives need not be distinguished at the phonemic level. Although this contrast is present in only a few languages, it is very interesting, particularly as Bonan, Osage, and Zhongu have little relation in terms of language family.

The aspirated plosive is the most common among the complex plosives, representing more than 40% of the total in Figure 3-6. Moreover, 65 types of complex plosives are accompanied by aspiration, which is much more numerous than complex plosives combined with other secondary articulations. The list of the aspirated plosives is summarized in Table 3-8 according to the five types of (2) in 3.2.

There are a variety of types of aspirated complex plosives. The most diverse aspirated plosives are type-(b), followed by type-(a). There are few aspirated plosives in type-(c, e). However, most of the high-frequency aspirated plosives in Table 3-9 belong to type-(a). The type-(a) aspirated plosives represent approximately 92% of the total aspirated plosives. In other words, the type-(a) aspirated plosives account for more than nine of ten aspirated plosives in languages worldwide.

Table 3-8. List of aspirated plosives

a.	Single secondary articulation	p^{h}, b^{h}, ${}^{h}p$, t̪^{h}, d̪^{h}, ${}^{h}\text{t̪}$, t^{h}, d^{h}, ${}^{h}t$, ʈ^{h}, ɖ^{h}, ȶ^{h}, c^{h}, ɟ^{h}, k^{h}, g^{h}, ${}^{h}k$, q^{h}, ɢ^{h}, ʔ^{h}, kp^{h}, gb^{h}
b.	Multiple secondary articulations	p^{hw}, p^{hj}, ${}^{m}p^{h}$, ${}^{m}b^{h}$, ${}^{m\text{ʔ}}p^{h}$, ${}^{m}p^{jh}$, t̪^{hw}, t̪^{hj}, ${}^{n}\text{t̪}^{h}$, ${}^{n}\text{d̪}^{h}$, t^{hw}, t^{hj}, ${}^{n}t^{h}$, ${}^{n}d^{h}$, ${}^{n\text{ʔ}}t^{h}$, ${}^{n}t^{hj}$, ${}^{\text{ɳ}}\text{ʈ}^{h}$, ${}^{\text{ɳ}}\text{ɖ}^{h}$, ȶ^{hw}, c^{hw}, ${}^{\text{ɲ}}c^{h}$, ${}^{\text{ɲ}}\text{ɟ}^{h}$, k^{hw}, k^{hj}, k^{hwj}, ${}^{\text{ŋ}}k^{h}$, ${}^{\text{ŋ}}g^{h}$, ${}^{\text{ŋ}}k^{hw}$, ${}^{\text{ŋ}}k^{hj}$, q^{hw}, q^{hj}, ${}^{\text{N}}q^{h}$, ${}^{\text{N}}\text{ɢ}^{h}$, ${}^{\text{N}}q^{hw}$
c.	Glottal action	t̤^{h}, k̤^{h}
d.	Liquid-colored release	p^{hl}, p^{hr}, ${}^{m}p^{hl}$, t^{hl}, ${}^{n}t^{hl}$, k^{hl}, k^{hr}
e.	Tenseness	none

32 The languages in which preaspirated and postaspirated plosives exist as allophones of one phoneme were known before. Blevins (2004: 90) took Icelandic and Uduk (=Twampa) as examples.

The type-(c) aspirated plosives are found only in Chantyal, which belongs to the Sino-Tibetan language family. According to Noonan (2005: 3), Chantyal has a very specific opposition in the plosive with the involvement of three laryngeal features: vibration of the vocal folds, aspiration, and breathiness.[33] For example, velar plosives, which are the most complex in Chantyal, include a voiceless plain plosive (k), a voiced plain plosive (g), a voiceless aspirated plosive (k^h), a voiceless breathy voice (k̤), a voiced breathy voice (g̈), a voiceless aspirated breathy voice (k̤^{h}). In most languages, the breathy voice consonant is realized as voiced, but in Chantyal, the voiced and voiceless breathy-voice plosives form a phonological opposition. This situation is so unique that it is difficult to find other examples. Adding aspiration to breathy voice with complicated phonation type by glottal action places a tremendous burden on articulation. Therefore, it is natural that type-(c) aspirated plosives are rare.

The type-(d) aspirated plosive is characterized by its liquid-colored release. The complex plosives in type-(d) are so infrequent that they appear only in five or fewer languages. There is no aspirated plosive belonging to type-(e). Fortis plosives such as /pp, tt, kk/ are accompanied by tension in the larynx, and as a result, there seems to be no aspirated fortis plosive.

The high-frequency aspirated plosives among the complex plosives in Table 3-8 are shown in Table 3-9. Table 3-9 shows the ranking and proportions of each aspirated plosive based on how many languages have each one. The most frequent aspirated plosive, /k^h/, appears in 831 of the 4,356 languages, or approximately one-fifth. The top five aspirated plosives comprise more than 70% of the total, and the rest have a very small proportion. For example, even if the percentages of aspirated plosives from the 11th to 20th are summed, that figure does not approach any one of the top three. In addition, only the top three aspirated plosives appear in more than 10% of the 4,356 languages.

All top 10 aspirated plosives in Table 3-9 are type-(a) plosives in Table 3-8. Among the type-(b) aspirated plosives in Table 3-8, /k^{hw}/ occupies the highest proportion at 1.6%, whereas the other type-(b)

33 In Noonan (2005: 3), 'breathy voice' is referred to as 'murmured', but the two can be regarded as the same.

Table 3-9. High-frequency aspirated plosives

Ranking	Plosive	Frequency	Percentage
1	k^{h}	831	22.8%
2	p^{h}	784	21.5%
3	t^{h}	644	17.7%
4	t̪^{h}	240	6.6%
5	ʈ^{h}	173	4.7%
6	b^{h}	112	3.1%
7	q^{h}	106	2.9%
8	c^{h}	104	2.9%
9	g^{h}	104	2.9%
10	ɖ^{h}	75	2.1%
11	d̪^{h}	67	1.8%
12	k^{hw}	57	1.6%
13	d^{h}	49	1.3%
14	p^{hj}	29	0.8%
15	k^{hj}	23	0.6%
16	^{m}p^{h}	21	0.6%
16	t^{hj}	21	0.6%
18	^{n}t^{h}	20	0.5%
19	ɟ^{h}	18	0.5%
20	p^{hw}	12	0.3%

aspirated plosives constitute less than 1%. In addition, no type-(c, d) aspirated plosive in Table 3-8 is included in Table 3-9.

The frequency ranking of the aspirated plosives in Table 3-9 is expected to coincide with that of the plain plosives from which the aspiration is removed. However, such does not seem to be the case. The top 10 high-frequency plain plosives are as follows.[34]

(7) Top 10 high-frequency plain plosives
k > p > t > b > g > d > ʔ > t̪ > d̪ > c

34 The list of high-frequency plosives and their proportions are given in 5.1.

When comparing (7) with Table 3-9, except for /k, p, t/ and /k^{h}, p^{h}, t^{h}/, the rankings of the plain and aspirated plosives do not match. There are several good reasons for this discrepancy. The frequency of voiced /b, g, d/ is very high among the plain plosives, but the frequency of aspirated /b^{h}, g^{h}, d^{h}/ is inevitably lower because aspiration much less frequently accompanies the voiced plosive.[35] In addition, the glottal plosive /ʔ/ has difficulty with aspiration accompaniment because it involves closure of the larynx.[36] For these reasons, the frequency rankings of the plain plosives and of corresponding aspirated plosives are difficult to set in parallel.

Now let us examine the number of aspirated plosives in each language. As shown in Table 3-10, 79.3% of all languages have no aspirated plosive. Although aspiration is the most frequent secondary articulation, only approximately 20% of languages have the aspirated plosive as a phoneme. Among languages with the aspirated plosives, the proportion of languages with three or four such phoneme is very high. This seems to be related to the fact that many languages have three or four places of articulation for the plosive. That is, the aspirated plosives tend to be articulated at all of these places in many languages.

Although rare, some languages have more than 10 aspirated plosives. Languages such as Diandongbei-Large Flowery Miao, Hmong Njua, Northern Guiyang Hmong, Northern Huishui Hmong, Hmong Daw, Horned Miao and Western Xiangxi Miao have 12 to 16 aspirated plosives. All of these languages belong to the Hmong-Mien language family located in Asia, and have a large-scale consonant system that

35 For this reason, the relative frequency ratio of the voiced aspirated plosive compared to the voiceless aspirated plosive is much lower than that of the voiced plain plosive compared to the voiceless plain plosive. Adding the ratio of the voiced aspirated plosive to Figure 3-3 to illustrate, the relative frequency ratio of the voiced plosive produces the following:

BI		DE		AL		RE		PA		VE		UV		LB	
b	b^{h}	d̪	d̪^{h}	d	d^{h}	ɖ	ɖ^{h}	ɟ	ɟ^{h}	g	g^{h}	ɢ	ɢ^{h}	gb	gb^{h}
0.79	0.14	0.69	0.28	0.71	0.08	0.85	0.43	0.89	0.17	0.65	0.13	0.11	0.02	0.95	0.67

The value represents the relative frequency ratio of the voiced plosive, given the frequency of corresponding voiceless plosive is '1'. The voiced aspirated plosive is much less frequent than the voiced plain plosive.

36 The aspirated glottal plosive has been reported to exist in only one language, which will be discussed later.

Table 3-10. Number of aspirated plosives in languages

Number of aspirated plosives	Number of languages	Percentage
0	3,453	79.3%
1	33	0.8%
2	62	1.4%
3	371	8.5%
4	201	4.6%
5	77	1.8%
6	32	0.7%
7	19	0.4%
8	68	1.6%
9	4	0.1%
10	19	0.4%
12	4	0.1%
13	2	0.0%
16	1	0.0%

exceeds twice the average of most languages. For reference, an inventory of aspirated plosives in Western Xiangxi Miao, which has the greatest number of aspirated plosives, is as follows.[37]

(8) Aspirated plosives in Western Xiangxi Miao

bilabial	alveolar	velar	uvular
p^h, p^{hj}, $^mp^h$, $^mp^{hj}$	t^h, t^{hj}, $^nt^h$, $^nt^{hj}$	k^h, k^{hj}, $^ŋk^h$, $^ŋk^{hj}$	q^h, q^{hw}, $^Nq^h$, $^Nq^{hw}$

Western Xiangxi Miao has a very special system in which the aspirated plosives have four-way opposition at four places of articulation. The aspirated plosives are combined with other secondary articulations such as nasalization, labialization, and palatalization to create a total of 16 aspirated plosives. Western Xiangxi Miao has 63 consonants, of which 31 consonants are plosives. Approximately half of the plosives are aspirated, forming a unique system that is difficult to find in other

37 The list in (8) is based on the analysis of Sposato (2015: 59).

languages.

Next, I will examine the frequency of aspirated plosives by the place of articulation. Figure 3-7 shows the proportions of the aspirated plosives by the place of articulation based on the frequency of the languages in which these plosives appear. In Figure 3-7, the proportions by place of articulation, from largest to smallest, are 'velar>bilabial>alveolar>dental>retroflex>uvular>palatal...'. This order is generally consistent with the order of proportion or frequency for the plosive shown in Figure 2-1 or Figure 2-2.

However, there are two distinct differences. One is that the glottal plosive is rarely accompanied by aspiration. Glottal plosives are not uncommon, as seen in Figure 2-1 and 2-2, but the glottal aspirated plosive has been reported to occur only in Wuding-Luquan Yi, a member of the Sino-Tibetan language family. There is a clear articulatory reason for this rarity. In the articulation of the glottal plosive, closure of the larynx occurs, which reduces the size of the glottis and the amount of airflow. It is very difficult to realize aspiration under this condition. The aspirated glottal plosive requires two incompatible actions of the vocal folds, so it cannot be expected to appear in many languages.[38]

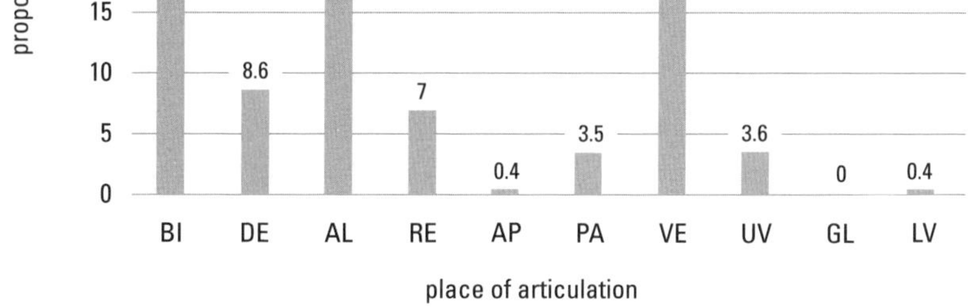

Figure 3-7. Proportion of aspirated plosives by place of articulation

38 In this respect, Wuding-Luquan Yi is a very special exception. According to Namkung (1996: 231), Wuding-Luquan Yi has both the glottal plain plosive /ʔ/ and the glottal aspirated plosive /ʔʰ/.

Another difference is that in the labiovelar plosive, which is a double-articulated plosive, the rate at which aspiration accompanies the plosive is very low. As shown in Figure 3-2, the frequency of the labiovelar plain plosive is higher than that of the retroflex plain plosive, but the overall proportion of the aspirated labiovelar plosive is significantly lower than that of the aspirated retroflex plosive in Figure 3-7. The labiovelar plosive is very rarely combined with other secondary articulations except for nasalization. This characteristic suggests that there may be phonetic reasons for preventing the double-articulated plosive from being accompanied by secondary articulation.

Finally, a few comments must be made on the voiced aspirated plosive. First, the voiced aspirated plosive is phonetically similar to the voiced breathy-voice plosive. Therefore, depending on the discussion, two types of plosives may or may not be distinguished. For this reason, consonants that are almost the same phonetically are analyzed as a voiced aspirated plosive or a voiced breathy-voice plosive for each language. Incorporating the breathy-voice plosive into the voiced aspirated plosive increases both the frequency and proportion of the voiced aspirated plosive.[39] However, this book accepts the original phonological analysis as it is, and draws a distinction between the voiced aspirated plosive and the voiced breathy-voice plosive.

Second, languages with the voiced aspirated plosive are biased by language family and region. The voiced aspirated plosive is concentrated in the Indo-European and Sino-Tibetan language families. In the Atlantic-Congo, the largest language family, only a few languages, including Okpamheri, have the voiced aspirated plosive. Moreover, for the Austronesian language family, which is similar to the Atlantic-Congo in size, none of the more than 700 languages included in the survey have the voiced aspirated plosive. The distributional bias according to the language family is clear. Regionally, the voiced aspirated plosive appears mainly in Asian languages.

Third, many of the languages with the voiced aspirated plosive have a four-way opposition in the manner of articulation for the plosive. That

39 For example, /d̤/ and /g̈/ appear in 16 and 18 languages, respectively, so when they are incorporated into $/d^h/$ and $/g^h/$, the ranking of $/d^h, g^h/$ in Table 3-9 becomes higher.

is, they have a phonological opposition of 'voiceless unaspirated : voiced unaspirated : voiceless aspirated : voiced aspirated', formed by the combination of two distinctive features, [±voiced] and [±aspirated]. The voiced aspirated plosive implies the existence of a specific four-way opposition.[40] There are only a few exceptional languages to this tendency, such as Nyangbo, Southern Mfumte, and Tafi.[41] These languages have only /b^h/ as a voiced aspirated plosive. Voiceless aspirated plosives do not appear in these languages at all. Therefore, it is highly likely that these languages did not originally have phonological opposition by [±aspirated]. The fact that these languages are spoken in Africa, not Asia, also supports this assumption. As seen above, voiced aspirated plosives are common in Asian languages.

3.5.2. Nasalization

Nasalization is a secondary articulation in which a nasal color is added to the edge of primary articulation through the fall of the velum. Nasalization is superimposed mainly in vowels, but can be combined with the consonant as a secondary articulation. Nasalization accompanying the plosive is commonly placed in front of the primary articulation, and the resulting complex plosive can be called a prenasalized plosive. Most of the complex plosives with nasalization fall into this type. However, a very few languages have a postnasalized plosive where nasalization is added to the back of the primary articulation.[42] According to Shimizu (1979: 21), in pronouncing postnasalized plosives, the release of velic closure precedes that of oral closure.[43] Postnasalized plosives are also

40 This is very interesting in that the individual phoneme implies the existence of multi-way opposition beyond that of other phonemes.

41 All of these languages are spoken in western Africa near the equator, so they are relatively close geographically.

42 Nasalization is marked by a superscript of the nasal stop where the primary articulation is made. Depending on the position of nasalization, its diacritic is added in front or back.

43 According to Laver (1994: 227~228), stops can be classified into the following six categories according to the velic state: simplex oral stop, simplex nasal stop, complex prenasal oral stop, complex postnasal oral stop, complex preoccluded nasal stop, and complex postoccluded nasal stop. Among them, the complex prenasal oral stop corresponds to the prenasalized plosive and the complex postnasal oral stop to the postnasalized plosive.

called nasally released plosives, and there are approximately five known languages with such plosives as a phoneme.

(9) Languages with the postnasalized plosive
 a. Mumuye: /b^{m}, t^{n}, d^{n}, $gb^{ŋm}$/
 b. Nemi: /p^{m}, p^{mw}, t^{n}, $c^{ɲ}$, $k^{ŋ}$/
 c. Pangseng: /b^{m}, t^{n}/
 d. Gaa: /$k^{ŋ}$, $g^{ŋ}$/
 e. Iatmul: /$k^{ŋ}$/

The number of postnasalized plosives in (9) varies by language. Nemi has five postnasalized plosives, whereas Iatmul has only one. No language has been found with a phonological opposition solely by the position of nasalization. For example, Iatmul has both the prenasalized plosive /^{ŋ}g/ and the postnasalized plosive /$k^{ŋ}$/, but these two nasalized plosives are not contrasted only by the position of nasalization because they also differ in [±voiced]. In other languages, either the prenasalized plosive or postnasalized plosive appears at one place of articulation. The languages in (9a, c, d) belong to the Atlantic-Congo language family and are spoken in eastern Nigeria. However, the languages in (9b, e) do not have much in common in terms of language family and are completely different from those in (9a, c, d).

The frequency and proportion of the nasalized plosive is the second highest after aspirated plosives among complex plosives with secondary articulation. In addition, there are 91 types of nasalized plosives, reflecting considerably more diversity than the aspirated plosives, which have only 65 types. The list of nasalized plosives is summarized in Table 3-11 according to the five types of (2) in 3.2.

The nasalized plosives in Table 3-11 are the most diverse of the complex plosives accompanied by secondary articulation. The most nasalized plosives appear in type-(b), followed by type-(a), but the overall proportion is the highest in type-(a) at 86.5%. This pattern is not significantly different from the aspirated plosive. The fact that the nasalized plosives do not appear much in type-(c) and that there is no nasalized plosive in type-(e) are also akin to the aspirated plosive. The type-(d) nasalized plosive is more diverse than that of the aspirated plosive.

Type-(c) nasalized plosives are found only in Chopi, a language

Table 3-11. List of nasalized plosives

a.	Single secondary articulation	^{m}p, ^{m}b, ^{ŋ}b, p^{m}, b^{m} ^{n}t̪, ^{n}d̪, ^{n}t, ^{n}d, t^{n}, d^{n}, ^{ɳ}ʈ, ^{ɳ}ɖ, ^{n}ᶑ, ^{ɲ}c, ^{ɲ}ɟ, c^{ɲ}, ^{ŋ}k, ^{ŋ}g, k^{ŋ}, g^{ŋ}, ^{N}q, ^{N}ɢ, ^{N}ʔ, ^{ŋm}kp, ^{ŋm}gb, gb^{ŋm}, ^{mn}bd
b.	Multiple secondary articulations	^{m}p^{h}, ^{m}b^{h}, ^{mʔ}p, ^{mʔ}p^{h}, ^{m}p^{w}, ^{m}b^{w}, ^{m}p^{j}, ^{m}b^{j}, ^{m}p^{hj}, p^{mw}, ^{n}t̪^{h}, ^{n}d̪^{h}, ^{n}t̪^{j}, ^{n}d̪^{j}, ^{n}t̪^{w}, ^{n}d̪^{w}, ^{n}t^{h}, ^{n}d^{h}, ^{nʔ}t, ^{nʔ}d, ^{nʔ}t^{h}, ^{n}t^{w}, ^{n}d^{w}, ^{n}t^{j}, ^{n}d^{j}, ^{n}t^{hj}, ^{ɳ}ʈ^{h}, ^{ɳ}ɖ^{h}, ^{ɳʔ}ʈ, ^{ɲ}c^{h}, ^{ɲ}ɟ^{h}, ^{ŋ}k^{h}, ^{ŋ}g^{h}, ^{ŋʔ}k, ^{ŋʔ}g, ^{ŋ}k^{w}, ^{ŋ}g^{w}, ^{ŋ}k^{j}, ^{ŋ}g^{j}, ^{ŋ}k^{hw}, ^{ŋ}k^{hj}, ^{ŋ}g^{wj}, ^{N}q^{h}, ^{N}ɢ^{h}, ^{N}q^{w}, ^{N}q^{hw}, ^{N}ʔ^{w}
c.	Glottal action	^{m}b̤, ^{n}d̤, ^{ŋ}g̈
d.	Liquid-colored release	^{m}p^{l}, ^{m}b^{l}, ^{m}p^{hl}, ^{m}b^{r}, ^{n}d̪^{r}, ^{n}d̪^{rw}, ^{n}d^{r}, ^{n}d^{rw}, ^{n}t^{l}, ^{n}d^{l}, ^{n}t^{hl}, ^{ŋ}g^{r}, ^{ŋm}gb^{r}
e.	Tenseness	none

of the Atlantic-Congo language family in Africa. According to Nurse & Philippson (2003: 615), Chopi has a very complicated plosive system that employs the opposition of aspiration, nasalization, and breathiness.[44]

(10) Plosive inventory of Chopi

	BI	AL	VE
PL	p, p^{h}, b̤, ^{m}b, ^{m}b̤	t, t^{h}, d̤, ^{n}d, ^{n}d̤	k, k^{h}, g̈, ^{ŋ}g, ^{ŋ}g̈

In Chopi, there is a proportional five-way opposition at the three places of articulation. Moreover, there are not only many opposed members, but also a unique type of phonological opposition. That is, three voiced plosives are phonologically contrasted by nasalization and breathiness. In addition, both voiceless and voiced plosives appear, but there are no contrastive pairs that are opposed only by [±voiced]. This system is seldom found in other languages. As reviewed in Chapter 5, the most common phonological opposition in the plosive is formed by [±voiced]. Although Chopi has as many as five opposed plosives in each place of articulation, there is no contrastive pair by [±voiced].

The high-frequency plosives among the nasalized plosives in Table 3-11 are shown in Table 3-12, which contains the same contents as in Table 3-9. Like the aspirated plosive, a few of the top-level plosives account for most of the total, and the type-(a) complex plosives in Table

44 Chopi has three implosive stops in addition to the plosives of (10).

Table 3-12. High-frequency nasalized plosives

Ranking	Plosive	Frequency	Percentage
1	^{m}b	608	21.2%
2	^{ŋ}g	592	20.7%
3	^{n}d	550	19.2%
4	^{ŋ}k	122	4.3%
5	^{m}p	117	4.1%
6	^{n}t	114	4.0%
7	^{ŋm}gb	102	3.6%
8	^{ŋ}g^{w}	96	3.4%
9	^{ɲ}ɟ	84	2.9%
10	^{n}d̪	80	2.8%
11	^{m}b^{w}	43	1.5%
12	^{ŋ}k^{h}	23	0.8%
13	^{m}p^{h}	21	0.7%
14	^{n}t^{h}	20	0.7%
15	^{ɲ}c	19	0.7%
16	^{n}ɖ	17	0.6%
16	^{n}t̪	16	0.6%
18	^{n}d^{j}	16	0.6%
19	^{m}b^{j}	14	0.5%
20	^{ŋ}g^{j}	12	0.4%

3-11 have a high frequency. However, there is one remarkable difference between the nasalized plosives in Table 3-12 and the aspirated plosive in Table 3-9. Among the nasalized plosives, the frequency of voiced plosives is much higher than that of voiceless plosives. This is the complete opposite of the aspirated plosive. In Table 3-9, the top five aspirated plosives are all voiceless and account for more than 70% of the total. By contrast, in Table 3-12, all the top three nasalized plosives are voiced and constitute more than 60% of the total.

This characteristic is revealed even by directly comparing the frequency of the voiced and voiceless nasalized plosives. For example, in contrastive pairs such as '^{m}p : ^{m}b', '^{n}t : ^{n}d', and '^{ŋ}k : ^{ŋ}g', the frequency of the voiced nasalized plosive is almost fivefold higher than that of the voiceless nasalized plosive. As seen in Figure 3-3 and footnote 87, generally, the frequency of the voiced plosive is much lower than that of the voiceless plosive, whereas the voiced nasalized plosive has a predominantly higher frequency than the voiceless opposite. This trend seems to be closely related to the fact that nasalization as a secondary articulation is phonetically similar to nasal consonants, which, similarly to other sonorant consonants, are generally realized with the vibration of the vocal folds. Therefore, voiced plosive have more advantages than voiceless plosives when accompanied by nasalization.[45]

Now let's look at the number of nasalized plosives each language has. As shown in Table 3-13 below, 84.4% of languages have no nasalized plosive. This is a higher value compared to the aspirated plosive whose percentage of absence is 79.3%. The lower the frequency and proportion of certain secondary articulation, the higher the proportion of languages that do not have a plosive accompanied by such secondary articulation. Among languages with nasalized plosives, the proportion of languages with three or four is very high, which is similar to the aspirated plosive.

Nasalization is less frequent than aspiration, but the maximum number of nasalized plosives in a language is comparable to that of aspirated plosives. In Table 3-13, there are five languages with more than 15 nasalized plosives. Of these five languages, Western Xiangxi Miao and Diandongbei-Large Flowery Miao belong to the Hmong-Mien language family, and the rest belong to the Atlantic-Congo language family. All of these languages have over 60 consonants and over 30 plosives. There are as many as 20 nasalized plosives in Soga, which is the most of any language.[46]

(11) Nasalized plosives in Soga

Bilabial	Dental	Alveolar	Palatal	Velar
^{m}p, ^{m}b, ^{m}p^{w}, (^{m}b^{w}), ^{m}p^{j}, (^{m}b^{j})	^{n}t̪, ^{n}d̪, ^{n}d̪^{w}, ^{n}d̪^{j}	^{n}t, ^{n}d, ^{n}t^{w}, ^{n}d^{w}, ^{n}t^{j}, ^{n}d^{j}	^{ɲ}c, ^{ɲ}ɟ	^{ŋ}k, ^{ŋ}g, ^{ŋ}k^{w}, ^{ŋ}g^{w}

45 However, in the case of plosives accompanied by both nasalization and aspiration, the voiceless dominate over the voiced. For example, 'mp^{h} (21), nt^{h} (20), ŋk^{h} (23)' are more frequent than 'mb^{h} (3), nd^{h} (4), ŋg^{h} (4)'. This indicates that the phonetic conditions for the realization of aspiration take precedence over those of nasalization.

46 Soga has two marginal phonemes, /^{m}b^{w}, ^{m}b^{j}/. Including these marginal phonemes, there are 22 nasalized plosives in Soga. The list of the nasalized plosives in Soga is based on Nabirye et al. (2016: 220).

Table 3-13. Number of nasalized plosives in languages

Number of nasalized plosives	Number of languages	Percentage
0	3,676	84.4%
1	24	0.6%
2	31	0.7%
3	240	5.5%
4	185	4.2%
5	66	1.5%
6	77	1.8%
7	17	0.4%
8	22	0.5%
9	3	0.1%
10	2	0%
11	1	0%
12	4	0.1%
13	3	0.1%
15~	5	0.1%

The nasalized plosives of Soga in (11) are notable for two reasons. First, Soga has 40 plosives, of which 20 are nasalized plosives, constituting fully 50% of the total plosives.[47] Second, the nasalized plosive has a contrast of [±voiced]. For example, contrastive pairs such as '^{m}p : ^{m}b' and '^{n}t : ^{n}d' appear in (11). This opposition itself is not particularly rare, but it is seldom found that both voiceless and voiced nasalized plosives are opposed at all five places of articulation as in Soga.

Now, I will examine the proportion of nasalized plosives by the place of articulation. Figure 3-8 was created in the same way as Figure 3-7 but with the target changed from the aspirated plosive to the nasalized plosive. Figures 3-7 and 3-8 reflect the same high proportion of the complex plosives at the major places of articulation. Because the glottal plosive has a limitation on its combination with secondary

47 Given that the number of consonants in Soga is 68, the proportion of the plosive itself is also very high. As will be seen in 5.1, the greater the number of consonants in a language, the lower the proportion of the plosive is, but Soga reflects a completely different situation.

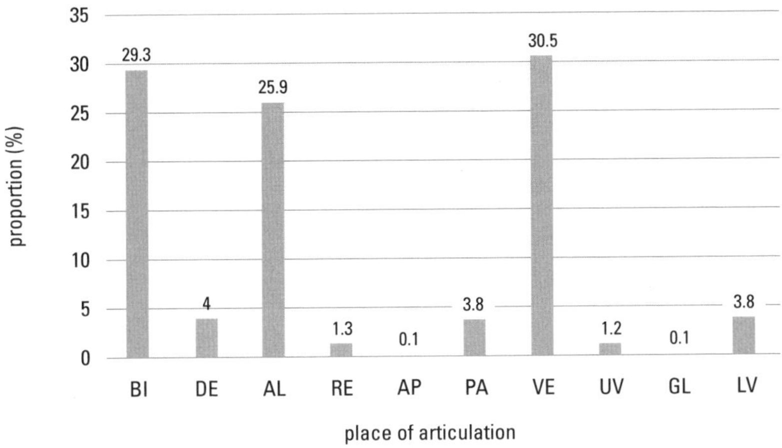

Figure 3-8. Proportion of nasalized plosives by place of articulation

articulations, the proportion of the glottal nasalized plosive in Table 3-8 is very low. In addition, the proportion of the retroflex nasalized plosive is also low compared to that of the retroflex plain plosive.

Finally, I would like to briefly deal with a very special nasalized plosive. The place of nasalization as a secondary articulation and the place of the primary articulation are homorganic. This trait is revealed in the IPAs for the nasalized plosive, which are shown in Table 3-11. Here, the place of articulation of diacritics for nasalization coincides with the place of the primary articulation.[48] However, it has been reported that a very specific exception exists in Ngbaka Minagende, a language of the Atlantic-Congo language family. According to Englund (1963: 8), Ngbaka Minagende has the homorganic 'ᵐb' and the heterorganic 'ᵑb' as separate phonemes. Moreover, contrastive pairs parallel to this are also found in the implosive stop.[49] Ngbaka Minagende is the only language that has these incredible contrastive pairs.

48 For convenience, the diacritic of nasalization for the dental nasalized plosive is marked with the alveolar nasal /n/ instead of the dental nasal /n̪/.

49 These contrastive pairs appear only in the bilabial plosive.

3.5.3. Labialization

Labialization is a secondary articulation in which lip rounding is added to the primary articulation. Unlike aspiration or nasalization, it does not matter whether the labialization is placed in the front or back of the primary articulation. There is no case in which phonemes contrast according to the positions of labialization. However, it is customary to add ‘^{w}’, a diacritic of labialization, behind the consonant. Labialized plosives account for 16.8% of the complex plosive accompanied by secondary articulation. This value is never low. There are 60 types of labialized plosives, reflecting slightly less diversity than aspirated plosives. The list of the labialized plosives is summarized in Table 3-14 according to the five types of (2) in 3.2.

The frequency or proportion of the labialized plosive according to the types is not significantly different from that of the aspirated or nasalized plosives. However, it is different from the previous two classes in that there are two type-(e) labialized plosives. Type-(e) is related to the adjustment of the larynx, and unlike aspiration or nasalization, labialization occurs far from the larynx, so it seems that the labialized plosives can exist in type-(e). Nevertheless, each of two type-(e) labialized plosives appears only in one language: /kk^{w}/ in Koalib-Rere and /gg^{w}/ in Northern Paiute.

Among the labialized plosives in Table 3-14, the high-frequency plosives that appear in more than 10 languages are given in Table 3-15. As shown in Table 3-15, there are some characteristics that are not found in the high-frequency aspirated or nasalized plosives. First, the frequency and proportion of /k^{w}/ and /g^{w}/, which are velar plosives, are very high compared to other labialized plosives. In other secondary articulations,

Table 3-14. List of labialized plosives

a.	Single secondary articulation	p^{w}, b^{w}, $t̪^{w}$, $d̪^{w}$, t^{w}, d^{w}, $ʈ^{w}$, $ƫ^{w}$, c^{w}, $ɟ^{w}$, k^{w}, g^{w}, q^{w}, $ɢ^{w}$, $ʔ^{w}$, kp^{w}, gb^{w}
b.	Multiple secondary articulations	p^{hw}, $p^{wɣ}$, $b^{wɣ}$, ${}^{m}p^{w}$, ${}^{m}b^{w}$, ${}^{ʔ}b^{w}$, p^{mw}, $t̪^{hw}$, ${}^{n}t̪^{w}$, ${}^{n}d̪^{w}$, t^{hw}, t^{hj}, d^{hj}, ${}^{ʔ}d^{w}$, ${}^{n}t^{w}$, ${}^{n}d^{w}$, $ƫ^{hw}$, c^{hw}, k^{hw}, $k^{ʔw}$, k^{wj}, g^{wj}, k^{hwj}, ${}^{ŋ}k^{w}$, ${}^{ŋ}g^{w}$, ${}^{ŋ}k^{hw}$, ${}^{ŋ}g^{wj}$, $k^{wʕ}$, q^{hw}, ${}^{ɴ}q^{w}$, ${}^{ɴ}q^{hw}$, $q^{wʕ}$, ${}^{ɴ}ʔ^{w}$
c.	Glottal action	$k̰^{w}$, $g̈^{w}$
d.	Liquid-colored release	$t̪^{rw}$, $d̪^{rw}$, t^{rw}, d^{rw}, ${}^{n}d^{rw}$, k^{lw}
e.	Tenseness	kk^{w}, gg^{w}

Table 3-15. High-frequency labialized plosives

Ranking	Plosive	Frequency	Percentage
1	k^w	562	37.0%
2	g^w	256	16.9%
3	p^w	121	8.0%
4	$^ŋg^w$	96	6.3%
5	b^w	94	6.2%
6	q^w	67	4.4%
7	k^{hw}	57	3.8%
8	$^mb^w$	43	2.8%
9	t^w	37	2.4%
10	$ʔ^w$	24	1.6%
11	d^w	18	1.2%
12	p^{hw}	12	0.8%
13	t̪^{w}	11	0.7%
14	$^nd^w$	11	0.7%
15	$^ŋk^w$	11	0.7%
16	q^{hw}	10	0.7%

the complex plosives at the three major places of articulation (bilabial, alveolar, velar) show a similarly high frequency and proportion. However, in the case of labialization, two labialized velar plosives exceed 50% of the total, and such a case is not found otherwise.

Second, the ranks of complex plosives accompanied by two secondary articulations, such as /$^ŋg^w$, k^{hw}, $^mb^w$/, are relatively high. None of the aspirated plosives with two secondary articulations are in the top 10, and two nasalized plosives with two secondary articulations are. In contrast, there are three labialized plosives with two secondary articulations in the top 10, and their rankings are also higher. The fact that the rank and frequency of plosives accompanying multiple secondary articulations are higher in Table 3-15 is noticeable when compared to Table 3-9 or 3-12.

Third, the labialized glottal plosive is included in the top 10. As we have confirmed several times earlier, the glottal plosive does not favor combination with secondary articulation, and in reality, such complex plosives do not appear frequently. However, the glottal plosive accompanied by labialization poses an exception, as it occurs with relative high frequency.

The next topic for consideration is the number of the labialized plosives in all languages. In Table 3-16, 84.9% of languages have no labialized plosive, which is similar to that of the nasalized plosive (84.4%). The distribution in Table 3-16 reveals a distinct difference from the aspirated and nasalized plosives. For the aspirated and nasalized plosives, languages with three or four plosives occupied the highest proportion. This fact was interpreted to mean that aspirated and nasalized plosives tend to appear in all the major places of articulation including the bilabial, alveolar, and velar. By contrast, in the case of the labialized plosive, the proportion of languages with one or two such plosives is very high. This data suggests that even if there are some labialized plosives in a language, it is very likely that they will not appear at all the major places of articulation. This finding is exactly in line with the fact that in Table 3-15 above and Figure 3-9 below, the labialized plosive is concentrated in a specific place of articulation, i.e., the velar.

Although rare, some languages have more than 10 labialized plosives. The language with the most labialized plosives is Diriku, which has 13.[50]

Table 3-16. Number of labialized plosives in languages

Number of labialized plosives	Number of languages	Percentage
0	3,697	84.9%
1	235	5.4%
2	235	5.4%
3	80	1.8%
4	61	1.4%
5	12	0.3%
6	16	0.4%
7	8	0.2%
8	5	0.1%
9	2	0.0%
10~	5	0.1%

50 Diriku is spoken in south-central Africa. The list of the labialized plosives for Diriku is taken from Möhlig (2005: 24) that clearly demonstrates the phonemic status by presenting the labialized plosives with their minimal pairs.

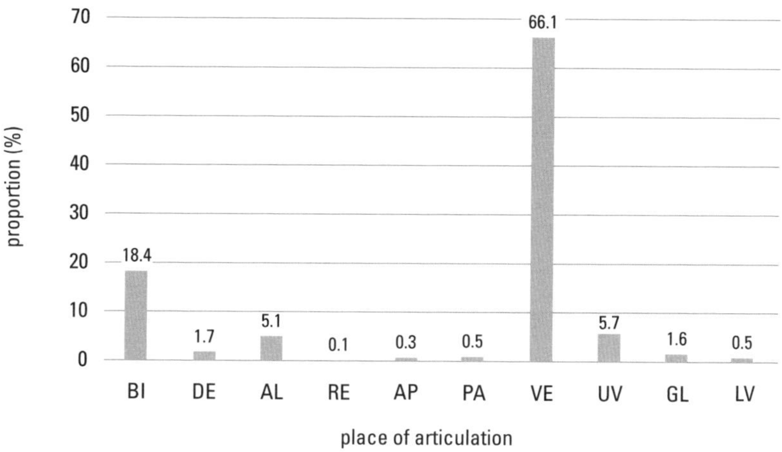

Figure 3-9. Proportion of labialized plosives by place of articulation

(12) Labialized plosives in Diriku

Bilabial	Dental	Alveolar	Velar
p^{w}, b^{w}, $^{m}p^{w}$, $^{m}b^{w}$	t̪^{w}	t^{w}, d^{w}, $^{n}t^{w}$, $^{n}d^{w}$	k^{w}, g^{w}, $^{ŋ}k^{w}$, $^{ŋ}g^{w}$

As shown in (12), Diriku has labialized plosives with four-way opposition at three of the four places of articulation. The four series are opposed by voicedness and nasalization. In addition, there is a dental labialized plosive, so there is a phonological contrast between the dental and alveolar in the labialized plosive.

Now, I will consider the proportion of the labialized plosive by the place of articulation. In Figure 3-9 above, the proportion of the velar labialized plosive is exceptionally high, which is a natural result considering that the velar plosives were ranked first and second in the list of high-frequency labialized plosives (Table 3-15). In general, labialized plosives are common in peripheral zones such as the velar and bilabial, and less in central zones such as the retroflex and palatal. The frequency of the retroflex or palatal plosives itself is not low, but the frequency with which these consonants accompany labialization is very low.

3.5.4. Palatalization

Palatalization is a secondary articulation in which a palatal color is added by raising the front part of the tongue toward the palate while maintaining the primary place of articulation.[51] Palatalization as a secondary articulation needs to be distinguished from palatalization as a phonological rule that changes the primary place of articulation itself. Palatalization as a secondary articulation only causes a change in the height of the tongue, leaving the primary place of articulation as it is. Consonants with palatalization as the secondary articulation are 'palatalized', whereas consonants whose primary place of articulation is changed to the palatal are 'palatal'.

Like labialization, it does not matter whether palatalization is placed in the front or back of the primary articulation, and it is customary to add 'ʲ', a diacritic of palatalization, behind the consonant. It is not that there have been no reports of the existence of prepalatalization occurring in front of the primary articulation. For example, Kaytetye, an Australian language, has many disagreements in phonemic analysis, but the fact that the prepalatalized plosive exists is common in all discussions. According to Brown & Ogilvie (2009: 586), Kaytetye has the prepalatalized nasal and lateral as well as /ʲt/, which is an alveolar prepalatalized plosive. Each of these prepalatalized consonants is opposed to a plain consonant without palatalization. However, there is no known language in which prepalatalized and postpalatalized consonants exist as separate phonemes by the position of palatalization.

Palatalization is a relatively well-known secondary articulation, but it constitutes just 8.5% of complex plosives accompanied by secondary articulation. These values are lower than those of aspiration, nasalization, and labialization. There are 41 types of palatal plosives, which is relatively small compared to the more than 60 types for other plosives previously examined, including the aspirated plosive. The list of palatalized plosives is summarized in Table 3-17 according to the five types of (2) in 3.2.

The list of palatalized plosives in Table 3-17 is relatively simple in terms of quantity and quality. There is no type-(c, d, e) palatalized

51 The front part of the tongue here refers to the laminal vicinity.

Table 3-17. List of palatalized plosives

a.	Single secondary articulation	pʲ, bʲ, t̪ʲ, d̪ʲ, tʲ, dʲ, ʲt, ʈʲ, ɖʲ, cʲ, ɟʲ, kʲ, gʲ, qʲ, ʔʲ, kpʲ, gbʲ
b.	Multiple secondary articulations	pʰʲ, ˀbʲ, ᵐpʲ, ᵐbʲ, ᵐpʰʲ, t̪ʰʲ, ⁿt̪ʲ, ⁿd̪ʲ, tʰʲ, tʷʲ, dʷʲ, ˀdʲ, ⁿtʲ, ⁿdʲ, ⁿtʰʲ, kʰʲ, kʷʲ, gʷʲ, kʰʷʲ, ᵑkʲ, ᵑgʲ, ᵑkʰʲ, ᵑgʷʲ, qʰʲ
c.	Glottal action	None
d.	Liquid-colored release	None
e.	Tenseness	none

plosive. Palatalization cannot be accompanied by complex plosives with glottal action or liquid-colored release. Secondary articulations to be examined later, including palatalization, are infrequent, so these types are, comparatively, very poor.

Among the palatalized plosives in Table 3-17, the high-frequency plosives that appear in more than 10 languages are shown in Table 3-18. As expected, in Table 3-18, the palatalized plosives that occupy the upper ranks are those in which the plain plosive in the major places

Table 3-18. High-frequency palatalized plosives

Ranking	Plosive	Frequency	Percentage
1	tʲ	119	15.5%
2	kʲ	111	14.5%
3	pʲ	92	12.0%
4	gʲ	72	9.4%
5	bʲ	68	8.9%
6	dʲ	57	7.4%
7	t̪ʲ	35	4.6%
8	d̪ʲ	30	3.9%
9	pʰʲ	29	3.8%
10	kʰʲ	23	3.0%
11	tʰʲ	21	2.7%
12	ⁿdʲ	16	2.1%
13	ᵐbʲ	14	1.8%
14	ᵑgʲ	12	1.6%
15	ʔʲ	10	1.3%

of articulation is accompanied by palatalization. The most remarkable feature in Table 3-18 is that many of the alveolar plosives (including dental plosives) are included in the upper ranks: /tʲ/ ranks the highest, and /dʲ, t̪ʲ, d̪ʲ/ also has a relatively high frequency. In the case of other secondary articulations that have been previously examined, the frequency of velar or bilabial plosives is higher than that of alveolar plosives, but in palatalization, the frequency of alveolar plosives is higher.[52]

The next topic for discussion is the extent to which the palatalized plosive appears in all languages. It is shown in Table 3-19. Just as palatalization constitutes a low proportion of secondary articulation, the proportion of languages without any palatalized plosives is 93.3%, much higher than that of other secondary articulations. If a language has a palatalized plosive, it is very likely to have one or two such plosives, similarly to the labialized plosive. However, since the palatalized plosive, unlike the labialized plosive, is not biased toward a specific place of articulation, it is not clear whether the implications are the same.

Few languages have numerous palatalized plosives, but some

Table 3-19. Number of palatalized plosives in languages

Number of palatalized plosives	Number of languages	Percentage
0	4,065	93.3%
1	102	2.3%
2	96	2.2%
3	28	0.6%
4	25	0.6%
5	8	0.2%
6	14	0.3%
7	4	0.1%
8	5	0.1%
9	2	0.0%
10	3	0.1%
11~	4	0.1%

52 In particular, the frequency of the alveolar plosive is very low in labialization.

languages have more than 10. Three (Western Xiangxi Miao, Maang, Maonan) of four languages with 11 or more palatalized plosives, are spoken in Asia. Of these, Maonan has the most palatalized plosives, with 15. According to the analysis by Lu (2008: 79), Maonan has the following palatalized plosives.

(13) Palatalized plosives in Maonan:

Bilabial	Alveolar	Velar
p^j, b^j, p^{hj}, $^mb^j$, $^?b^j$	t^j, d^j, t^{hj}, $^nd^j$, $^?d^j$	k^j, g^j, k^{hj}, k^{wj}, k^{hwj}

In Maonan, five palatalized plosives appear at each of the three major places of articulation. The phonological opposition of the palatalized plosives differs depending on the place of articulation. In the bilabial and alveolar, five-way opposition of the same character appears, but there is a difference in the velar. The plosives common to the three places of articulation are a voiceless palatalized plosive (p^j, t^j, k^j), a voiced palatalized plosive (b^j, d^j, g^j), and a voiceless aspirated palatalized plosive (p^{hj}, t^{hj}, k^{hj}).

Now, I will consider the proportion of the palatalized plosive by the place of articulation. Figure 3-10 shows that the alveolar (including the dental) plosives accounts for the highest percentage of the palatalized

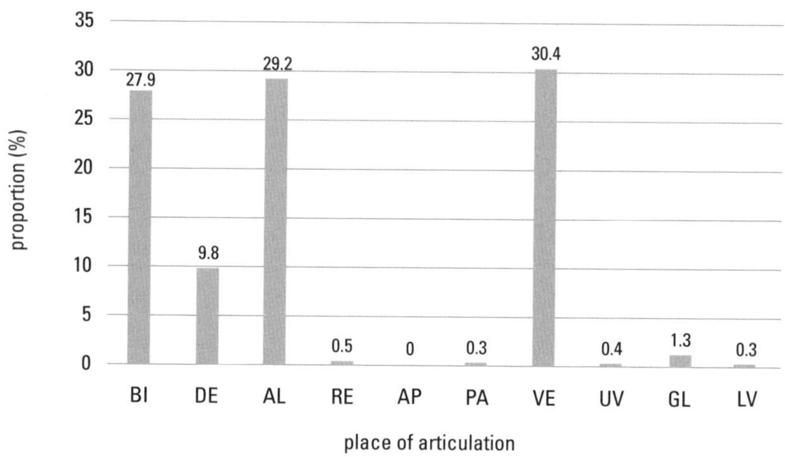

Figure 3-10. Proportion of palatalized plosives by place of articulation

plosives. This result reflects the ranking of the high-frequency palatalized plosives in Table 3-18. However, many palatalized plosives are also found in other major places of articulation, such as the bilabial and velar.

A prominent trend in Figure 3-10 is that the palatalized plosive hardly appears in places other than three major places of articulation, that is, the bilabial, alveolar (including dental), and velar. Of course, in the case of other secondary articulations, these three major places occupy an overwhelmingly high proportion. However, the degree is much more severe in the palatalized plosive.

3.5.5. Pharyngealization

Pharyngealization is a secondary articulation that narrows the passage around the pharynx by contracting the tongue root. Whether pharyngealization precedes or follows primary articulation has no function in discriminating pharyngealized plosives. A representative example of the pharyngealized consonant is the emphatic consonant, which is frequently found in the Semitic language family, a subfamily of the Afro-Asiatic. The phonetic characteristic of the emphatic consonant is sometimes described as occurring through velarization instead of pharyngealization.[53] However, the view that interprets the emphatic consonant as a pharyngealized consonant is more prevalent.

The type and proportion of the pharyngealized plosive are quite limited. The pharyngealized plosive constitutes just 1.3% of complex plosives with secondary articulation, similarly to the laryngealized plosive. However, there are only 13 types of pharyngealized plosives, much fewer than laryngealized plosives. The list of the pharyngealized plosives is summarized in Table 3-20 according to the five types of (2) in 3.2.

In Table 3-20, it is remarkable that the type-(a) pharyngealized plosive is more diverse than type-(b). For the other secondary articulations examined earlier, many more plosives belong to type-(b) than to type-(a), but the pharyngealized plosive does not display such a pattern. This situation is the same for laryngealization and velarization

53 As noted by Laver (1994: 327), the acoustic effects of the velarization and pharyngealization are similar.

Table 3-20. List of pharyngealized plosives

a.	Single secondary articulation	pˤ, bˤ, t̪ˤ, d̪ˤ, tˤ, dˤ, kˤ, gˤ, qˤ, ɢˤ, ʔˤ
b.	Multiple secondary articulations	kʷˤ, qʷˤ
c.	Glottal action	none
d.	Liquid-colored release	none
e.	Tenseness	none

whose frequency is very low, which will be examined later. Through this finding, it seems possible to generalize that type-(b) is more diverse than type-(a) in the case of plosives with high-frequency secondary articulations. If the frequency of secondary articulation is low, such trend is not valid.

Among the pharyngealized plosives in Table 3-20, the high-frequency plosives that appear in more than 10 languages are shown in Table 3-21 below. In Table 3-21, the place of articulation in the high frequency pharyngealized plosives is limited to the dental or alveolar. Pharyngealized plosives in other places of articulation appear in fewer than 10 languages. This restriction on the place of articulation is as severe as that for the labialized plosive.

The number of pharyngealized plosives in each language is shown in Table 3-22, according to which most languages have no pharyngealized plosives. The proportion of languages with one or two pharyngealized plosives is relatively high. The most frequent inventory of the pharyngealized plosive in languages is /tˤ, dˤ/ or /t̪ˤ, d̪ˤ/. For example, eight languages, including Awjilah, contain /t̪ˤ, d̪ˤ/, and 13 languages, including Alfayfiyah, contain /tˤ, dˤ/. Only a few languages have three or more pharyngealized plosives. Khwarshi-Inkhoqwari, a language of the Nakh-Daghestanian language family, has five, which is the most pharyngealized plosives of any language. According to Khalilova (2009: 13), the pharyngealized plosives in Khwarshi-Inkhoqwari are as follows.[54]

(14) Pharyngealized plosives in Khwarshi-Inkhoqwari

BI	VE	UV
pˤ, bˤ	kˤ, gˤ	qˤ

54 Khwarshi-Inkhoqwari also has two pharyngealized ejectives, /p'ˤ/ and /k'ˤ/.

Table 3-21. High-frequency pharyngealized plosives

Ranking	Plosive	Frequency	Percentage
1	tˤ	31	27.4%
2	t̪ˤ	19	16.8%
3	dˤ	17	15.0%
4	d̪ˤ	13	11.5%

Table 3-22. Number of pharyngealized plosives in languages

Number of pharyngealized plosives	Number of languages	Percentage
0	4,298	98.7%
1	20	0.5%
2	27	0.6%
3	6	0.1%
4	4	0.1%
5	1	0%

With regard to the pharyngealized plosive, Khwarshi-Inkhoqwari has two characteristics. One is that Khwarshi-Inkhoqwari belongs to the Nakh-Daghestanian language family, not the Semitic language family where the pharyngealized plosives are most common.[55] The other is that none of the pharyngealized plosives in Khwarshi-Inkhoqwari are dental or alveolar. As seen in Table 3-21, the high-frequency pharyngealized plosives are dental or alveolar, but the pharyngealized plosives in Khwarshi-Inkhoqwari deviate from this trend.

The proportion of the pharyngealized plosives by the place of articulation is presented in Figure 3-11. As mentioned earlier, many pharyngealized plosives are concentrated on the dental or alveolar. The pharyngealized plosive has many restrictions on the place of articulation. There are six places of articulation in which any pharyngealized plosive occurs, which is considerably less than the plosives with other secondary articulations. It is also unusual that uvular pharyngealized plosives

55 The region where Khwarshi-Inkhoqwari is spoken is not far from the region where the languages of the Semitic language family are spoken.

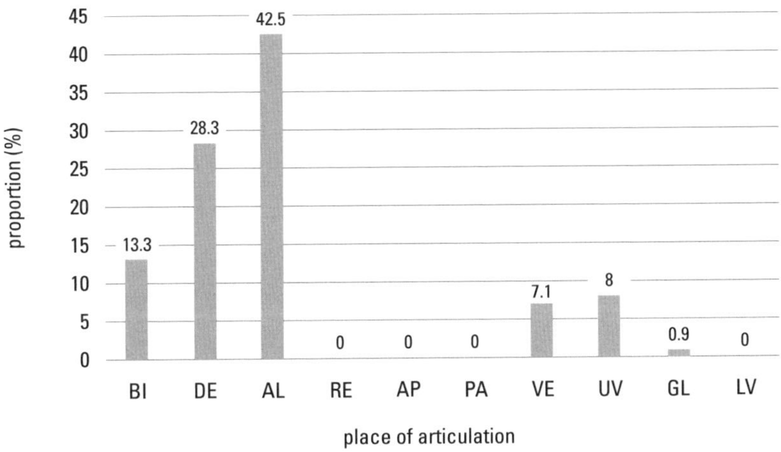

Figure 3-11. Proportion of pharyngealized plosives by place of articulation

are more common than velar pharyngealized plosives. Although the frequency of the uvular plain plosive is significantly lower than that of the velar plain plosive, the pharyngealized plosive is found more often in the uvular.

3.5.6. Laryngealization

Laryngealization is a secondary articulation in which a strong constriction or closure of the larynx is added to the edge of the primary articulation. There is disagreement about the range of laryngealized plosives. The laryngealized plosive may include only the plosive in which the constriction, not closure, of the larynx occurs, or it may include all the plosives in which the constriction or closure of the larynx occurs. In general, a creaky voice is presented as a representative example of a laryngealized consonant, but in this book, only plosives that are accompanied by closure at the larynx or stronger constriction than the creaky voice are included among the laryngealized plosives for the convenience of typological discussion.[56] The addition of 'ˀ', a superscript

56 The creaky voice is classified as a separate category from the secondary articulation.

indicating the glottal plosive, when representing the laryngealized plosive, reflects this view. Laryngealization in this sense is sometimes referred to as glottalization.[57]

The laryngealized plosive occupies a low proportion of the complex plosives with secondary articulation. Additionally, there are very few types of laryngealized plosives, just 28. Moreover, there are only five laryngealized plosives that appear in more than 10 languages. Laryngealization belongs to the minor class among secondary articulations.

Laryngealization can be placed in front or back of the primary articulation. Aspiration is overwhelmingly frequent to be realized behind the primary articulation, whereas nasalization is most common in front of the primary articulation. For the laryngealization, however, both positions are similarly frequent. In any case, there is no language in which two laryngealized plosives are opposed by the position of the laryngealization.

The laryngealization placed in front of the primary articulation is prelaryngealization, and the plosive accompanying such laryngealization is a prelaryngealized plosive.[58] As shown in Table 3-23 below, the prelaryngealized plosives are mostly voiced, and there is a limitation that prelaryngealization can accompany the voiceless plosive only when it is nasalized. That is, the voiceless prelaryngealized plosive is always accompanid by nasalization. Examples are plosives such as /^{mʔ}p, ^{mʔ}p^{h}, ^{nʔ}t, ^{nʔ}t^{h}, ^{ɳʔ}ʈ, ^{ŋʔ}k/, as shown in Table 3-23. There is no exception among the data identified so far. However, it is not easy to clearly distinguish the prelaryngealized plosive from the implosive. Therefore, some of the consonants suggested as prelaryngealized plosive in this book may have to be classified as implosive.

The laryngealization placed behind the primary articulation is postlaryngealization, and the plosive accompanying such laryngealization is a postlaryngealized plosive. The postlaryngealized plosive may be

57 The plosives accompanied by glottalization are commonly referred to as glottalized or glottalic stops. However, caution is required because the glottalized stop may refer to the ejective or implosive instead of the plosive covered in this book. For example, in Campbell (1973: 44), the glottalic consonant encompasses both the ejective and implosive.

58 The terms ‘preglottalization’ and ‘preglottalized stop’ are also frequently used.

Table 3-23. List of laryngealized plosives

a.	Single secondary articulation	pˀ, bˀ, ˀb, t̪ˀ, ˀd̪, tˀ, dˀ, ˀd, ʈˀ, ˀɖ, ˀɟ, kˀ, gˀ, ˀg, qˀ
b.	Multiple secondary articulations	ˀbʲ, ᵐˀp, ᵐˀpʰ, ˀbʷ, ˀdʷ, ˀdʲ, ⁿˀt, ⁿˀtʰ, ⁿˀd, ᶯˀʈ, kˀʷ, ᵑˀk, ᵑˀg
c.	Glottal action	none
d.	Liquid-colored release	none
e.	Tenseness	none

voiceless or voiced. It is difficult to distinguish the postlaryngealized plosive from the ejective. The majority of those phonemes classified as voiceless glottalized plosives in the description of individual languages and not explicitly identified as ejective are nonetheless ejectives rather than laryngealized plosives. This is largely the case with the voiceless glottalized stops in the languages of the indigenous people of North America. The laryngealized plosives in this book are limited to plosives that have been confirmed as neither implosives nor ejectives. For example, Nevin (1998: 53) revealed that Achumawi has laryngealized stops, which are not ejectives.[59] Only these plosives are included among the laryngealized plosives.

The list of laryngealized plosives is summarized in Table 3-23 according to the five types of (2) in 3.2. Like the pharyngealized plosive, the laryngealized plosive appears only in type-(a, b). However, the laryngealized plosive is more diverse than the pharyngealized plosive. In Table 3-23, it is remarkable that type-(a) and type-(b) reflect similar levels of diversity. As mentioned earlier, this pattern deviates the general trend that type-(b) is more diverse than type-(a), and is found in secondary articulation with low frequency, such as pharyngealization and laryngealization.

Among the laryngealized plosives in Table 3-23, the high-frequency plosives that appear in more than 10 languages are shown in Table 3-24 below. Only five laryngealized plosives appear in more than 10

59 In Achumawi, there is a three-way opposition between a voiceless plain plosive, a voiceless aspirated plosive, and a voiceless laryngealized plosive at four places of articulation. The three-way opposition with the same character as Achumawi is found only in a few languages, including Korean.

languages. The most common laryngealized plosive, /ˀb/, is found in 21 languages. Compared to the high-frequency plosives in other secondary articulations, this frequency is very low, and, consequently, the number of laryngealized plosives in each language is also very low.

In Table 3-25, most languages have no laryngealized plosive. Less than 1% of languages have the laryngealized plosive. The proportion of languages with two or three laryngealized plosives is relatively high, but it is difficult to ascribe these any significant meaning because their absolute frequency is very low. Only three languages have more than five laryngealized plosives: Maonan, T'en and Luopohe Hmong, which are found in Asia and are not geographically far from one another. Of these, Luopohe Hmong has six laryngealized plosives, the most of any language. According to Niederer (1998: 112), Luopohe Hmong has the following laryngealized plosives.

(15) Laryngealized plosives in Luopohe Hmong

Bilabial	Alveolar	Retroflex	Velar
ᵐˀp, ᵐˀpʰ	ⁿˀt, ⁿˀtʰ	ᶯˀʈʰ	ᵑˀk

Table 3-24. High-frequency laryngealized plosives

Ranking	Plosive	Frequency	Percentage
1	ˀb	21	18.4%
2	ˀd	16	14.0%
3	kˀ	13	11.4%
4	pˀ	11	9.6%
4	tˀ	11	9.6%

Table 3-25. Number of laryngealized plosives in languages

Number of laryngealized plosives	Number of languages	Percentage
0	4,315	99.1%
1	5	0.1%
2	12	0.3%
3	15	0.3%
4	6	0.1%
5	2	0.0%
6	1	0.0%

Laryngealized plosives in Luopohe Hmong occur at four places of articulation and demonstrate a fairly complicated pattern. No laryngealized plosive is accompanied by laryngealization alone. Nasalization always accompanies laryngealization, and there are even three complex plosives that combine three secondary articulations, that is, aspiration, nasalization, and laryngealization. In addition, it is unusual that Luopohe Hmong has only voiceless prelaryngealized plosives because the prelaryngealized plosives are more often voiced. As such, the laryngealized plosives in Luopohe Hmong are unique.

Finally, the proportion of the laryngealized plosives by the place of articulation is shown in Figure 3-12. Predictably, most laryngealized plosives are found in three major places of articulation: bilabial, alveolar, and velar. Remarkably, however, the velar laryngealized plosive is relatively uncommon. Overall, laryngealization rarely appears in plosives articulated in the back of the oral cavity. This is probably because the back of the oral cavity is close to where laryngealization occurs. If there is little distance between the primary articulation and secondary articulation, it is possible for the phonetic effect of the secondary articulation to be reduced. In addition, the fact that double-articulated plosives are never accompanied by laryngealization cannot be overlooked.

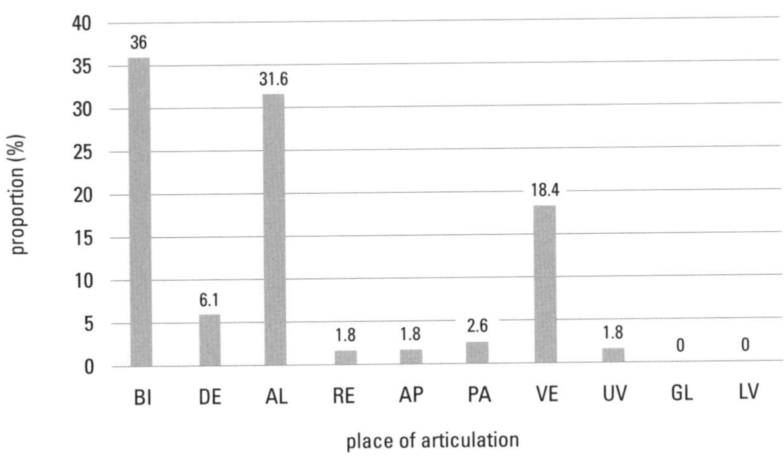

Figure 3-12. Proportion of laryngealized plosives by place of articulation

3.5.7. Velarization

Velarization is a secondary articulation that lifts the back of the tongue toward the velar. Even if velarization occurs, the gap between the tongue and the velar does not become sufficiently narrow to cause a strong stricture. As pointed out earlier, the acoustic effects of velarization are akin to those of pharyngealization because the distance between the velar and pharynx are relatively close, and their articulators, the dorsum and tongue root, are also similar. This commonality is also reflected in the fact that, similarly to pharyngealization, the distribution of velarization is very limited. Despite their similarities, however, there are more restrictions on velarization than pharyngealization.

Only nine languages have at least one velarized plosive, of which six have only one velarized plosive, and the other three have two velarized plosives. There are no known languages with more than three velarized plosives. Five of the nine languages with the velarized plosive belong to the Oceanic language family, which is a subfamily of the Austronesian, and they are spoken in 'Papunesia' among the six macroareas classified by GLOTTOLOG. The four languages that do not belong to this category are Arab languages, and their velarized plosives are so-called emphatic consonants. Therefore, there is ample room to reinterpret their secondary articulation as pharyngealization rather than velarization. Considering this possibility, not only is the frequency of the velarized plosive very low, it is also very biased by the language family and region.

The types and frequency of the velarized plosive are shown in Table 3-26. There are only six types of velarized plosives in Table 3-26, none of which appears in four or more languages.[60] In addition, the place of articulation for the velarized plosive is limited to the front of the oral cavity, such as the bilabial and alveolar (including dental). As a result, the farther away from the velar, the easier for velarization to accompany the plosive. Nonetheless, velarization is so infrequent that there is no need for further discussion here.

60 As before, the numbers in parentheses indicate the number of languages in which the plosive appears.

Table 3-26. Types and frequency of velarized plosives

a.	Single secondary articulation	pˠ(3), t̪ˠ(1), tˠ(3), dˠ(2)
b.	Multiple secondary articulations	pʷˠ(2), bʷˠ(1)
c.	Glottal action	none
d.	Liquid-colored release	none
e.	Tenseness	none

3.6. Types of multiple secondary articulations

In 3.5, I examined the seven types of secondary articulation accompanying the plosive in detail. As confirmed several times, some of the complex plosives are accompanied by two or more secondary articulations, that is, multiple secondary articulations. In this section, only the plosives accompanied by multiple secondary articulations are targeted, and the combination types of secondary articulation will be examined. Multiple secondary articulations can be divided into two categories, i.e. a combination of either two or three secondary articulations. There is no case in which four or more secondary articulations are accompanied by a single plosive. This is fully understandable given the extreme articulatory complexity of such a plosive.

I will now consider the types in which two secondary articulations are combined. The combination of two of the seven secondary articulations can create up to 21 types. The list of complex plosives for each type is as follows. The number in parentheses indicates the number of languages in which the plosive appears.

(16) Combination types of two secondary articulations:
- a. Aspiration + nasalization: ᵐpʰ (21), ᵐbʰ (4), ᵐpʰˡ (2), ⁿt̪ʰ (3), ⁿd̪ʰ (1), ⁿtʰ (20), ⁿdʰ (3), ⁿtʰˡ (1), ᶯʈʰ (6), ᶯɖʰ (2), ᶮcʰ (3), ᶮɟʰ (2), ᵑkʰ (23), ᵑgʰ (4), ᶰqʰ (9), ᶰɢʰ (1)
- b. Aspiration + labialization: pʰʷ (12), t̪ʰʷ (1), tʰʷ (4), ȶʰʷ (2), cʰʷ (1), kʰʷ (57), qʰʷ (10)
- c. Aspiration + palatalization: pʰʲ (29), t̪ʰʲ (2), tʰʲ (21), kʰʲ (23), qʰʲ (1)
- d. Aspiration + laryngealization: none
- e. Aspiration + pharyngealization: none

f. Aspiration + velarization: none

g. Nasalization + labialization: $^{m}\text{p}^{w}$ (5), $^{m}\text{b}^{w}$ (43), p^{mw} (1), $^{n}\text{t̪}^{w}$ (1), $^{n}\text{d̪}^{w}$ (3), $^{n}\text{d̪}^{rw}$ (1), $^{n}\text{t}^{w}$ (2), $^{n}\text{d}^{w}$ (11), $^{n}\text{d}^{rw}$ (1), $^{\text{ŋ}}\text{k}^{w}$ (11), $^{\text{ŋ}}\text{g}^{w}$ (96), $^{\text{N}}\text{q}^{w}$ (1), $^{\text{N}}\text{ʔ}^{w}$ (1)

h. Nasalization + palatalization: $^{m}\text{p}^{j}$ (6), $^{m}\text{b}^{j}$ (14), $^{n}\text{t̪}^{j}$ (1), $^{n}\text{d̪}^{j}$ (7), $^{n}\text{t}^{j}$ (4), $^{n}\text{d}^{j}$ (16), $^{\text{ŋ}}\text{k}^{j}$ (1), $^{\text{ŋ}}\text{g}^{j}$ (12)

i. Nasalization + laryngealization: $^{m\text{ʔ}}\text{p}$ (1), $^{n\text{ʔ}}\text{t}$ (1), $^{n\text{ʔ}}\text{d}$ (1), $^{\text{ŋʔ}}\text{k}$ (1), $^{\text{ŋʔ}}\text{g}$ (1)

j. Nasalization + pharyngealization: none

k. Nasalization + velarization: none

l. Labialization + palatalization: t^{wj} (1), d^{wj} (1), k^{wj} (7), g^{wj} (3)

m. Labialization + laryngealization: $^{\text{ʔ}}\text{b}^{w}$ (1), $^{\text{ʔ}}\text{d}^{w}$ (1), $\text{k}^{\text{ʔ}w}$ (2)

n. Labialization + pharyngealization: $\text{k}^{w\text{ʕ}}$ (1), $\text{q}^{w\text{ʕ}}$ (2)

o. Labialization + velarization: $\text{p}^{w\text{ɣ}}$ (2), $\text{b}^{w\text{ɣ}}$ (1)

p. Palatalization + laryngealization: $\text{b}^{\text{ʔ}j}$ (3), $\text{d}^{\text{ʔ}j}$ (3)

q. Palatalization + pharyngealization: none

r. Palatalization + velarization: none

s. Laryngealization + pharyngealization: none

t. Laryngealization + velarization: none

u. Pharyngealization + velarization: none

(16a) is a combination type of aspiration and nasalization. It is one of the representative types in (16). Since aspiration and nasalization are the most frequent secondary articulations, the combination of the two is also the most abundant, both quantitatively and qualitatively. The complex plosives in (16a) appear at many places of articulation. In the (16a) type, the frequency of the voiceless plosive is much higher than that of the voiced plosive. While the voiceless plosive is advantageous for aspiration to be realized, the voiced plosive is advantageous for nasalization. The complex plosives that are combined with these two secondary articulations are much more voiceless. This fact suggests that the complex plosive in (16a) follows the tendency of aspiration, not nasalization.

(16b) is a type that combines aspiration and labialization. This type is more extreme than (16a), so there are no examples of voiced plosives, only of voiceless plosives. This is also true for (16c), a combination of aspiration and palatalization. In (16), there are three types that include aspiration: (a, b, c). As shown in (16), when one of the two secondary articulations is aspiration, there is a strong bias toward the voiceless plosive. Additionally, the place of articulation of the plosives in (16b) is concentrated on the velar. This bias is consistent with the fact that the velar is most often accompanied by labialization, as shown in Figure 3-9.

There is no complex plosive in (16d, e, f). Aspiration and laryngealization in (16d) are secondary articulations that adjust the larynx differently. Since it is difficult for one articulatory organ to work differently at the same time, type-(16d) is not found in any language. The absence of (16e) is similar. The larynx, where aspiration is created, and the pharynx, where pharyngealization is created, are quite close. In addition, pharyngealization itself is very limited in its ability to combine with other secondary articulations to produce a complex plosive. The velarization of (16f) also cannot be created with various types because of the many restrictions on its combination with other secondary articulations.

(16g) is a combination type of nasalization and labialization. It is one of the main types along with (16a). Complex plosives of this type are found in many places of articulation. Unlike (16a, b, c), (16g) appears more in the voiced plosive than in the voiceless plosive, which is because nasalization as a secondary articulation is combined more often with the voiced plosive than the voiceless plosive. Therefore, except for the case in which nasalization is combined with aspiration, the complex plosive accompanied by both nasalization and one of the other secondary articulations is more frequent in the voiced plosive than in the voiceless plosive. Among the complex plosives in (16g), /$^{m}b^{w}$/ and /$^{ŋ}g^{w}$/ are the most frequent compared to other complex plosives in (16).

(16h) is a type combining nasalization and palatalization. Compared to (16g), its frequency is low and it contains less variety. However, like (16g), the frequency of the voiced plosive is higher than that of the voiceless plosive. The languages with the most complex plosives belonging to (16h) are Soga, Diriku, and Kwangali, languages of the Atlantic-Congo language family. These languages have four complex plosives in (16h).[61] Diriku, for example, has /$^{m}p^{j}$, $^{m}b^{j}$, $^{n}t̪^{j}$, $^{n}d̪^{j}$/.[62]

---

61 The complex plosives of type-(16h) in these three languages are articulated in the bilabial or alveolar (including dental), not in the velar.

62 According to Möhlig (2005: 24), in Diriku, there is a 12-way phonological opposition in the bilabial and alveolar plosives, which is very unusual. As

(16i) is type that combines nasalization and laryngealization. Although complex plosives of this type occur at several places of articulation, they are extremely infrequent. The plosives in (16i) are all prelaryngealized and are found in Luopohe Hmong and San Martín Itunyoso Triqui. Luopohe Hmong has only voiceless complex plosives, /^{mʔ}p, ^{nʔ}t, ^{ŋʔ}k/, whereas San Martín Itunyoso Triqui has only voiced complex plosives, /^{nʔ}d, ^{ŋʔ}g/. These two languages are not related in terms of language family or region, and their plosives in (16i) are also mutually exclusive.

No plosive has been reported for type-(16j, k). For nasalization to occur, the uvular must be involved in the articulatory process. However, even in pharyngealization and velarization, the articulator or point of articulation adjacent to the uvular play a main function in articulation. Due to this articulatory overlap, type-(16j, k) plosives seem unlikely to exist.

(16l~16u) are types in which infrequent secondary articulations are combined. There are few cases with a plosive that meets the conditions, and such cases are very rare. Since the frequency of each secondary articulation itself is low, this is a natural result.

The proportions of the complex plosives accompanied by two secondary articulations in (16) are given in Figure 3-13. The percentages shown in Figure 3-13 were calculated by using the sum of the language in which the complex plosives in (16) appear as the denominator and the sum of the languages in which each type of the plosive appears as the numerator. The proportions of each type show a considerable difference. (16g) is the highest, accounting for approximately one-third of the total. In addition, (16a, b, c, h) comprise 10% or more. However, the other types have far lower percentages.

Figure 3-13 reveals four characteristics. First, as expected, the types in which high-frequency secondary articulations are combined account for a much higher proportion than the types that do not involve such combination. The complex plosives that are combined with two secondary articulations among the four main secondary articulations

---

shown in the inventory /p, b, p^w, b^w, p^j, b^j, ^{m}p, ^{m}b, $^m p^w$, $^m b^w$, $^m p^j$, $^m b^j$, t, d, t^w, d^w, t^j, d^j, ^{n}t, ^{n}d, $^n t^w$, $^n d^w$, $^n t^j$, $^n d^j$/, nasalization, labialization, and palatalization are involved in the opposition. Contrary to expectations, aspiration, which is the most frequent secondary articulation, is not found.

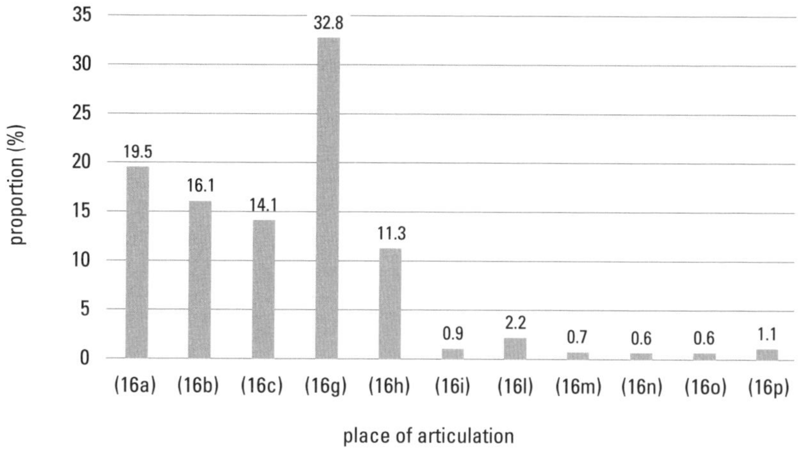

Figure 3-13. Proportion of the complex plosives in (16)

(aspiration, nasalization, labialization, and palatalization) exceed 90% of the total.

Second, of the 21 candidate types in which two of the seven secondary articulations can be combined, only 11, or approximately half, actually appear. In other words, there are many restrictions on the combination of two secondary articulations. The fact that the plosive is accompanied simultaneously by two secondary articulations is an articulatory burden that limits the possible types of combination. Therefore, it is difficult to expect the combination of low-frequency secondary articulations.

Third, the ranking of the activeness of participation in the combination of the secondary articulation does not coincide with the proportional rankings of secondary articulation. As shown in Figure 3-6, secondary articulation, ranked by overall percentage, proceeds as follows: 'aspiration > nasalization > labialization > palatalization > laryngealization > pharyngealization > velarization'. However, counting the number of secondary articulations in each type of (16) results in the following frequency ranking: 'labialization (6) > nasalization = palatalization (4) > aspiration = laryngealization (3) > pharyngealization = velarization (1)'.[63] Labialization can be combined with six types of secondary

63 The numbers in parentheses indicate in how many types secondary articulation

articulation except for itself, whereas aspiration and nasalization can combine only three or four. This hierarchy is significantly different from proportional rankings shown in Figure 3-6.

The inconsistency between the preferences in the combination of the secondary articulation and the proportional rankings of the secondary articulation itself is also revealed in other aspect. Figure 3-14 below shows the result of calculating the percentage of complex plosives by the type of secondary articulation, with the same method as Figure 3-13.

As shown here, 64.6% of the total plosives include nasalization in the combination of two secondary articulations, and 53% include labialization.[64] In contrast, aspiration, which is the most frequent among the secondary articulations, is included in the combination of secondary articulation by only 49.7%. This rate is lower than that of labialization. Although it is difficult to clearly understand the reason for this, it may be explained by the possibility that secondary articulation created at both edges of the oral cavity, that is, the lips and velum, is more advantageous in combination with other secondary articulations than such articulation

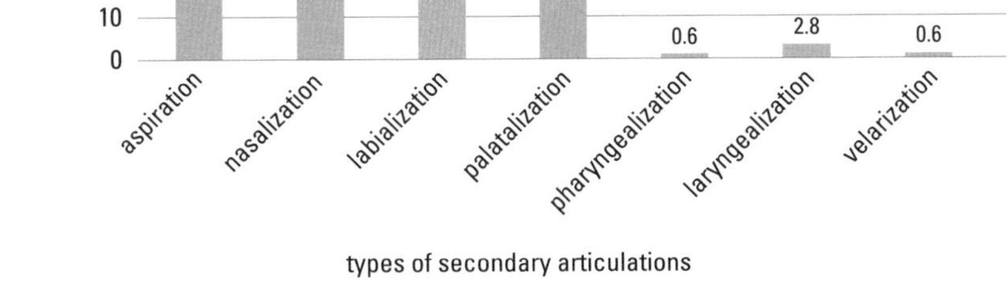

Figure 3-14. Proportion of the secondary articulations in (16)

appears.

64 In Figure 3-14, one complex plosive may be calculated multiple times. For example, a plosive in which nasalization and labialization are combined is calculated twice, once as nasalization and once as labialization. As a result, the sum of percentages in Figure 3-14 exceeds 100.

related to laryngeal action.

Fourth, no double-articulated plosive combine with two secondary articulations. Multiple secondary articulations can accompany only a single-articulated plosive and cannot accompany a double-articulated plosive such as /kp, gb/. In addition, although the glottal plosive is a single-articulated plosive, /$^{ŋ}ʔ^{w}$/, which appears in Psikye, is the only complex plosive that combines with multiple secondary articulations.[65]

Finally, I examine the complex plosive that is combined with three secondary articulations. There are only nine types of such plosive, and their frequency is so low that they appear only in one or two languages.

(17) Complex plosives with three secondary articulations

$^{mʔ}p^{h}$ (1), $^{m}p^{hj}$ (2), $^{nʔ}t^{h}$ (1), $^{n}t^{hj}$ (1), $^{ɳʔ}ʈ^{h}$ (1), k^{hwj} (1), $^{ŋ}k^{hj}$ (1), $^{ŋ}g^{wj}$ (2), $^{ɴ}q^{hw}$ (1)

Of the nine plosives in (17), as many as seven have been reported to exist in only one language. It is very likely that aspiration or nasalization is included among the three secondary articulations in (17). Aspiration or nasalization are found in eight of these nine plosives. By contrast, no plosive is combined with pharyngealization or velarization. It is remarkable that labialization, which demonstrates an advantage regarding the combination of two secondary articulations, appears only in three types of these plosives. The language with the most complex plosives in (17) is Western Xiangxi Miao, an Asian language of the Hmon-Mien language family. According to Sposato (2015: 59), there are four complex plosives accompanied by three secondary articulations in Western Xiangxi Miao: /$^{m}p^{hj}$, $^{n}t^{hj}$, $^{ŋ}k^{hj}$, $^{ɴ}q^{hw}$/. All of these plosives are voiceless, and include aspiration and nasalization in the three secondary articulations.

65 According to Smith (1969: 43), in Psikye, there are three glottal plosives: /ʔ, $ʔ^{w}$, $^{ŋ}ʔ^{w}$/.

Chapter 4

DESCRIPTION OF PLOSIVES

In this chapter, I will describe the phonetic characteristics of each plosive. There are 293 types of plosives found in the languages referenced in this book. Several issues, including the phonetic category and frequency, will be discussed. After the plosives are classified according to the place of articulation, an overview of the general characteristics at each place of articulation is provided, and then the individual plosives are described.

4.1. Bilabial plosives

4.1.1. Overview

The bilabial plosive, along with the alveolar and velar plosives, belongs to the major place of articulation. Bilabial plosives are very frequent and include many types. The list of bilabial plosives is summarized in Table 4-1.

Table 4-1. List of bilabial plosives

a.	Plain	p, b
b.	Single secondary articulation	p^{h}, b^{h}, ${}^{h}p$, ${}^{m}p$, ${}^{m}b$, ${}^{ŋ}b$, p^{m}, b^{m}, $p^{ʔ}$, $b^{ʔ}$, ${}^{ʔ}b$, p^{w}, b^{w}, p^{j}, b^{j}, $p^{ɣ}$, $p^{ʕ}$, $b^{ʕ}$
c.	Multiple secondary articulations	p^{hw}, p^{hj}, ${}^{ʔ}b^{w}$, ${}^{ʔ}b^{j}$, ${}^{m}p^{h}$, ${}^{m}b^{h}$, $p^{wɣ}$, $b^{wɣ}$, ${}^{mʔ}p$, ${}^{mʔ}p^{h}$, ${}^{m}p^{w}$, ${}^{m}b^{w}$, ${}^{m}p^{j}$, ${}^{m}b^{j}$, ${}^{m}p^{hj}$, p^{mw}
d.	Glottal action	p̈, b̤, p̃, b̰, ^{m}b̤
e.	Liquid-colored release	p^{r}, b^{r}, p^{l}, b^{l}, p^{hr}, p^{hl}, ${}^{m}b^{r}$, ${}^{m}p^{l}$, ${}^{m}b^{l}$, ${}^{m}p^{hl}$
f.	Tenseness	pp, bb, b̥

Table 4-2. Top 10 bilabial plosives

Ranking	Plosive	Frequency	Ranking	Plosive	Frequency
1	p	3,829	6	^{m}p	117
2	b	3,105	7	b^{h}	112
3	p^{h}	784	8	b^{w}	94
4	^{m}b	608	9	p^{j}	92
5	p^{w}	121	10	b^{j}	68

The high-frequency plosives in the top 10 among the bilabial plosives in Table 4-1 are given in Table 4-2. The frequencies in Table 4-2 reflect in how many languages each plosive appears. Two plain plosives are ranked first and second, followed by plosives accompanying major secondary articulations such as aspiration, nasalization, labialization, and palatalization. The 10 bilabial plosives in Table 4-2 consist of five contrastive pairs by [±voiced], such as 'p : b, p^{h} : b^{h}, ^{m}p : ^{m}b, p^{w} : b^{w}, p^{j} : b^{j}'. Except for /^{m}p, ^{m}b/, which are prenasalized, voiceless plosives are more frequent than voiced plosives.

Table 4-3 provides the number of bilabial plosives in the world's languages. As shown in Table 4-3, the average number of bilabial plosives is 2.1, and this average remains similar when excluding the

Table 4-3. Number of bilabial plosives in languages

Number of bilabial plosives	Number of languages	Percentage
0	57	1.3%
1	1,113	25.6%
2	2,085	47.8%
3	693	15.9%
4	317	7.3%
5	32	0.7%
6	34	0.8%
7	7	0.2%
8	8	0.2%
9	5	0.1%
10~	5	0.1%

languages without the bilabial plosive. Most languages, constituting 47.8% or nearly half the total, have two bilabial plosives. Languages with five or more bilabial plosives represent only approximately 2%. There are also 57 languages that do not have a bilabial plosive at all, of which 35 belong to the Otomanguean, Iroquoian, and Athabaskan-Eyak-Tlingit language families spoken in North America. In addition to these three language families, languages of the Caddoan and Salishan language families spoken in North America often do not have bilabial plosives. Therefore, the absence of the bilabial plosives reveals a bias in the region or language family.

The language with the most bilabial plosives is Diriku, which has been mentioned several times in this book. According to Möhlig (2005: 24), Diriku has as many as 12 bilabial plosives.

(1) Bilabial plosives in Diriku

p, b, p^w, b^w, p^j, b^j, ^mp, ^mb, $^mp^w$, $^mb^w$, $^mp^j$, $^mb^j$

Among the bilabial plosives of Diriku in (1), some match the high-frequency plosives in Table 4-2, but others do not. For example, high-frequency aspirated plosives do not exist in Diriku. Instead, it has complex plosives such as /$^mp^w$, $^mb^w$, $^mp^j$, $^mb^j$/.

Now, targeting languages in which bilabial plosives exist, I will attempt to determine the general pattern based on the number of bilabial plosives. The types and frequencies of the inventory appearing in the 1,113 languages with one bilabial plosive are provided in Table 4-4. The most common plosive in Table 4-4 is /p/. Of the 1,113 languages, 728, or 65.4%, have a /p/ as the only bilabial plosive, which is a lower percentage than expected. In other words, approximately one-third of the total have bilabial plosives other than /p/. In particular, there are many languages that have the voiced plain plosive /b/. Considering that voiceless plosives are unmarked compared to voiced plosives, it is surprising that so many languages have /b/ instead of /p/ as their only

Table 4-4. Types and frequency of single bilabial plosive inventories

Inventory	p	b	^mb	p^h	b^w	^mp	^ʔb
Number of languages	728	355	25	2	1	1	1

Table 4-5. Types and frequency of two-way bilabial plosive inventories

Inventory	p, b	p, p^h	p, ^mb	p, p^w	b, ^mb	b, p^h	b, b^w
Number of languages	1,687	150	119	29	27	19	11

bilabial plosive.

There are 2,085 languages with two bilabial plosives. Table 4-5 is a list of the inventories that are common in these languages. The seven inventories in Table 4-5 are each found in more than 10 languages. Of the languages with two bilabial plosives, 1,687 languages, which constitute the absolute majority, have /p, b/ in their inventories. This means that the most common inventory in languages with two bilabial plosives consists of two plain plosives opposed by [±voiced].[1] /p, b/ is distributed evenly in many languages without any bias in the region or language family.

As shown in Table 4-5, /p, p^h/ and /p, ^mb/ are highly frequent and occur in more than 100 languages. The former (p, p^h) is very common in the Sino-Tibetan language family, whereas none of the Austronesian language family, one of the two largest language families, include /p, p^h/ in their inventories. By contrast, the latter (p, ^mb) is found in many languages of the Austronesian and Nuclear Trans New Guinea language families spoken in the Papunesia area. Languages with /p, p^h/ and /p, ^mb/ are complementary in terms of language family or region.

The frequency rankings in Table 4-5 are closely related to those of the bilabial plosive in Table 4-2. Generally, the inventory of two-way plosives includes /p/ as an essential element along with other high-frequency bilabial plosives, as shown in Table 4-2. Interestingly, the frequency rankings of bilabial plosives in Table 4-2 coincide with those of the inventories in Table 4-5. For example, in Table 4-2, the frequency ranking is 'b > p^h > ^mb > p^w >...'. If the bilabial plosives are added to /p/ in this order, the result is '/p, b/ > /p, p^h/ > /p, ^mb/ > /p, p^w/, which is the same as the frequency ranking given in Table 4-5.

Next, I will consider the common inventories in languages with

1 The contrast with the same character as 'p : b' can also be found in '^mp : ^mb'. Among the languages with two bilabial plosives, two African languages, Ngando-Lalia and Shanjo, have /^mp, ^mb/.

Table 4-6. Types and frequency of three-way bilabial plosive inventories

Inventory	Type-(a)	Type-(b)	Type-(c)	Type-(d)
	p, b, p^h	p, b, $^m b$	p, p^h, $^m b$	p, p^h, $^m p$
Number of languages	355	237	10	10

three bilabial plosives. There are 693 languages with three bilabial plosives. Among the inventories of the bilabial plosive in these languages, the above four appear in more than 10 languages.

There are significant differences in the frequencies of the four inventories in Table 4-6. Types-(a) and (b) are found in many languages, but types-(c) and (d) are each found in only 10 languages. The regional distribution of types-(a) and (b) is clearly distinguished. Type-(a) commonly appears in languages of the Austroasiatic, Sino-Tibetan, and Tai-Kadai language families, which are spoken in Asia. In contrast, type-(b) appears in many African languages belonging to the Atlantic-Congo and Central Sudanic language families. These two high-frequency types are composed of /p, b/, which are plain plosives, and /p^h/ or /$^m b$/, which are also high-frequency bilabial plosives. Compared to this, types-(c) and (d), which are infrequent, are based on contrast by [±aspirated], so they include a contrastive pair such as /p, p^h/.

In Table 4-6, the high-frequency and the low-frequency types are related to whether there is an opposition by [±voiced]. This aspect of Table 4-6 is not irrelevant to the frequency order in Table 4-5. As shown in Table 4-6, inventories that consist of /p, b/, the most frequent in Table 4-5, and other high-frequency bilabial plosives are also frequent, whereas inventories that do not contain /p, b/ are infrequent. In other cases to be considered later, most of the inventories with three or more plosives at one place of articulation include a contrastive pair by [±voiced].

There are 317 languages with four bilabial plosives. Table 4-7 provides a list of the common inventories in these languages. Table 4-7 present seven inventories that appear in more than 10 languages. Compared with Table 4-6, the number of types has increased, but the frequency of each type has decreased. Types-(a) and (f) can be regarded as virtually the same class, considering the phonetic similarity between the voiced aspirated plosive and breathy voice.[2]

The inventories of bilabial plosives in Table 4-7 show a strong bias toward a specific language family, regardless of the size of the language

Table 4-7. Types and frequency of four-way bilabial plosive inventories

Inventory	Type-(a)	Type-(b)	Type-(c)	Type-(d)	Type-(e)	Type-(f)	Type-(g)
	p, b, p^h, b^h	p, b, ^mp, ^mb	p, b, p^h, ^mb	p, b, p^j, b^j	p, b, p^w, b^w	p, b, p^h, b̤	p, p^h, p^j, p^{hj}
Number of languages	102	59	27	26	25	13	10

family. Type-(a) is most often found in the Indo-European language family, followed by the Sino-Tibetan language family, and is rarely found in any other language family. By contrast, type-(b) appears mainly in languages of the Atlantic-Congo and Austronesian language families, which are the two largest language families. Languages with type-(c) are common in the Sino-Tibetan language family. Type-(d) appears frequently in the Indo-European language family but also in Mongolic and Uralic language families. Type-(e) is mainly seen in the Austronesian language family, and type-(g) is seen in Asian languages including the Sino-Tibetan language family. Inventories containing aspirated plosives tend to appear in Asian languages, and inventories without aspirated plosive tend to appear in the Austronesian language family.

A clear trend is reflected in Table 4-7. First, most of the inventories are based on the contrast by [±voiced]. That is, they include a contrastive pair 'p : b'. In Table 4-7, except for type-(g), which is the least frequent, all others have a contrastive pair by [±voiced]. This feature has already been seen in Table 4-6. It has long been known that the voicedness is very important in the contrast of the plosive, and this fact is once again supported by various aspects of the large-scale language data here.

Second, the more frequent the inventory is, the more likely it is to maximize optimal opposition. The four-way contrast can ideally be distinguished by a combination of two distinctive features. Most of the inventories in Table 4-7 have such a system. That is, among the inventories in Table 4-7, all except for type-(c) have maximized opposition.[3] To describe the opposition of type-(c), three distinctive features, [±voiced],

2 These two types share similar distribution in language family and region.
3 As mentioned earlier, type-(a) and (f) can be regarded as the same.

[±aspirated], and [±nasalized], are necessary, but the other types can be described by two distinctive features.[4] The two distinctive features required for each type are as follows.

(2) Distinctive features required for the bilabial plosives in Table 4-7

Type-(a)	Type-(b)	Type-(d)	Type-(e)	Type-(g)
p, b, p^h, b^h	p, b, ^mp, ^mb	p, b, p^j, b^j	p, b, p^w, b^w	p, p^h, p^j, p^{hj}
[±voiced], [±aspirated]	[±voiced], [±nasalized]	[±voiced], [±palatalized]	[±voiced], [±labialized]	[±aspirated], [±palatalized]

As seen in (2), it is possible to capture with two distinctive features all the opposing relations of the bilabial plosives. This is the result of maximizing phonological opposition through the use of as few distinctive features as possible. Type-(g) is not commonly known and includes /p^{hj}/, the only complex plosive accompanied by two secondary articulations. However, since type-(g) is very efficient and simple in terms of phonological opposition, it could have been included in Table 4-7. Clearly, inventories in which high frequency plosives form a systematic and efficient opposition are preferred. This result again confirms the importance of opposition in the phonological system.

None of the inventories composed of five or more bilabial plosives appear in more than 10 languages. Therefore, the discussion on the commonly preferred inventory types according to the number of bilabial plosives ends here.[5] Instead, based on the discussion so far, I will deal with a slightly different topic. It is possible to establish an activeness hierarchy of distinctive features through the inventories of the bilabial plosives that appear repeatedly in many languages. To simplify the discussion, the following activeness hierarchy can be proposed, targeting the three distinctive features, [±voiced], [±aspirated], and

4 For convenience, the distinctive feature indicating the secondary articulation is set to reflect each secondary articulation as it is. For example, nasalization is marked with [±nasalized], and labialization with [±labialized]. This is merely to express the phonological contrast in simple terms and will not hinder the discussion here.

5 The scope of discussion on other places of articulation is also limited to those languages with four plosives.

[±nasalized].

(3) Activeness hierarchy of [±voiced], [±aspirated], and [±nasalized]
[±voiced] > [±aspirated] > [±nasalized]

The higher a distinctive feature is ranked within the activeness hierarchy, the more likely it is that the contrastive pair by that distinctive feature appears in numerous languages. For example, in an inventory with two bilabial plosives, /p, b/, in which the highest [±voiced] is involved, appears most often, followed by /p, p^h/, in which [±aspirated] is involved. Of course, some supplemental discussion of the activeness of distinctive features is necessary. Even if [±aspirated] is involved in the contrast, /b, b^h/ is infrequent compared to /p, p^h/. In addition, the inventory in which [±nasalized] is involved should be /p, ^{m}p/ or /b, ^{m}b/, but in reality, /p, ^{m}b/ is more frequent. There is a good reason for this, since aspirated plosives are much more often voiceless, whereas nasalized plosives are more often voiced. However, the activeness hierarchy in (3) alone cannot clearly explain these points. Nonetheless, with minor modifications, the activeness hierarchy of a distinctive feature can be very useful for various phonological oppositions.

The hierarchy in (3) is also valid for the frequency rankings of the inventories with three or more bilabial plosives. To describe the three or four opposed members, at least two distinctive features are needed. In this case, the choice of the two distinctive features generally follows the activeness hierarchy of (3). According to (3), the most preferred combination is expected to be '[±voiced], [±aspirated]', the second '[±voiced], [±nasalized]', and the third '[±aspirated], [±nasalized]'. Comparing this prediction with the frequency rankings of the inventories in Table 4-6 or Table 4-7 shows that the hierarchy in (3) has a very high explanatory power. Some minor discrepancies can be sufficiently resolved through further refinement.

When there are two or more bilabial plosives, the inventory of bilabial plosives is not randomly selected, but follows a certain principle. This tendency is found not only in the bilabial, but also in other places of articulation. As a result, as will be seen in 5.3, it is possible to establish the preferred plosive inventories that appear widely across languages.

4.1.2. Description of the bilabial plosives

Based on the classification of the types in Table 4-1, the description of individual bilabial plosives begins with the plain plosives, followed by the plosives accompanied by secondary articulation, breathy/ creaky voice, etc. This is also the case for the plosives at other places of articulation.

/p/

Voiceless, plain. This plosive appears in 3,829 languages. It is the most frequent (87.9%, 3,829/4,356) of the bilabial plosives and the second most frequent among all plosives. Languages without /p/ are often found in the Atlantic-Congo and Afro-Asiatic language families. In particular, 88 of the 219 languages in the Afro-Asiatic language family do not have /p/, which reflects a distinct trend. In the Atlantic-Congo language family, 106 of the 718 languages do not have /p/. This plosive is unaspirated by classification, but is sometimes accompanied by light aspiration, depending on the language. If the aspiration accompanying /p/ is slightly stronger, even if there is only one bilabial plosive, it is analyzed as /pʰ/ instead of /p/, like in Jizhao and Tojolabal.[6]

/b/

Voiced, plain. This plosive appears in 3,105 languages. It is the fourth most frequent (71.3%) among all plosives and the second frequent among the bilabial plosives. In particular, /b/ is the most frequent among the voiced plosives. /b/ forms a contrastive pair with /p/ by [±voiced]. The contrastive pair 'p : b' is found in 2,672 languages, meaning that in 86.1% of 3,105 languages with /b/, /b/ implies the presence of /p/. Unlike /p/, /b/ is not less commonly found in languages belonging to the Atlantic-Congo and Afro-Asiatic language families. Instead, more than 70% of the languages of Algic, Athabaskan-Eyak-Tlingit, and Salishan language families in North America do not have /b/.

6 If there is only one bilabial plosive in a language, it can be analyzed as a plain /p/ rather than an aspirated /pʰ/ at the phonological level, even though it has strong aspiration. It is possible to describe the phonetic aspiration in terms of allophone.

/pʰ/

Voiceless, postaspirated. This plosive appears in 784 languages, and is the second most frequent (18.0%) among all aspirated plosives. This plosive appears in many language families, but is especially common in the Sino-Tibetan. Of the 784 languages with /pʰ/, 345 are in the Sino-Tibetan language family. Moreover, 95% of the 363 languages in the Sino-Tibetan language family include /pʰ/.

/bʰ/

Voiced, postaspirated. This plosive appears in 112 languages. The distribution of /bʰ/ is concentrated in two language families: 75 in the Indo-European language family, and 29 in the Sino-Tibetan language family. Among the 112 languages with /bʰ/, 103 languages also have /pʰ/, so the contrast by [±voiced] appears in 92.0% (103/112) of the total. This percentage is higher than that of 'p : b' (86.1%). In particular, 91.1% of languages with /bʰ/ have a four-way opposition such as 'p : b : pʰ : bʰ'.[7] The voiced aspirated plosive in other places of articulation also implies a very high rate of the four-way opposition with the same character.[8] Interestingly, individual phonemes imply the existence of multi-way opposition.

/ʰp/

Voiceless, preaspirated. This plosive appears in six languages, but they share nothing in common, such as the language family or region. This plosive is different from /pʰ/ in that the position of aspiration is in front of the primary articulation. In Osage, Bonan, and Zhongu, /pʰ/ and /ʰp/ exist as separate phonemes, so they have a phonological opposition created by the position of aspiration. So far, there are no known languages with /ʰb/, a voiced opposite of /ʰp/. This is also true for other preaspirated voiceless plosives.

/ᵐp/

Voiceless, prenasalized. This plosive appears in 117 languages. In

7 If languages in which the breathy voice /b̤/ appears instead of /bʰ/ are included, the rate becomes higher.

8 For example, languages with /dʰ/, a voiced alveolar aspirated plosive, have four-way opposition without exception.

general, the frequency of the voiceless obstruent is higher than that of the voiced obstruent, but when accompanied by nasalization, the opposite is true. Therefore, /ᵐp/ is also infrequent compared to /ᵐb/. This difference suggests that the implication relationship should also be examined in reverse direction. In other words, in the case of the nasalized plosive, it is necessary to examine to what extent the presence of the voiceless plosive implies the existence of the voiced opposite. In 83 of the 117 languages with /ᵐp/, /ᵐb/ appears, and the two consonants form a contrastive pair by [$\pm$voiced]. The presence of /ᵐp/ implies the existence of /ᵐb/, in 70.9% (83/117) of these languages. Approximately half (47.0%) of the languages in which /ᵐp/ appears belong to the Atlantic-Congo language family.

/ᵐb/

Voiced, prenasalized. There are 608 languages that have this plosive, making it five times more frequent than the voiceless /ᵐp/. The plosive /ᵐb/, like /ᵐp/, appears most often in the Atlantic-Congo language family, but it is also widespread in other language families. Regionally, it is evenly distributed across various areas, such as Asia, Africa, Papua New Guinea, and the Americas.

/ᵑb/

Voiced, prenasalized. Except for /ᵑb/, which is heterorganic, the nasalized plosives are homorganic, i.e., the places of primary and secondary articulation are the same. The plosive /ᵑb/ appears only in Ngbaka Minagende. Specially, according to Englund (1963: 8), /ᵑb/ and /ᵐb/ exist as separate phonemes in this language. Ngbaka Minagende is unique in that it include not only a /ᵑb/ but also a contrastive pair such as 'ᵐb : ᵑb'.[9]

/pᵐ/

Voiceless, postnasalized. This plosive appears only in Nemi. All of the postnasalized plosives are infrequent and appear in very few languages. The plosive /pᵐ/ is distinguished from /ᵐp/ by the position of

9 Ngbaka Minagende also has two prenasalized implosives, /ᵐɓ, ᵑɓ/, as separate phonemes.

nasalization, but there is no language in which both /p^{m}/ and /^{m}p/ exist as separate phonemes. In other words, the position of nasalization is not involved in phonological contrast.

/b^{m}/

Voiced, postnasalized. This plosive is a voiced opposite of /p^{m}/ and appears only in Mumuye and Pangseng. The two languages are closely related both by language family and region. The contrast between /b^{m}/ and /^{m}b/ is parallel to the contrast between /p^{m}/ and /^{m}p/. There is no case where both /b^{m}/ and /^{m}b/ exist in one language as separate phonemes.

/p^{w}/

Voiceless, labialized. This plosive appears in 121 languages, and is one of the most frequent plosives with secondary articulation. The plosive /p^{w}/ is particularly common in the Austronesian language family, as 68 of 121 languages with /p^{w}/ belong to that.

/b^{w}/

Voiced, labialized. This plosive appears in 94 languages, 55 of which also have /p^{w}/. That is, a contrastive pair by [±voiced] appears in those 55 languages. Like /p^{w}/, /b^{w}/ is frequent in the Austronesian language family, where it appears in 50 of 94 languages belonging to that.

/p^{j}/

Voiceless, palatalized. This plosive appears in 92 languages. /p^{j}/ is rare in the Austronesian language family, one of the largest language families, as only Nahavaq, Nalögo, and Patep have /p^{j}/. This proportion is in stark contrast to /p^{w}/, which is common in the Austronesian language family.

/b^{j}/

Voiced, palatalized. This plosive appears in 68 languages, 54 of which have a contrastive pair, 'p^{j} : b^{j}'. Like /p^{j}/, this plosive is rare in the Austronesian language family. Among the Austronesian languages, only North Ambrym, Dambi, and Kumalu have /b^{j}/. Interestingly, these languages do not overlap with other Austronesian languages, which have /p^{j}/. Languages of the Austronesian language family rarely have bilabial palatalized plosives, and even when they occur, there is no contrast by [±voiced].

/pˤ/

Voiceless, pharyngealized. This plosive appears in six languages, three of which belong to the Afro-Asiatic language family. /pˤ/ is one of the emphatic consonants found in many languages of the Afro-Asiatic language family.

/bˤ/

Voiced, pharyngealized. This plosive appears in nine languages, seven of which belong to the Afro-Asiatic language family. Voiced /bˤ/ is more frequent than voiceless /pˤ/. The contrastive pair 'pˤ : bˤ' is found in four languages, including Ubykh.

/pˀ/

Voiceless, postlaryngealized. This plosive appears in 11 languages. Languages with /pˀ/ often do not follow the general pattern. Of these 11 languages, only Chol and Emberá-Tadó have both /p/ and /b/ which are the most frequent bilabial plosives, whereas six have /pʰ/, which is relatively infrequent. No language has /pˀ/ as its only bilabial plosive. Languages with /pˀ/ have two or three bilabial plosives.

/bˀ/

Voiced, postlaryngealized. This plosive appears in three languages, which do not overlap at all with languages that have /pˀ/. In other words, there is no language in which the bilabial postlaryngealized plosives are opposed by only [±voiced]. /bˀ/ is often confused with the implosive /ɓ/, so it requires attention.

/ˀb/

Voiced, prelaryngealized. This plosive differs from /bˀ/ in its position of laryngealization, which is in front of the primary articulation. /ˀb/ appears in 21 languages, and is thus more frequent than /bˀ/. Prelaryngealization is more common than postlaryngealization in voiced plosives.

/$p^ɣ$/

Voiceless, velarized. This plosive appears in three languages: Aneityum and Pollapese in the Austronesian language family and Assyrian Neo-Aramaic in the Afro-Asiatic language family. In particular, Aneityum and Pollapese have only four plosives overall, one of which is /$p^ɣ$/, a very infrequent plosive. Its voiced opposite, /$b^ɣ$/, is not found in any language.

/p^{hw}/

Voiceless, postaspirated, labialized. This plosive appears in 12 languages. While the aspirated /p^h/ or labialized /p^w/ tend to appear in few language families, /p^{hw}/, which is accompanied by both aspiration and labialization, does not show such bias. All the 12 languages with /p^{hw}/ have /p, p^h, p^w/, so the more complicatedly articulated plosive perfectly implies the presence of less complicatedly articulated plosives. Its voiced opposite, /b^{hw}/, does not appear in any language.

/p^{hj}/

Voiceless, postaspirated, palatalized. This plosive appears in 29 languages. Unlike /p^{hw}/, which does not show a bias in language family, /p^{hj}/ appears mostly in Asian languages belonging to the Sino-Tibetan, Tai-Kadai, and Hmong-Mien language families. That is, the distribution of /p^{hj}/ is similar to that of /p^h/ accompanied only by aspiration. Its voiced opposite, /b^{hj}/, does not appear in any language.

/$^mp^h$/

Voiceless, postaspirated, prenasalized. This plosive appears in 21 languages, many of which belong to the Sino-Tibetan, Hmong-Mien, and Atlantic-Congo language families. Languages with this plosive have at least three bilabial plosives, although Kwangali and Nyanja, members of the Atlantic-Congo, have 10. The presence of /$^mp^h$/ implies the existence of /p^h/ in 16 of these 21 languages (76.2%), but /$^mp^h$/ implies the existence of /^mp/ in only 10 langages (47.6%).[10] The rate at which the plosive accompanied by two secondary articulations implies the existence

10 The fact that the percentage of implication is less than 50% indicates that the implicational relationship can not be established.

of plosive accompanied by one secondary articulation, varies according to the type of secondary articulation.

/$^{m}b^{h}$/

Voiced, postaspirated, prenasalized. This plosive is a voiced opposite of /$^{m}p^{h}$/ and appears in four languages, including Gepo. All of these languages are spoken in Asia. No language is known to include both /$^{m}b^{h}$/ and /$^{m}p^{h}$/, i.e., the distribution of these twi plosives is mutually exclusive.

/^{mʔ}p/

Voiceless, prenasalized, prelaryngealized. This plosive appears only in Luopohe Hmong, which includes a considerable number of plosives, with 23. When only laryngealization is combined with the voiceless plosive, the possible type is limited to postlaryngealization. However, /^{mʔ}p/ is accompanied by prelaryngealization, not postlaryngealization. It is not known whether this characteristic is due to the nasalization in /^{mʔ}p/.

/$^{m}p^{w}$/

Voiceless, prenasalized, labialized. This plosive appears in five languages, three of which belong to the Atlantic-Congo language family. Languages with /$^{m}p^{w}$/ have a total of four or more bilabial plosives, which is significantly above the average. All five languages have /p^{w}/, and four have /^{m}p/. In general, a language that includes a plosive accompanied by two secondary articulations is likely to have a plosive accompanied by one of them.

/$^{m}b^{w}$/

Voiced, prenasalized, labialized. This plosive is the voiced opposite of /$^{m}p^{w}$/ and appears in 43 languages, making it quite frequent compared to other complex plosives of the same type. This plosive shows a bias in language family, with 30 of these 43 languages belonging to the Austronesian language family. Only Kwangali and Diriku have both the voiced /$^{m}b^{w}$/ and the voiceless /$^{m}p^{w}$/. Overall, plosives accompanied by multiple secondary articulations tend not to show the contrast by [±voiced] in a language.

/p^{mw}/

Voiceless, postnasalized, labialized. This plosive is a very rare complex plosive in that nasalization follows primary articulation. /p^{mw}/ appears only in Nemi, which has another postnasalized plosive, /p^{m}/. The voiced opposite of /p^{mw}/, that is /b^{mw}/, is not found in any language.

/$^{m}p^{j}$/

Voiceless, prenasalized, palatalized. This plosive appears in six languages, four of which belong to the Atlantic-Congo language family and two to the Hmong-Mien language family. Languages with /$^{m}p^{j}$/ have at least six bilabial plosives, which is well above average.

/$^{m}b^{j}$/

Voiced, prenasalized, palatalized. This plosive is a voiced opposite of /$^{m}p^{j}$/. /$^{m}b^{j}$/ appears in 14 languages, which is more than the voiceless /$^{m}p^{j}$/. The reason why voiced plosives are more frequent than voiceless oppposites is due to the characteristics of nasalized plosives. Among the languages that have /$^{m}b^{j}$/, only Kwangali and Diriku also have the voiceless /$^{m}p^{j}$/. In the case of complex plosives accompanied by multiple secondary articulations, the ratio for the voiced plosive to imply the presence of the voiceless opposite is quite low.

/$p^{wɣ}$/

Voiceless, labialized, velarized. This plosive appears only in Pingelapese and Satawalese, which are members of the Austronesian language family and are also geographically close.

/$b^{wɣ}$/

Voiced, labialized, velarized. This plosive is a voiced opposite of /$p^{wɣ}$/ and appears only in Carolinian, a language of Austronesian language family. Carolinian also include /$p^{wɣ}$/ as a marginal phoneme. Bilabial plosives accompanying velarization are rare and are mainly found in the Austronesian language family. In particular, plosives that are combined with both labialization and velarization, whether voiced or voiceless, exist only in the bilabial and does not appear in other places of articulation.

/$^{ʔ}b^{w}$/

Voiced, prelaryngealized, labialized. This plosive is found only in T'en, which is spoken in Southwestern China. Its voiceless opposite, /$^{ʔ}p^{w}$/, is not found in any language.

/$^{ʔ}b^{j}$/

Voiced, prelaryngealized, palatalized. This plosive is found in three languages, T'en, Tày, and Maonan, all of which are members of the Kam-Tai, a subfamily of the Tai-Kadai language family. Its voiceless opposite, /$^{ʔ}p^{j}$/, is not found in any language.

/$^{m}p^{hj}$/

Voiceless, postaspirated, prenasalized, palatalized. This plosive is combined with three secondary articulations and appears only in Northern Guiyang Hmong and Western Xiangxi Miao, which are in the Hmong-Mien language family. These two languages have a large number of bilabial plosives: Northern Guiyang Hmong has ten and Western Xiangxi Miao seven. Having a complicated articulatory plosive means that there is a high probability that a phonetically simpler plosive will exist, so the large number of bilabial plosives in these languages is fully predictable. The voiced opposite of /$^{m}p^{hj}$/, /$^{m}b^{hj}$/, is not found in any language.

/$^{mʔ}p^{h}$/

Voiceless, postaspirated, prenasalized, prelaryngealized. This plosive appears only in Luopohe Hmong. Of the bilabial plosives, only /$^{m}p^{hj}$/ and /$^{mʔ}p^{h}$/ are combined with three secondary articulations, and these two consonants are commonly accompanied by aspiration and nasalization. The existence of /$^{mʔ}p^{h}$/ is somewhat doubtful, since it is accompanied by both aspiration and laryngealization, which are largely incompatible. Niederer (1998), which reported the existence of /$^{mʔ}p^{h}$/, did not offer a phonologically detailed analysis of Luopohe Hmong, so the existence of this consonant cannot be certain.

/p̤/

Voiceless, breathy-voice. This plosive only appears in Chantyal, a language of the Sino-Tibetan language family. Because the breathy-voice plosive is generally voiced, the voiceless /p̤/ is both very special and extremely rare. The inventory of plosives for Chantyal presented in Noonan (2005: 3) includes /b̤/ in addition to /p̈/, so the two breathy-voice plosives show opposition by [±voiced].[11] The appearance of this phonological contrast in the same language is highly unusual.

/b̤/

Voiced, breathy-voice. This plosive appears in 19 languages and is clearly distinguished from /p̈/, which appears in only one language. Again, it can be seen that the breathy-voice plosive is generally voiced. Nine of the 19 languages with /b̤/, or nearly half, belong to the Sino-Tibetan language family. In addition, /b̤/ also appears in the Indo-European and Atlantic-Congo language families. This distribution is largely consistent with that reflected in Ladefoged & Maddieson (1996: 57-58).

Three-quarters of languages with /b̤/ also have /p, b, p^h/. That is, four-way opposition appears in the bilabial plosive. Depending on the discussion, /b̤/ is sometimes analyzed as /b^h/, a voiced aspirated plosive. As seen before, most of languages with /b^h/ have four-way opposition such as ‘p : b : p^h : b^h’. Thus, the breathy-voice plosive /b̤/ has a similar pattern to the voiced aspirated plosive /b^h/.

/p̃/

Voiceless, creaky-voice. This plosive appears only in Siona-Tetete, a language of the Tucanoan language family. Siona-Tetete also has a creaky-voice plosive in the alveolar and velar. The creaky voiced sound is usually voiced, although it accompanies the irregular and incomplete vibration of the vocal folds, but /p̃/ is voiceless. Ladefoged & Maddieson (1996: 53) pointed out that the creaky voice has been reported to exist in several language families, but is described as preglottalized or implosive instead of creaky voice due to scholarly disagreements. The extremely low frequency of /p̃/ seems to be related to this tradition.

11 In Noonan (2005: 3), /p̈/ is described as a murmured stop with voiceless onset and is transcribed as ‘pɦ’, whereas /b̤/ is transcribed as ‘bɦ’ and explained as a ‘murmured stop’.

/b̰/

Voiced, creaky-voice. This plosive appears only in Fyer, a language of the Afro-Asiatic language family. Fyer is unrelated to Siona-Tetete, in which /p̃/ is reported to exist, in terms of both language family and region. There is no known language with a phonological opposition between /b̰/ and /p̃/.

/ᵐb̤/

Voiced, prenasalized, breathy-voice. This plosive appears only in Chopi, a language of the Atlantic-Congo language family. Chopi has a total of six breathy-voice plosives, three of which are accompanied by nasalization. The five bilabial plosives of this language include /ᵐb, b̤, ᵐb̤/, so the voiced plosives have a very complicated three-way opposition by nasalization and breathiness. According to Nurse & Philippson (2003: 615), Chopi does not have /b/, the most unmarked voiced plosive in the bilabial.

/pʳ/

Voiceless, trill-released (or flap-released). This plosive appears in four languages, three of which are members of the Sino-Tibetan and Hmong-Mien language families, and is thus distributed mainly in Asian languages. Unlike plain plosives, /pʳ/ incorporates the characteristics of nonlateral liquids such as trills or flaps into the release. In general, there are more trill-released plosives than flap-released plosives.[12]

/bʳ/

Voiced, trill-released (or flap-released). This plosive is a voiced opposite of /pʳ/ and appears in three languages, which all have /pʳ/ as well as /bʳ/.

/pˡ/

Voiceless, lateral-released. This plosive appears in seven languages, with strong bias in region and language family. Six of these seven languages are spoken in Asia, five of which belong to the Hmong-Mien

12 The flap-released plosive /ⁿdʳ/ has been reported to be found in Nyindrou, a language of the Austronesian language family.

language family. The articulation of /p^l/ is the same as that of the /p/ until the stage of closure and hold, but in the release, the airflow passes to the lateral channel of the tongue.

/b^l/

Voiced, lateral-released. This plosive appears in Thou-Kathu and Peve. Its voiceless opposite, /p^l/, appears mainly in the Hmong-Mien language family, but neither Thou-Kathu nor Peve belong to this language family. Interestingly, among the languages of the Hmong-Mien language family, no language has /b^l/. By contrast, Thou-Kathu and Peve have both /p^l/ and /b^l/, that is, a contrastive pair by [±voiced].

/p^{hr}/

Voiceless, postaspirated, trill-released (or flap-released). This plosive appears in Pochuri Naga and Queyu, which belong to the Sino-Tibetan language family. These two languages also have /p^r/, which lacks aspiration. That is, /p^r/ and /p^{hr}/ are opposed to each other by [±aspirated]. Its voiced opposite, /b^{hr}/, is not found in any language.

/p^{hl}/

Voiceless, postaspirated, lateral-released. The defining characteristic of /p^{hl}/ occurs in the final articulatory stage, where aspiration and lateral release are found. This plosive appears in four languages of the Hmong-Mien and Sino-Tibetan language families of Asia. All four languages have /p^l/ in addition to /p^{hl}/, and there is contrast by [±aspirated]. In particular, Thou-Kathu has three bilabial lateral-released plosives, /p^l, b^l, p^{hl}/, which is a very rare system. The voiced opposite of /p^{hl}/, /b^{hl}/, is not found in any language.

/$^mb^r$/

Voiced, prenasalized, trill-released (or flap-released). This plosive appears in Peve and Lele (Papua New Guinea), which are not related by either language family or region. Lele (Papua New Guinea), which is a member of the Austronesian language family with tends to have simple plosive inventory, has as many as eight plosives. However, compared to other languages with trill-released plosives, the inventory of Lele (Papua New Guinea) is quite small. For example, of the six languages with one or more bilabial trill-released plosives, the remaining five languages excluding Lele (Papua New Guinea) have an average of 17.4 plosives. No language has /$^{m}p^{r}$/, a voiceless opposite of /$^{m}b^{r}$/.

/$^{m}p^{l}$/

Voiceless, prenasalized, lateral-released. This plosive appears in four languages belonging to the Hmong-Mien language family. All of these languages also have /p, p^{l}, ^{m}p/, which complicates the opposition of the bilabial plosive.

/$^{m}b^{l}$/

Voiced, prenasalized, lateral-released. This plosive is a voiced opposite of /$^{m}p^{l}$/ and appears in Peve and Hmong Daw, which are unrelated by both language family and region. Peve also has /$^{m}b^{r}$/, so there is a contrast by release type.[13] Languages that include both /$^{m}p^{l}$/ and /$^{m}b^{l}$/ have not been reported.

/$^{m}p^{hl}$/

Voiceless, postaspirated, prenasalized, lateral-released. This plosive goes through a very complicated articulatory process in that it is combined with two secondary articulations and has an unusual release type. /$^{m}p^{hl}$/ appears in Horned Miao and Northern Huishui Hmongthe, which are members of the Hmong-Mien language family. These two languages have four bilabial lateral-released plosives, /p^{l}, p^{hl}, $^{m}p^{l}$, $^{m}p^{hl}$/, which form systematic opposition by [±aspirated] and [±nasalized]. In addition, /p, p^{h}, ^{m}p, $^{m}p^{h}$/ also exist in these languages. As a result, both central-released and lateral-released plosives have four-way opposition. Such a situation is extremely rare, and no other examples are known.

/pp/

Voiceless, fortis. In languages that include the 'tense : lax' phonological opposition in consonants, the concept of 'fortis' is used when referring to tense consonants. Since there is no separate IPA to transcribe the fortis consonant, it is a long-standing convention to use geminate forms. As mentioned earlier, fortis consonants have a

13 Peve has many contrastive pairs by the type of release, such as 'p^{l} : p^{r}', 'b^{l} : b^{r}', 't^{l} : t^{r}', and 'd^{l} : d^{r}'.

stronger tension and a longer closure duration. However, it is difficult to determine an intrinsic phonetic characteristic that can distinguish fortis from other consonants, and there is no guarantee that consonants described as fortis are the same for each language. Therefore, simply grouping the fortis consonants of several languages into the same phonetic class is likely to produce inaccuracies. The label 'fortis', which has been used so far, may refer to a kind of cover phonemes that encompass slightly different consonants.

The bilabial fortis plosive /pp/ appears in six languages and is not found in large language families such as Atlantic-Congo and Austronesian. All the languages with /pp/ have a contrastive pair 'p : pp'. Specifically, Quapaw, a language of the Siouan language family in North America, has /p, b, pʰ/ in addition to /pp/ and shows a complicated opposition.

/bb/

Voiced, fortis. This plosive is a forits, but is voiced, which clearly shows that the distinction between fortis and lenis differs from that between voiceless and voiced consonants. That is, the voiceless consonant cannot be equated with the fortis, nor the voiced consonant with the lenis. /bb/ appears in Northern Paiute and Wolio, which are not related by either language family or region. In addition to /bb/, Northern Paiute and Wolio have /p, b/. These two languages have a contrastive pair 'p : b' by [±voiced] and a contrastive pair 'b : bb' by [±tensed]. No known language has both /pp/ and /bb/ as separate phonemes.

/b̥/

Devoiced. The subscript '˳' of /b̥/ is a diacritic for devoicing, so /b̥/ may look the same as the voiceless plosive /p/ at first glance, but some languages require the use of /b̥/, not /p/.[14] Fleischer & Schmid (2006: 244) describes /p/ and /b̥/ as separate consonants in Swiss German. In Scaraffiotti (2011: 12), /b, pʰ, b̥/ are given as the bilabial plosives in Xhosa.

14 /p/ and /b̥/ are not distinguished by the feature system of Chomsky & Halle (1968) but are distinguished by that of Halle & Stevens (1971). That is, they have different values in [±slack glottis] and [±stiff glottis].

Voiceless plain plosives may be analyzed as devoiced plosives. Korean is the representative example of this approach. Korean is very well known for its special three-way opposition in the obstruent. Voiceless unaspirated plosives in Korean, such as /p, t, k/ are sometimes interpreted as /b̥, d̥, g̊/, and referred to as lenis. In Lagefoged & Maddieson (1996: 64), /b̥/ is also used to indicate a slack voiced bilabial plosive in Javanese, which seems to be a different usage from that in Korean.

4.2. Linguolabial plosives

4.2.1. Overview

The linguolabial plosive is articulated with the tongue tip touching the upper lip. As seen in Chapter 2, the linguolabial plosive is mainly found in languages spoken in Central Vanuatu. A total of seven languages have a linguolabial plosive, of which six meet this condition. The only exception is Hungworo, an African language.

There are only three types of linguolabial plosives: the plain plosive /p̼, b̼/ and nasalized /ᵐb̼/. Among the symbols for the linguolabial plosive, some, such as /p̼, b̼/, which is adopted here, indicate the point of articulation, while others, such as /t̼, d̼/, indicate the articulator.

4.2.2. Description of the linguolabial plosives

/p̼/

Voiceless, plain. This plosive appears in five languages and is the most frequent of the linguolabial plosives. All of these languages except for Hungworo have /p̼/ as their only linguolabial plosive.

/b̼/

Voiced, plain. This plosive appears in Hungworo and Tutuba. Hungworo has /p̼/ in addition to /b̼/, so it is the only language that shows a contrast by [±voiced] in the linguolabial plosive.

/ᵐb̼/

Voiced, prenasalized. This plosive is the only consonant in the linguolabial plosive that is accompanied by secondary articulation. /ᵐb̼/ appears only in Nese.

4.3. Dental plosives

4.3.1. Overview

As seen in Chapter 2, there are far more languages with either the dental or alveolar plosives than languages with both. In the former, the classification of the same consonant as a dental or alveolar plosive differs, depending on the discussion. Even phonemic descriptions that classify a place of articulation as coronal or apical without clearly identifying whether it is dental or alveolar are sometimes found. For this reason, some of the dental plosives may need to be reanalyzed as alveolar, or conversely, some of the alveolar plosives as dental. In this book, the original analysis is followed, but if the place of articulation is marked unclearly, it is consistently classified as alveolar, considering its relatively high frequency. It is necessary to consider this background in

Table 4-8. List of dental plosives

a.	Plain	t̪, d̪
b.	Single secondary articulation	t̪ ʰ, d̪ʰ, ʰt̪, ⁿt̪, ⁿd̪, t̪ˀ, ˀd̪, t̪ʷ, d̪ʷ, t̪ʲ, d̪ʲ, t̪ˤ, d̪ˤ, t̪ˠ
c.	Multiple secondary articulations	t̪ʰʷ, t̪ʰʲ, ⁿt̪ʰ, ⁿd̪ʰ, ⁿt̪ʷ, ⁿd̪ʷ, ⁿt̪ʲ, ⁿd̪ʲ
d.	Glottal action	d̪̤
e.	Liquid-colored release	t̪ʳ, d̪ʳ, t̪ʳʷ, d̪ʳʷ, ⁿd̪ʳ, ⁿd̪ʳʷ
f.	Tenseness	t̪t̪

Table 4-9. Top 10 dental plosives

Ranking	Plosive	Frequency	Ranking	Plosive	Frequency
1	t̪	908	6	t̪ʲ	35
2	d̪	678	7	d̪ʲ	30
3	t̪ʰ	240	8	t̪ˤ	19
4	ⁿd̪	80	9	ⁿt̪	16
5	d̪ʰ	67	10	d̪ˤ	13

Table 4-10. Number of dental plosives in languages

Number of dental plosives	Number of languages	Percentage
0	3,334	76.5%
1	267	6.1%
2	474	10.9%
3	151	3.5%
4	119	2.7%
5	2	0%
6	6	0.1%
8~	3	0.1%

the typological review of the dental plosive.

The list of dental plosives is summarized in Table 4-8. The types of dental plosives are similar to the major plosives, such as the bilabial, alveolar, and velar plosives, except that there is no dental plosive accompanied by three secondary articulations. The top 10 high-frequency plosives among the dental plosives in Table 4-8 are given in Table 4-9.

As expected, two plain plosives are in the top position, and the aspirated plosives are also highly ranked. The fact that the pharyngealized plosives are included instead of the labialized plosives among the high-frequency plosives is different from the other places of articulation. The 10 dental plosives in Table 4-9 consist of five contrastive pairs by [±voiced], such as 't̪ : d̪, t̪ʰ : d̪ʰ, ^{n}t̪ : ^{n}d̪, t̪ʲ : d̪ʲ, t̪ˤ : d̪ˤ'.

The number of dental plosives in world's languages is shown in Table 4-10. Based on Table 4-10, the average number of dental plosives in all languages is 0.5. This frequency is so low that one dental plosive appears in every two languages. However, when languages without dental plosives are excluded, the average number rises to 2.2. This difference is because many languages do not have any dental plosives. The high proportion of languages with no dental plosive is related to the low proportion of languages with both dental and alveolar plosives. Many languages have either a dental or an alveolar plosive, and in such cases, are much more likely to have an alveolar plosive rather than a dental plosive. As a result, the proportion of languages without a dental plosive is bound to be high. If a language has any dental plosive, the number is most often two (10.9%), followed by one (6.1%) and three (3.5%). The proportion of languages with five or more dental plosives drops sharply.

The languages in which more than eight dental plosives appear are Soga, Southern Ma'di, and Kwangali, all of which are spoken in Africa. According to Möhlig (1997: 216~218), Kwangali has 12 dental plosives (t̪, d̪, t̪ʷ, d̪ʷ, t̪ʲ, d̪ʲ, ⁿt̪ʰ, ⁿd̪, ⁿt̪ʷ, ⁿd̪ʷ, ⁿt̪ʲ, ⁿd̪ʲ). In addition to the plain plosive, there are a variety of dental plosives that are combined with nasalization, labialization, and palatalization. The phonological opposition of dental plosives in Kwangali is parallel to that of bilabial plosives in Diriku, which has the most bilabial plosives.[15] However, even though Möhlig (1997: 216~218) categories the 12 dental plosives into the same group, /t̪, d̪/ was described as alveodental, and /ⁿt̪ʰ, ⁿd̪/ as alveolar. Because of this uncertainty, excluding Kwangali, Southern Ma'di, which belongs to the Central Sudanic language family, has the most dental plosives, with 10. According to Andersen (1986: 194~195), the dental plosives of Southern Ma'di are as follows.

(4) Dental plosives in Southern Ma'di

t̪, d̪, t̪ʷ, ⁿd̪, t̪ʳ, d̪ʳ, ⁿd̪ʳ, t̪ʳʷ, d̪ʳʷ, ⁿd̪ʳʷ

Dental plosives in Southern Ma'di are characterized by a large number of trill-released plosives. Six of its ten dental plosives are of this type. Dental aspirated plosives, however, which occur frequently in other languages, are not found in this language.

The discussion will now turn to the patterns that generally appear according to the number of dental plosives. The types and frequencies of the plosives appearing in the 267 languages with one dental plosive are presented below. In Table 4-11, approximately 90% of the 267 languages with one dental plosive have /t̪/ and the remaining 10% have /d̪/. Only

Table 4-11. Types and frequency of single dental plosive inventories

Inventory	t̪	d̪	t̪ʰ	ⁿd̪	d̪ˤ
Number of languages	238	26	1	1	1

15 The phonological description of both languages is based on Möhlig (1997).

Table 4-12. Types and frequency of two-way dental plosive inventories

Inventory	t̪, d̪	t̪, t̪ʰ	t̪, ⁿd̪	d̪, t̪ʰ
Number of languages	381	52	17	8

three languages pose an exception. Since voiceless plain plosives are the most common and most frequent, the results in Table 4-10 reflect this trend well.

There are 474 languages with two dental plosives. Table 4-12 provides a list of the inventories that are common in these languages. Each inventory in Table 4-12 appears in more than five languages. The frequency of /t̪, d̪/ is overwhelmingly high. The frequency rankings of the remaining inventories parallel to those of the bilabial plosive. In the case of the bilabial plosive, the contrastive pair by [±aspirated], /p, pʰ/, showed a bias toward the Sino-Tibetan language family, whereas /t̪, t̪ʰ/ did not, being evenly distributed in several language families. However, /t̪, t̪ʰ/ are not found in the Austronesian language family, nor is the bilabial plosive.

The next topic to consider is the preferred inventory in languages with three dental plosives. Table 4-13 presents inventories of the dental plosive that appear in five or more languages. More than half of the 151 languages with three dental plosives have type-(a). When there are three plosives in one place of articulation, the most preferred inventory consists of voiceless plain, voiced plain, and voiceless aspirated plosives. Type-(a) matches exactly this. Type-(a) appears overwhelmingly in the Sino-Tibetan language family and, to some extent, in the Indo-European language family. Geographically, it is mainly found in Asian languages. Type-(b), an inventory composed of voiceless plain, voiced plain, and voiced prenasalized plosives, is the second most frequent after type-(a) in most places of articulation. Type-(b) is mainly found in African languages such as the Atlantic-Congo and Afro-Asiatic language families, and this is the same as the bilabial plosive.

Table 4-13. Types and frequency of three-way dental plosive inventories

Inventory	Type-(a)	Type-(b)	Type-(c)
	t̪, d̪, t̪ʰ	t̪, d̪, ⁿd̪	t̪, d̪, d̪ˤ
Number of languages	87	32	7

Table 4-14. Types and frequency of four-way dental plosive inventories

Inventory	Type-(a)	Type-(b)	Type-(c)	Type-(d)
	t̪, d̪, t̪ʰ, d̪ʰ	t̪, d̪, t̪ʲ, d̪ʲ	t̪, d̪, t̪ˤ, d̪ˤ	t̪, d̪, t̪ʰ, ^{n}d̪
Number of languages	65	17	11	5

There are 119 languages with four dental plosives. Table 4-14 provide the inventories of the dental plosive that appear in five or more languages. Type-(a), whose members are opposed by two distinctive features, [±voiced] and [±aspirated], comprises the majority type. The inventory with the same characteristics as type-(a) is also the most frequent in other places of articulation. In contrast, the type with opposition by [±voiced] and [±nasalized] which is very frequent in other places of articulation, that is, /t̪, d̪, ^{n}t̪, ^{n}d̪/, is not found in Table 4-14. Inventories in Table 4-14 commonly include /t̪, d̪/, and other plosives with secondary articulation are added. As in the case of the bilabial plosive, excluding type-(d), which is the least frequent in Table 4-14, all other types form a system in which two distinctive features are combined to maximize the contrast. For example, type-(b) uses [±voiced] and [±palatalized], and type-(c) [±voiced] and [±pharyngealized].

The inventories of the dental plosive with four-way opposition have a clear bias regarding language family. Type-(a) is most common in the Indo-European language family, followed by the Sino-Tibetan. Most languages with type-(a) belong to these two language families. Type-(b) including the palatalized plosive is often seen in the Uralic language family. Type-(c) with the pharyngealized plosive is mainly found in the Berber or Semitic language families, which are subbranches of the Afro-Asiatic language family. Thus, when the plosive has multiple oppositions at one place of articulation, the inventory is evidently biased toward a specific language family.

Through examination of the inventories of the dental plosive discussed above from the perspective of phonological opposition, the activeness hierarchy, which is similar to that of (3) in 4.1.1, can be established. If there are two or three dental plosives in languages, the activeness hierarchy of '[±voiced] > [±aspirated] > [±nasalized]' operates without exception, as seen in Table 4-12 and 4-13. However, there is a slight difference in languages with four dental plosives. In

Table 4-14, the activeness hierarchy of '[±voiced] > [±aspirated]' is still valid, but [±nasalized] is less active than [±palatalized] or [±pharyngealized].

4.3.2. Description of the dental plosives

/t̪/

Voiceless, plain. This plosive appears in 980 languages and is evenly distributed without bias by language family or region. /t̪/ is unaspirated, but sometimes accompanied by light aspiration in some languages. If the aspiration accompanying /t̪/ is a little stronger, even if there is only one bilabial plosive, it is analyzed as /t̪ʰ/ instead of /t̪/, like in Suena, a language spoken in Papua New Guinea.

/d̪/

Voiced, plain. This plosive appears in 678 languages. /d̪/ forms a contrastive pair with /t̪/ by [±voiced]. Among the languages with /d̪/, 639 languages also have /t̪/. In other words, approximately 94% of languages with /d̪/ have a contrastive pair by [±voiced]. This ratio of implication is higher than that for other places of articulation.[16]

/t̪ʰ/

Voiceless, postaspirated. This plosive appears in 240 languages. /t̪ʰ/ is most often found in languages of the Sino-Tibetan language family. However, among the languages of the Austronesian, one of the largest language families, only some languages, such as Haroi, Madurese, Nengone, and Yuaga, have this consonant as a phoneme.

/d̪ʰ/

Voiced, postaspirated. This plosive appears in 67 languages. The distribution of /d̪ʰ/ is concentrated in two language families, Indo-European and Sino-Tibetan. Within the Indo-European language family, many languages of the Indo-Iranian subfamily have /d̪ʰ/. As a result, /d̪ʰ/ is found mainly in Asian languages. Tariana, which belongs to the

16 The rate at which the voiced plain plosive implies the presence of voiceless plain plosive is covered in 5.2.

Arawakan language family spoken in South America, is the only non-Asian language that has /d̪^{h}/. Among the 67 languages with /d̪^{h}/, all other languages except Kachi Koli have four-way opposition such as /t̪, d̪, t̪^{h}, d̪^{h}/. The rate at which the voiced /d̪^{h}/ implies not only the voiceless opposite /t̪^{h}/ but also the existence of a four-way opposition is very high.

/^{h}t̪/

Voiceless, preaspirated. This plosive is different from /t̪^{h}/ in that the position of aspiration is in front of the primary articulation. /^{h}t̪/ appears only in Osage, a language of the Siouan language family spoken in North America. In Osage, /t̪^{h}/ and /^{h}t̪/ exist as separate phonemes. Its voiced opposite, /^{h}d̪/, is not found in any language.

/^{n}t̪/

Voiceless, prenasalized. This plosive appears in 16 languages, of which only seven also have /^{n}d̪/. The ratio for /^{n}t̪/ to imply the presence of voiced opposite /^{n}d̪/ is somewhat lower than that for other places of articulation.

/^{n}d̪/

Voiced, nasalized. There are 80 languages with /^{n}d̪/, making it five times more frequent than the voiceless /^{n}t̪/.

/t̪^{w}/

Voiceless, labialized. This plosive appears in 11 languages. Its frequency is much lower than that of the bilabial labialized plosive or velar labialized plosive. In addition to /t̪^{w}/, plosives articulated in the nonperipheral area of the oral cavity, such as the alveolar and palatal, are generally less frequently combined with labialization.

/d̪^{w}/

Voiced, labialized. This plosive appears in eight languages, six of which also have /t̪^{w}/. Like /t̪^{w}/, /d̪^{w}/ does not show a bias toward a specific language family or region. However, /d̪^{w}/ does not appear in large language families in Asia such as the Sino-Tibetan.

/t̪^{j}/

Voiceless, palatalized. This plosive appears in 35 languages, which represents a much higher frequency than /t̪ʷ/ accompanied by labialization. Peripheral plosives, such as bilabial or velar plosives, are more often combined with labialization than palatalization, but in nonperipheral plosives, such as dental and alveolar plosives, palatalization tends to be more common than labialization. In large language families such as the Atlantic-Congo and Austronesian, only a few languages have /t̪ʲ/, whereas in the Uralic language family, which is small in size, there are relatively many languages with this consonant.

/d̪ʲ/

Voiced, palatalized. This plosive appears in 30 languages and is not considerably different from /t̪ʲ/, which appears in 35 languages. It is uncommon for voiced plosives to have a frequency similar to their voiceless opposites.[17] Of the 30 languages that have /d̪ʲ/, 22 also have /t̪ʲ/. The plosive /d̪ʲ/, like /t̪ʲ/, is often found in the Uralic language family.

/t̪ˤ/

Voiceless, pharyngealized. This plosive appears in 19 languages, which is a high frequency considering that the size of dental plosives is not large. For example, /t̪ˤ/ appears in many more languages than the bilabial /pˤ/ or the velar /kˤ/. Of these 19 languages, 17 belong to the Afro-Asiatic language family. /t̪ˤ/ appears mainly in Arabic languages.

/d̪ˤ/

Voiced, pharyngealized. This plosive appears in 13 languages, 12 of which also have /t̪ˤ/. In other words, the rate at which the voiced plosive implies the presence of voiceless plosive is quite high. Like /t̪ˤ/, /d̪ˤ/ appears mainly in the Afro-Asiatic language family.

/t̪ˀ/

Voiceless, postlaryngealized. This plosive appears in four languages, three of which are spoken in North America. Its voiced opposite, /d̪ˀ/, is not found in any language.

---

17 Comparing 'pʲ, tʲ, kʲ' and 'bʲ, dʲ, gʲ', the frequency of the voiceless plosive is much higher than that of the voiced plosive.

/^{ʔ}d̪/

Voiced, prelaryngealized. This plosive is the only dental plosive in which laryngealization precedes primary articulation. /^{ʔ}d̪/ appears in Haroi, Pwo Northern Karen and Tampuan. Interestingly, the inventory of dental plosives for these three languages is the same as /t̪, t̪^{h}, ^{ʔ}d̪/.[18] These three languages belong to different language families, but they are spoken in the Indochina Peninsula. The voiceless opposite of /^{ʔ}d̪/, /^{ʔ}t̪/, is not found in any language.

/t̪^{ɣ}/

Voiceless, velarized. This plosive appears only in Andalusian Arabic. /t̪^{ɣ}/ may be reinterpreted as a pharyngealized plosive. Its voiced opposite, /d̪^{ɣ}/, is not found in any language.

/t̪^{hw}/

Voiceless, postaspirated, labialized. This plosive appears only in Lezgian, which also has /t̪^{h}/. Therefore, there is a phonological opposition by [±labialized]. Its voiced opposite, /d̪^{hw}/, is not found in any language.

/t̪^{hj}/

Voiceless, postaspirated, palatalized. This plosive appears in Chimborazo Highland Quichua and Halh Mongolian. These two languages share /t̪^{h}, t̪^{j}/ in common, and there are at least four series, /t̪, t̪^{h}, t̪^{j}, t̪^{hj}/, opposed by [±aspirated] and [±palatalized]. However, since Chimborazo Highland Quichua belongs to the Quechuan language family and Halh Mongolian to the Mongolic language family, respectively, they share little in terms of linguistic genealogy. The voiced opposite of /t̪^{hj}/, /d̪^{hj}/, is not found in any language.

/^{n}t̪^{h}/

Voiceless, postaspirated, prenasalized. This plosive appears in three languages, which have at least three dental plosives. Nyemba and Kwangali in the Atlantic-Congo language family have three and twelve

18 Phonemic analysis of these three languages was conducted by different researchers.

dental plosives, respectively, and Hmong Njua in the Hmong-Mien language family has four dental plosives.

/^{n}d̪^{h}/

Voiced, postaspirated, prenasalized. This plosive is a voiced opposite of /^{n}t̪^{h}/. /^{n}d̪^{h}/ appears only in Hmong Daw, a member of the Hmong-Mien family. Hmong Daw does not include /^{n}t̪^{h}/. There is no language that has both /^{n}t̪^{h}/ and /^{n}d̪^{h}/.

/^{n}t̪^{w}/

Voiceless, prenasalized, labialized. This plosive appears only in Kwangali, an African language. Kwangali has as many as 12 dental plosives, including /^{n}t̪^{h}, ^{n}t̪^{w}, ^{n}d̪^{w}, ^{n}t̪^{j}, ^{n}d̪^{j}/ which are accompanied by multiple secondary articulations.

/^{n}d̪^{w}/

Voiced, prenasalized, labialized. This plosive is a voiced opposite of /^{n}t̪^{w}/. Unlike /^{n}t̪^{w}/, which appears in only one language, /^{n}d̪^{w}/ appears in three. All three languages have /^{n}d̪/ which is not accompanied by labialization. However, there is no language other than Kwangali that has the contrastive pair '^{n}t̪^{w} : ^{n}d̪^{w}'.

/^{n}t̪^{j}/

Voiceless, prenasalized, palatalized. This plosive, like /^{n}t̪^{w}/, appears only in Kwangali.

/^{n}d̪^{j}/

Voiced, prenasalized, palatalized. This plosive is a voiced opposite of /^{n}t̪^{j}/. Unlike /^{n}t̪^{j}/, which appears only in one language, /^{n}d̪^{j}/ appears in seven, all of which also have /^{n}d̪/, which is not accompanied by palatalization. However, no language other than Kwangali has the contrastive pair '^{n}t̪^{j} : ^{n}d̪^{j}'.

/d̪̤/

Voiced, breathy-voice. This plosive appears in four languages, all of which are spoken in and around India, even though they all belong to different language families. All languages with /d̪̤/ also have /t̪, d̪, t̪^{h}/. That is, they have at least four series of dental plosive. The voiced opposite of /d̤/, /t̤/, is not found in any language.

/t̪^{r}/

voiceless, trill-released (or flap-released). This plosive is the same as the bilabial /p^{r}/, except for the place of articulation. It appears in Linngithigh and Southern Ma'di, which are geographically distant from those regions where languages with /p^{r}/ is mainly spoken.

/d̪^{r}/

Voiced, trill-released (or flap-released). This plosive is a voiced opposite of /t̪^{r}/ and appears only in Southern Ma'di, a language of the Central Sudanic language family. According to Andersen (1986: 194~197), Southern Ma'di has six dental trill-released plosives, including /t̪^{r}/ and /d̪^{r}/.

/^{n}d̪^{r}/

Voiced, prenasalized, trill-released (or flap-released). This plosive is the same as the bilabial /^{m}b^{r}/, except for the place of articulation. /^{n}d̪^{r}/ appears in Southern Ma'di and Linngithigh, both of which also have /^{n}d̪/. In other words, the voiced nasalized plosive in these languages shows the phonological opposition by the release type. The voiceless opposite of /^{n}d̪^{r}/, /^{n}t̪^{r}/, is not found in any language.

/t̪^{rw}/

Voiceless, labialized, trill-released (or flap-released). This plosive appears only in Southern Ma'di.

/d̪^{rw}/

Voiced, labialized, trill-released (or flap-released). This plosive is a voiced opposite of /t̪^{rw}/ and, like that phoneme, appears only in Southern Ma'di. As a result, Southern Ma'di is the only language that has the contrastive pair 't̪^{rw} : d̪^{rw}'.

/^{n}d̪^{rw}/

Voiced, prenasalized, labialized, trill-released (or flap-released). This plosive is arguably the most complicated dental plosive, as it is combined with not only two secondary articulations but also the addition of rhotic color in the release stage. It appears only in Southern Ma'di.

/t̪t̪/

Voiceless, fortis. This plosive is equivalent to the bilabial /pp/ and appears in Maranao, Quapaw, and Koalib-Rere, which are all geographically separated. These languages also share /pp/ in common.

4.4. Alveolar plosives

4.4.1. Overview

Along with bilabial and velar plosives, alveolar plosives form one of the major plosive groups and has high frequency. There are 58 types of alveolar plosives, making it the most diverse class as well.[19] The list of

Table 4-15. List of alveolar plosives

a.	Plain	t, d
b.	Single secondary articulation	t^{h}, d^{h}, ^{h}t, ^{n}t, ^{n}d, t^{n}, d^{n}, t^{ʔ}, d^{ʔ}, ^{ʔ}d, t^{w}, d^{w}, t^{j}, d^{j}, ^{j}t, t^{ʕ}, d^{ʕ}, t^{ɣ}, d^{ɣ}
c.	Multiple secondary articulations	t^{hw}, t^{hj}, t^{wj}, d^{wj}, ^{ʔ}d^{w}, ^{ʔ}d^{j}, ^{n}t^{h}, ^{n}d^{h}, ^{nʔ}t, ^{nʔ}t^{h}, ^{n}t^{w}, ^{n}d^{w}, ^{n}t^{j}, ^{n}d^{j}, ^{n}t^{hj}, ^{nʔ}d
d.	Glottal action	t̤, d̤, t̰, d̰, t̤^{h}, ^{n}d̤
e.	Liquid-colored release	t^{r}, d^{r}, t^{l}, d^{l}, t^{rw}, d^{rw}, t^{hl}, ^{n}d^{r}, ^{n}d^{rw}, ^{n}t^{l}, ^{n}d^{l}, ^{n}t^{hl}
f.	Tenseness	tt, dd, d̥

Table 4-16. Top 10 alveolar plosives

Ranking	Plosive	Frequency	Ranking	Plosive	Frequency
1	t	3,442	6	^{n}t	114
2	d	2,458	7	d^{j}	57
3	t^{h}	644	8	d^{h}	49
4	^{n}d	550	9	t^{w}	37
5	t^{j}	119	10	t^{ʕ}	31

19 Even if the discussion is expanded to include manners of articulation other than the plosive, it is unlikely that such various types will appear in one place of articulation.

alveolar plosives is summarized in Table 4-15.

Table 4-16 above shows the top 10 high-frequency alveolar plosives among those in Table 4-15. The phonological characteristics of the high-frequency plosives in Table 4-16 are not significantly different compared to those of other major places of articulation. The notable difference is that the labialized plosive is relatively uncommon, and the pharyngealized plosive is included in the list. Pharyngealized plosives are highly frequent in the dental and alveolar.

The number of alveolar plosives in world's languages is given in Table 4-17. Based on Table 4-17, the average number of alveolar plosives in all languages is 1.8, which is slightly lower than the bilabial or velar plosives. However, when excluding languages without alveolar plosives, the average number is 2.2, which is the same as the bilabial or velar plosives. In Table 4-17, languages with two alveolar plosives are the most common, and this result generally corresponds to the trend of other major places of articulation.

Diandongbei-Large Flowery Miao, Diriku, Maonan and Soga have the most alveolar plosives, with 12. (5) lists the alveolar plosives in these languages.

(5) Four languages with the most alveolar plosives

a. Diandongbei-Large Flowery Miao: /t, d, t^h, ^nt, nd, $^nt^h$, t^l, d^l, t^{hl},

Table 4-17. Number of alveolar plosives in languages

Number of alveolar plosives	Number of languages	Percentage
0	759	17.4%
1	785	18.0%
2	1,896	43.5%
3	631	14.5%
4	229	5.3%
5	20	0.5%
6	21	0.5%
7	4	0.1%
8	4	0.1%
9	1	0%
10~	6	0.1%

$^{n}t^{l}$, $^{n}d^{l}$, $^{n}t^{hl}$/

b. Diriku: /t, d, t^{w}, d^{w}, t^{j}, d^{j}, ^{n}t, ^{n}d, $^{n}t^{w}$, $^{n}d^{w}$, $^{n}t^{j}$, $^{n}d^{j}$/

c. Maonan: /t, d, t^{h}, t^{w}, t^{j}, d^{j}, t^{hj}, ^{n}d, $^{n}d^{j}$, ^{ʔ}d, $^{ʔ}d^{w}$, $^{ʔ}d^{j}$/

d. Soga: /t, d, t^{w}, d^{w}, t^{j}, d^{j}, ^{n}t, ^{n}d, $^{n}t^{w}$, $^{n}d^{w}$, $^{n}t^{j}$, $^{n}d^{j}$/

The four languages in (5) share two plain plosives /t, d/ and one nasalized plosive /^{n}d/ in common. Three of these languages, with the exception of Maonan, have six nasalized plosives, comprising fully half of the 12 alveolar plosives in their inventories. Notably, the aspirated plosive, which is the most frequent among the plosives with secondary articulation, does not appear at all in (5b, d).

Now, the discussion will determine what inventories commonly appear depending on the number of alveolar plosives. In Table 4-18, /t/ is overwhelmingly the most frequent, with /d/ occupying the next rank. This order is the same as that of the alveolar plosives in Table 4-16. However, the remaining plosives are slightly different. For example, according to Table 4-16, /t^{h}/ should have the next highest frequency after /t/ and /d/ in Table 4-18, but it does not.

There are 1,896 languages with two alveolar plosives, representing the highest proportion in Table 4-17. Table 4-19 shows the inventories of the alveolar plosives that are common in these languages. The pair /t, d/ appears in as many as 1,502 languages, showing the highest frequency. Inventories composed of two plain plosives are also most often found for other places of articulation. Except for /t, d/, the frequencies of /t, t^{h}/ and /t, ^{n}d/ are almost the same. The pair /t, t^{h}/, which has contrast by [±aspirated], appears frequently in the Sino-Tibetan language family. Of the large language families, such as the Atlantic-Congo and Austronesian language families, only a small fraction of the languages has /t, t^{h}/.

Table 4-18. Types and frequency of single alveolar plosive inventories

Plosive	t	d	t^{j}	^{n}d	t^{h}	t^{hj}	$t^{ʕ}$	$^{n}d^{r}$
Number of languages	664	109	4	3	2	1	1	1

Table 4-19. Types and frequency of two-way alveolar plosive inventories

Inventory	t, d	t, t^{h}	t, ^{n}d	t, t^{j}	d, t^{h}	t, ^{n}t
Number of languages	1,502	158	150	36	13	11

However, /t, ^{n}d/, which includes a nasalized plosive, is very common in these two language families. This characteristic is similar to the bilabial plosive in that different types of plosive inventories have an exclusive distribution by language family. In other words, there is a preferred opposition of the plosive according to the language family.

The frequency of /t, t^{j}/, which includes a palatalized plosive, is moderate. For plosives at places of articulation other than the alveolar, however, an inventory similar to /t, t^{j}/ is not found in many languages. The pair /t, t^{j}/ appears most often in languages belonging to the Pama-Nyungan language family. In the Uralic language family where many palatalized consonants are found, only Forest Nenets has this inventory.

There are 631 languages with three alveolar plosives. Table 4-20 lists the inventories that appear in more than 10 languages. In Table 4-20, type-(a) and (b) are very frequent compared to the other types. These two types consist of two plain plosives (t, d) and one complex plosive accompanied by a high-frequency secondary articulation (/t^{h}/ or /^{n}d/). Inventories with the same characteristics as types-(a) and (b) are also the most frequent in the bilabial and velar plosives.

The distributions of type-(a) and (b) are mutually exclusive based on language family. Type-(a) is mostly seen in Asian language families such as the Austroasiatic, Sino-Tibetan, and Tai-Kadai, while type-(b) is mainly seen in African language families such as the Atlantic-Congo and Afro-Asiatic. The difference between these types is which plosive is added to /t, d/. The aspirated plosive /t^{h}/ is common in the Sino-Tibetan and Tai-Kadai language families, and the prenasalized plosive /^{n}d/ is common in the Atlantic-Congo or Austronesian language families. This is related to the bias and mutual exclusivity of the type-(a) and (b) in Table 4-20. Among the remaining types, type-(c) and (e) also show a bias by language family. Type-(c) is found mostly in the Atlantic-Congo and type-(e) is found in the Afro-Asiatic. This distribution reflects the fact that rare plosives such as /^{n}t/ and /t^{ʕ}/ appear mainly in the corresponding language families.

Table 4-20. Types and frequency of three-way alveolar plosive inventories

Inventory	Type-(a)	Type-(b)	Type-(c)	Type-(d)	Type-(e)
	t, d, t^{h}	t, d, ^{n}d	t, ^{n}t, ^{n}d	t, t^{h}, ^{n}d	t, d, t^{ʕ}
Number of languages	289	228	16	16	16

Table 4-21. Types and frequency of four-way alveolar plosive inventories

Inventory	Type-(a)	Type-(b)	Type-(c)	Type-(d)	Type-(e)	Type-(f)
	t, d, ^{n}t, ^{n}d	t, d, t^{h}, d^{h}	t, d, t^{j}, d^{j}	t, d, t^{h}, ^{n}d	t, d, $t^{ʕ}$, $d^{ʕ}$	t, d, t^{h}, d̤
Number of languages	56	49	26	16	14	10

There are 229 languages with four alveolar plosives. Table 4-21 lists the inventories that appear in more than 10 languages. The most frequent type in Table 4-21 is type-(a), which has an opposition by [±voiced] and [±nasalized]. In the case of the bilabial plosive, the inventory corresponding to type-(b) is the most frequent. Of course, there is not much difference in frequency between these two types in Table 4-21. The phonological contrast of the most frequent inventories reveals differences according to the place of articulation. For example, in the case of the velar plosive, /k, g, k^{w}, g^{w}/, an inventory with contrasts by [±voiced] and [±labialized], is the most frequent, and its type is different from that of the bilabial or alveolar plosives. As a result, the most frequent four-way plosives at the three major places of articulation are all inconsistent.

However, the overall trend in Table 4-21 is similar to that of other places of articulation. First, a bias toward a specific language family of each type is revealed. Type-(a) appears mainly in the Atlantic-Congo, and type-(b) appears in the Indo-European or Sino-Tibetan language families. Next, the types based on the contrast by [±voiced] occur frequently. All the types in Table 4-21 have the contrastive pair 't : d'. Finally, types in which phonological contrast is optimized are preferred. If type-(f) is considered to be similar to type-(b), the remaining types, except for type-(d), have a four-way contrast that can be described by two distinctive features.[20]

The above discussion has helped elucidate the activeness hierarchy of distinctive features. Among the distinctive features, [±voiced], [±aspirated], and [±nasalized] are actively involved in phonological opposition, which is the same as other places of articulation. In particular, [±voiced] shows very high activeness in languages with

20 The combination of the two distinctive features can be referred to as presented in (2) of 4.1.1.

two or more alveolar plosives, so /t, d/, which is a contrastive pair by [±voiced], shows an overwhelmingly high frequency. However, the activeness hierarchy between [±aspirated] and [±nasalized] is not clear. When there are two or three alveolar plosives, [±aspirated] is more actively involved in phonological contrast than [±nasalized], but when there are four alveolar plosives, the degree of activeness is reversed. Comparing the fact that [±aspirated] has a higher activeness hierarchy than [±nasalized] in the bilabial or dental plosives, the hierarchy between the two distinctive features in the alveolar plosive is not fixed but unsettled.

4.4.2. Description of the alveolar plosives

/t/

Voiceless, plain. This plosive appears in 3,442 languages. Its frequency (79.0% of all languages) is the third highest among all plosives and the highest among alveolar plosives. Nonetheless, the frequency of /t/ is somewhat lower than that of other major plain plosives, /p/ or /k/, because plosives with similar places of articulation are divided into dental and alveolar depending on the discussion. If dental and alveolar plosives do not exist as separate phonemes, it is possible to group the two into the same class, in which case their frequency will be much higher. The plosive /t/ is unaspirated, but is sometimes accompanied by light aspiration, depending on the language. If the aspiration accompanying /t/ is slightly stronger, even if there is only one alveolar plosive, it is analyzed as /t^h/ instead of /t/, like in Jizhao and Tojolabal.[21]

/d/

Voiced, plain. This plosive appears in 2,458 languages. Of the languages with /d/, 94.5%, or 2,323 languages, have /t/, so there is a contrastive pair by [±voiced]. The percentage of /d/ implying the existence of voiceless opposite is higher than that of /b/ (86.1%) but lower than that of /g/ (96.1%).

21 The only bilabial plosive of these two languages is also /p^h/ instead of /p/.

/t^h/

Voiceless, postaspirated. This plosive appears in 644 languages and is the third most frequent among all aspirated plosives. /t^h/ appears in several language families but is most common in the Sino-Tibetan language family, which is home to 276 of these 644 languages.

/d^h/

Voiced, postaspirated. This plosive appears in 49 languages, and, surprisingly, all of these languages have four alveolar plosives, /t, d, t^h, d^h/. In other words, the existence of /d^h/ implies the existence of a four-way opposition by [±voiced] and [±aspirated] without exception. Like other voiced aspirated plosives, /d^h/ is very common in Asian languages.

/$^h t$/

Voiceless, preaspirated. This plosive is different from /t^h/ in the position of aspiration. /$^h t$/ appears in five languages, and there is no bias toward language families or regions. In Bonan and Zhongu, /t^h/ is also present in addition to /$^h t$/, so these two plosives are distinguished by the position of aspiration. No language with /$^h d$/, a voiced opposite of /$^h t$/, is currently known.

/$^n t$/

Voiceless, prenasalized. This plosive appears in 114 languages, many of which belong to the Atlantic-Congo and Austronesian language families. Voiced consonants are much more frequent than voiceless consonants among nasalized plosives, and this is also the case for alveolar nasalized plosives. Among the languages in which /$^n t$/ appears, 84 languages also have /$^n d$/, that is, a contrastive pair by [±voiced]. The percentage of languages in which /$^n t$/ implies the presence of /$^n d$/ is 73.7% (84/114).

/$^n d$/

Voiced, prenasalized. This plosive appears in 550 languages and is approximately five times more frequent than /$^n t$/. The plosive /$^n d$/, like /$^n t$/, appears in many languages of the Atlantic-Congo and Austronesian language families. However, in addition to these two language families, it is also widely seen in other language families, such as the Afro-Asiatic, Central Sudanic, and Nuclear Trans New Guinea.

/t^n/

Voiceless, postnasalized. This plosive appears in Pangseng, Mumuye, and Nemi. Of these, the first two languages are close in terms of language family and region, whereas Nemi is not. The position of nasalization distinguishes /t^n/ from /^nt/. No known language has both /^nt/ and /t^n/ as separate phonemes.

/d^n/

Voiced, postnasalized. This plosive is a voiced opposite of /t^n/ and appears only in Mumuye. This language also has /t^n/, so it is the only language in which there is a contrastive pair by [±voiced], 't^n : d^n'.

/t^w/

Voiceless, labialized. This plosive appears in 37 languages but occurs less frequently than /p^w/ or /k^w/, which have the same secondary articulation. It is common in African languages, including the Atlantic-Congo language family. While the bilabial /p^w/ appears often within the Austronesian language family, /t^w/ shows no such bias.

/d^w/

Voiced, labialized. This plosive is found in 18 languages. Like /t^w/, it appears in many African languages. Of the 18 languages with /d^w/, 14 also have the voiceless opposite /t^w/. In particular, all languages with /d^w/ also have /d/, which is not accompanied by labialization.

/t^j/

Voiceless, palatalized. This plosive appears in 119 languages, which is three times more frequent than /t^w/. In general, the frequency of the labialized plosive outperforms that of the palatalized plosive, but dental and alveolar plosives tend to be accompanied by more palatalization than labialization. The plosive /t^j/ is not biased toward a specific language family or region. Moreover, it appears more in the Otomanguean or the Pama-Nyungan language families than in the Atlantic-Congo or Austronesian language families, which are the most large-scale, so the distribution of /t^j/ is not related to the size of the language family.

/d^j/

Voiced, palatalized. This plosive appears in 57 languages and, like /t^j/, is not biased toward a language family or region. Of the 57 languages with /d^j/, 47 also have the contrastive pair 't^j : d^j'. Additionally, /d/ appears in 55 of these 57 languages, and the likelihood of /d^j/ implying the existence of /d/ not accompanied by palatalization is very high.

/^jt/

Voiceless pre-palatalized. This plosive is different from other palatalized plosives in that palatalization precedes primary articulation. The prepalatalized plosive has not been found in languages other than Kaytetye. According to Brown & Ogilvie (2009: 586), Kaytetye has /t, ^jt/ as alveolar plosives. However, no known language has both prepalatalized and postpalatalized plosives as separate phonemes.

/$t^ʕ$/

Voiceless, pharyngealized. This plosive appears in 31 languages and is the most frequent among the pharyngealized plosives. /$t^ʕ$/ is found mainly in languages belonging to the Afro-Asiatic language family and is one of the so-called emphatic consonants.

/$d^ʕ$/

Voiced, pharyngealized. This plosive appears in 17 languages and is the most frequent among the voiced pharyngealized plosives. Like /$t^ʕ$/, /$d^ʕ$/ is mainly distributed in languages of the Afro-Asiatic language family. Of the 17 languages with /$d^ʕ$/, 14 also have /$t^ʕ$/.

/$t^ˀ$/

Voiceless, postlaryngealized. This plosive appears in 11 languages, six of which also have an aspirated /t^h/. However, there are no other languages than Emberá-Tadó that have both /t/ and /d/, which are plain plosives with high frequency. That is, most languages with /$t^ˀ$/ do not follow the normal pattern of the plosive.

/$d^ˀ$/

Voiced, postlaryngealized. This plosive appears in two languages, Kakua and Tày. These two languages do not overlap with languages that has /$t^ˀ$/, a voiceless opposite of /$d^ˀ$/. There are no languages with alveolar postlaryngealized plosives that are opposed only by [$\pm$voiced].

/ˀd/

Voiced, prelaryngealized. This plosive is different from /dˀ/ in that laryngealization precedes primary articulation. /ˀd/ appears in 16 languages, making it more frequent than /dˀ/. It is found in many languages belonging to the Tai-Kadai language family. In contrast, it rarely appears in languages spoken in Africa. There is no language with both /ˀd/ and /dˀ/ as separate phonemes, which are opposed by the position of laryngealization.

/tˠ/

Voiceless, velarized. This plosive appears in three languages, all of which are Arabic languages. In that respect, /tˠ/ can also be seen as a kind of emphatic consonant. This is also true of its voiced opposite, /dˠ/.

/dˠ/

Voiced, velarized. This plosive appears in Kumzari and Standard Arabic, all of which are Arabic languages. These languages have the contrastive pair 'tˠ : dˠ'.

/ⁿtʰ/

Voiceless, postaspirated, prenasalized. This plosive appears in 20 languages, many of which are spoken in Asia. Languages with /ⁿtʰ/ have at least three alveolar plosives. The presence of /ⁿtʰ/ implies the existence of /tʰ/ in 17 of these 20 languages but implies the existence of /ⁿt/ in only 11. A significant difference exists in the ratio of implications between the plosives, depending on the type of secondary articulation.

/ⁿdʰ/

Voiced, postaspirated, prenasalized. This plosive is a voiced opposite of /ⁿtʰ/ and appears in three languages spoken in the Southwestern China. These three languages have similarities in the opposition of alveolar plosives. Gepo and Wumeng Nasu have /t, d, tʰ, ⁿdʰ/ in common, and South Wa has /ⁿd/ instead of /d/. None of languages with /ⁿdʰ/ have /ⁿtʰ/. In other words, there is no language that has both /ⁿtʰ/ and /ⁿdʰ/. This relationship is unusual compared to that of /dʰ/, the presence of which absolutely implies the existence of /tʰ/ in many languages.

/t^{hw}/

Voiceless, postaspirated, labialized. This plosive appears in four languages, three of which also have /t, t^h, t^w/, whose articulatory process is simpler than /t^{hw}/. Its voiced opposite, /d^{hw}/, is not found in any language.

/t^{hj}/

Voiceless, postaspirated, palatalized. This plosive appears in 21 languages and is quite frequent among the plosives accompanied by two secondary articulations. /t^{hj}/ appears mainly in Asian languages belonging to the Sino-Tibetan, Tai-Kadai, and Hmong-Mien language families. Its voiced opposite, /d^{hj}/, is not found in any language.

/$^nt^w$/

Voiceless, prenasalized, labialized. This plosive appears in Diriku and Soga. Although both languages belong to the Bantu language family, their subfamilies are different and the areas in which these two languages are used are very far apart. Surprisingly, however, both languages have the large inventory, which consists of twelve identical alveolar plosives.

/$^nd^w$/

Voiced, prenasalized, labialized. This plosive is a voiced opposite of /$^nt^w$/ and appears in 11 languages, making it more frequent than the voiceless /$^nt^w$/. All languages with /$^nd^w$/ have /nd/, but seven of these 11 languages have /d^w/. Interestingly, /$^mb^w$/, which is similar to /$^nd^w$/, appears mainly in the Austronesian language family, whereas /$^nd^w$/ does not appear in this language family. Instead, /$^nd^w$/ appears in African languages, including the Atlantic-Congo language family.

/$^nt^j$/

Voiceless, prenasalized, palatalized. This plosive appears in four languages. These languages have numerous alveolar plosives, including /t, t^j, ^nt, $^nt^j$/. Among them, South Tairora has the fewest alveolar plosives, with four, while the other three languages have eight or more.

/$^nd^j$/

Voiced, nasalized, palatalized. This plosive is a voiced opposite of /$^nt^j$/ and appears in 16 languages, making it more frequent than the voiceless /$^{n}t^{j}$/. That is, the frequencies of the voiced and voiceless plosives are reversed, which is a characteristic of the nasalized plosive. There is a variation in the rate at which /$^{n}d^{j}$/ implies the presence of phonetically simpler voiced alveolar plosives. For example, among languages with /$^{n}d^{j}$/, except for Yuaga, all other languages also have /^{n}d/, so the rate of implication between the two is high. However, of the 16 languages with /$^{n}d^{j}$/, 10 have /d/ and nine have /d^{j}/, so the rate of implications is relatively low.

/^{nʔ}t/

voiceless, prenasalized, prelaryngealized. This plosive appears only in Luopohe Hmong, a language spoken in Southwest of China. Luopohe Hmong has many plosives accompanied by nasalization and prelaryngealization at other places of articulation. As noted in the description of /^{mʔ}p/, when laryngealization is combined with nasalization, only a plosive in which laryngealization precedes the primary articulation is found.

/^{nʔ}d/

Voiced, prenasalized, prelaryngealized. This plosive is a voiced opposite of /^{nʔ}t/ and appears only in the San Martín Itunyoso Triqui, which is unrelated to Luopohe Hmong having the voiceless /^{nʔ}t/. There is no language with the contrastive pair '^{nʔ}t : ^{nʔ}d'.

/t^{wj}/

Voiceless, labialized, palatalized. This plosive is a voiceless plosive that is combined with labialization and palatalization. The combination of these two secondary articulations is very rare and is mainly found in the velar plosive. /t^{wj}/ appears only in Eastern Arrernte, an Australian language.

/d^{wj}/

Voiced, labialized, palatalized. This plosive is a voiced opposite of /t^{wj}/, but no language has both /t^{wj}/ and /d^{wj}/. It appears only in Awutu, a language spoken in Ghana. Awutu is unrelated to Eastern Arrernte, in which the voiceless /t^{wj}/ appears.

$/{}^{ʔ}d^{w}/$

Voiced, prelaryngealized, labialized. This consonant is a voiced plosive that is combined with labialization and prelaryngealization. It appears only in Maonan. Its voiceless opposite, $/t^{hj}/$, is not found in any language.

$/{}^{ʔ}d^{j}/$

Voiced, prelaryngealized, palatalized. This plosive, like $/{}^{ʔ}d^{w}/$, appears only in Maonan. This language is rich in voiced prelaryngealized plosives, including $/{}^{ʔ}d$, ${}^{ʔ}d^{w}/$. Its voiceless opposite, $/{}^{ʔ}t^{j}/$, is not found in any language.

$/{}^{n}t^{hj}/$

Voiceless, postaspirated, prenasalized, palatalized. This plosive appears only in Western Xiangxi Miao, which has more plosives of the same character as $/{}^{n}t^{hj}/$ in the bilabial and velar. Its voiced opposite, $/{}^{n}d^{hj}/$, is not found in any language.

$/{}^{nʔ}t^{h}/$

Voiceless, postaspirated, prenasalized, prelaryngealized. This plosive is found in only Luopohe Hmong, which also has $/{}^{mʔ}p^{h}/$. For an explanation of why the combination of secondary articulations seen in $/{}^{nʔ}t^{h}/$ is unnatural, refer to the description of $/{}^{mʔ}p^{h}/$ in 4.1.2.

/t̤ /

Voiceless, breathy-voice. This plosive appears only in Chantyal, a language of the Sino-Tibetan language family. Chantyal also has its voiced opposite, /d̤/, as a separate phoneme. For the specificity of the voiceless breathy-voice plosive, refer to the description of /p̈/ in 4.1.2.

/d̤/

Voiced, breathy-voice. This plosive appears in 16 languages and is more frequent than /t̤ / which appears in one language. /d̤/ is found in many languages of the Sino-Tibetan language family. Languages with /d̤/ usually have many alveolar plosives. Except for Manyika and Zulu, which have two, all others have four or more alveolar plosives.[22] However, Manyika and Zulu have more alveolar stops such as ejective, implosive, and click, so the presence of /d̤/ can be said to imply an inventory consisting of various alveolar stops.

/t̤ʰ/

Voiceless, postaspirated, breathy-voice. This plosive is special in two respects. One is that breathy-voice plosives are generally voiced, but /t̤ʰ/ is voiceless. The other is that the breathy voice itself includes some aspiration, but /t̤ʰ/ is accompanied by aspiration as an additional secondary articulation. /t̤ʰ/ appears only in Chantyal, which has a contrastive pair by [±aspirated], such as /t̤ : t̤ʰ/. Chantyal is unique in its opposition of the plosives by the vocal folds.[23]

/t̰/

Voiceless, creaky-voice. This plosive appears only in Siona-Tetete, which has several voiceless creaky-voice plosives. For the specificity of the voiceless creaky-voice plosive, refer to the description of 'p̰' in 4.1.2.

/d̰/

Voiced, creaky-voice. This plosive appears only in Fyer, which belongs to the Afro-Asiatic language family. There is no language that has both /t̰/ and /d̰/ as separate phonemes. This is also true for creaky-voice plosives in other places of articulation.

/ⁿd̤/

Voiced, prenasalized, breathy-voice. This plosive is highly uncommon in that the breathy-voice plosive is accompanied by secondary articulation. /ⁿd̤/ appears only in Chopi, which has more plosives similar to /ⁿd̤/ like /ᵐb̤, ᵑg̈/. In this language, there are voiced alveolar plosives such as /d̤, ⁿd, ⁿd̤/, but the most common /d/ is missing. This pattern is also found in the bilabial and velar plosives.

/tʳ/

Voiceless, trill-released (or flap-released). For this type of plosive, refer to the description of /pʳ/ in 4.1.2. /tʳ/ appears in five languages.

22 Languages of the Sino-Tibetan language family have the four series in common, such as /t, d, tʰ, d̤/.

23 An inventory of the plosive in Chantyal will be discussed in 5.5.

Unlike /p^r/, which is common in Asian languages, /t^r/ is not found in Asian languages.

/d^r/

Voiced, trill-released (or flap-released). This plosive appears in seven languages, making it more frequent than /t^r/. Notably, voiced plosive is more frequent than the voiceless plosive. The bilabial plosive /b^r/ is less frequent than /p^r/ and thus differs from /d^r/. Of the seven languages with /d^r/, four have a contrastive pair by [±voiced] such as 't^r : d^r'.

/t^l/

Voiceless, lateral-released. For this type of plosive, refer to the description of /p^l/ in 4.1.2. The plosive /t^l/ appears in nine languages. Unlike /p^l/, which is common mostly in Asian languages, /t^l/ is found throughout both Asian and African languages.[24]

/d^l/

Voiced, lateral-released. This plosive appears in four languages, which are widely scattered in Africa, Asia, and North America. Three of the four languages with /d^l/ have a contrastive pair by [±voiced] such as 't^l : d^l'.

/t^{rw}/

Voiceless, labialized, trill-released (or flap-released). This plosive is so rare that it appears only in Moru, a language of the Central Sudanic language family.

/d^{rw}/

voiced, labialized, trill-released (or flap-released). This plosive, like /t^{rw}/, appears only in Moru. As a result, Moru is the only language with the contrastive pair 't^{rw} : d^{rw}'.

/t^{hl}/

Voiceless, postaspirated, lateral-released. This plosive appears in seven languages and has similar distribution to /t^l/. All seven languages

24 /t^l/ also appears in Dogrib, a language spoken in North America.

with /t^{hl}/ have /t^h/, but five of these languages have /t^l/. There is no language with its voiced opposite, /d^{hl}/.

/$^nd^r$/

Voiced, prenasalized, trill-released (or flap-released). For this type of plosive, refer to the description of /$^mb^r$/ in 4.1.2. The plosive /$^nd^r$/ appears in nine languages, although none of them belong to the Atlantic-Congo, the largest language family. There is no language with its voiceless opposite, /$^nt^r$/.

/$^nd^{rw}$/

Voiced, prenasalized, labialized, trill-released (or flap-released). This consonant is a complex voiced plosive that is not only accompanied by two secondary articulations but also has a special release. It appears only in Moru. This language has several trill-released alveolar plosives, such as /t^r, d^r, t^{rw}, d^{rw}, $^nd^r$/.

/$^nt^l$/

Voiceless, prenasalized, lateral-released. This plosive appears in Diandongbei-Large Flowery Miao and Northern Huishui Hmong, members of the Hmong-Mien language family. These two languages have numerous alveolar plosives, with Diandongbei-Large Flowery Miao having 12 and Northern Huishui Hmong having six. The bilabial plosive /$^mp^l$/, which has the same features as /$^nt^l$/, is also found only in the Hmong-Mien language family.

/$^nd^l$/

Voiced, prenasalized, lateral-released. This plosive appears only in Diandongbei-Large Flowery Miao, a language of the Hmong-Mien language family. This language has the contrastive pair /$^nt^l$: $^nd^l$/.

/$^nt^{hl}$/

Voiceless, postaspirated, prenasalized, lateral-released. This consonant is a complex voiced plosive that is not only accompanied by two secondary articulations but also has a special release. It appears only in Diandongbei-Large Flowery Miao, which has many lateral-released alveolar plosives.

/tt/

Voiceless, fortis. For this type of plosive, refer to the description of /pp/ in 4.1.2. /tt/ appears in four apparently unassociated languages.

/dd/

Voiced, fortis. This plosive appears in two languages, neither of which has /tt/. Like the bilabial fortis plosive, no language has both voiceless and voiced alveolar fortis plosives. For the voiced fortis plosive, refer to the description of /bb/ in 4.1.2.

/d̥/

Devoiced. This plosive is distinguished from the voiceless /t/. For the devoiced plosive, refer to the description of /b̥/ in 4.1.2. /d̥/ appears in three languages. Among them, in Ter Saami and Swiss German, /d̥/ is phonologically opposed to /t/, but in Xhosa, it is not.[25]

4.5. Retroflex plosives

4.5.1. Overview

The retroflex plosive cannot be said to belong to the major place of articulation. It is less frequent than the glottal plosive or palatal plosive, and its types are not diverse. The list of retroflex plosives is summarized in Table 4-22 below.

There are few types of the retroflex plosives in Table 4-22, and the plosive frequency is very low. For example, among the 16 plosives in Table 4-22, only six appear in more than 10 languages, and eight are found in fewer than two languages. The retroflex plosives that appear in more than 10 languages are given in Table 4-23.

The list of high-frequency retroflex plosives follows the general pattern almost unchanged. The plain plosives 'ʈ, ɖ' are at the top, followed by those plosives accompanied by a high-frequency secondary

25 Xhosa has /tʰ/ as a phoneme instead of /t/. If /tʰ/ in Xhosa is reinterpreted as /t/, it can be said that all languages with /d̥/ have a contrast between /t/ and /d̥/.

Table 4-22. List of retroflex plosives

a.	Plain	ʈ, ɖ
b.	Single secondary articulation	$ʈ^{h}$, $ɖ^{h}$, $^{ɳ}ʈ$, $^{ɳ}ɖ$, $ʈ^{ʔ}$, $ʈ^{w}$, $ʈ^{j}$, $ɖ^{j}$
c.	Multiple secondary articulations	$^{ɳ}ʈ^{h}$, $^{ɳ}ɖ^{h}$, $^{ɳʔ}ʈ^{h}$
d.	Glottal action	ɖ̤
e.	Liquid-colored release	$ɖ^{r}$
f.	Tenseness	ʈʈ

Table 4-23. High-frequency retroflex plosives

Ranking	Plosive	Frequency	Ranking	Plosive	Frequency
1	ʈ	373	4	$ɖ^{h}$	75
2	ɖ	323	5	$^{ɳ}ɖ$	17
3	$ʈ^{h}$	173	6	$^{ɳ}ʈ$	10

Table 4-24. Number of retroflex plosives in languages

Number of retroflex plosives	Number of languages	Percentage
0	3,897	89.5%
1	175	4.0%
2	122	2.8%
3	69	1.6%
4	91	2.1%
5	1	0%
6	1	0%

articulation such as aspiration or nasalization.

The number of retroflex plosives is given in Table 4-24. Based on Table 4-24, the average number of retroflex plosives in all languages is small, at 0.2, because languages without any retroflex plosives make up nearly 90% of all languages. However, the average number of retroflex plosives in languages that include such phonemes is 2.2, which is not considerably different from that of other places of articulation.

Many languages have one or two retroflex plosives. However, unlike other places of articulation, more languages have one retroflex plosive than two. In addition, extremely few languages have more than five retroflex plosives. For bilabial, alveolar, and velar plosives, there are languages with more than 10 plosives, but for the retroflex, Urdu with five and Diandongbei-Large Flowery Miao with six represent a large inventory of retroflex plosives. For reference, the retroflex plosives in these two languages are given below. The list for Urdu is from Ismailee (1976) and that for Diandongbei-Large Flowery Miao is from Niederer (1998).

(6) Retroflex plosives in Urdu and Diandongbei-Large Flowery Miao
a. Urdu: /ʈ, ɖ, ʈ^{h}, ɖ̤, ^{n}ɖ/
b. Diandongbei-Large Flowery Miao: /ʈ, ɖ, ʈ^{h}, ^{n}ʈ, ^{n}ɖ, ^{n}ʈ^{h}/

Both languages have four plosives in common: /ʈ, ɖ, ʈ^{h}, ^{n}ɖ/. However, the overall phonological contrast differs between the two languages. Urdu has a breathy-voice plosive /ɖ̤/, so its contrast is similar to that of /ʈ, ɖ, ʈ^{h}, ɖ^{h}/ in which [±voiced] and [±aspirated] are involved. However, since /^{n}ɖ/ is included, a balanced contrast cannot be achieved. On the other hand, in Diandongbei-Large Flowery Miao, three distinctive features of [±voiced], [±aspirated], and [±nasalized] are almost equally involved in distinguishing the plosives. For example, there are two contrastive pairs by [±voiced] such as 'ʈ : ɖ' and '^{n}ʈ : ^{n}ɖ', two contrastive pairs by [±aspirated] such as 'ʈ : ʈ^{h}' and '^{n}ʈ : ^{n}ʈ^{h}', and three two contrastive pairs by [±nasalized] such as 'ʈ : ^{n}ʈ', 'ɖ : ^{n}ɖ', and 'ʈ^{h} : ^{n}ʈ^{h}'. The balance or efficiency of phonological contrast is better in Diandongbei-Large Flowery Miao than in Urdu.

Next, I will examine the commonly found types according to the number of retroflex plosives. The results for languages with one retroflex plosive are given in Table 4-25. The pattern in Table 4-25 is somewhat familiar. As expected, the frequency of plain plosives such as /ʈ/ and /ɖ/ is overwhelmingly high. Notably, however, the frequency of voiced plain /ɖ/ is relatively high compared to voiceless plain /ʈ/. This relationship is relevant to the smaller difference in frequency between /ʈ/ and /ɖ/ in Table 4-23. When there is only one plosive at one place of articulation,

Table 4-25. Types and frequency of single retroflex plosive inventories

Plosive	ʈ	ɖ	ʈ^{h}	^{ɳʔ}ʈ^{h}
Number of languages	95	78	1	1

Table 4-26. Types and frequency of two-way retroflex plosive inventories

Inventory	ʈ, ɖ	ʈ, ʈ^{h}	ʈ, ^{n}ʈ	ʈ, ^{n}ɖ
Number of languages	92	21	4	4

voiced plain plosives can frequently be found in the palatal in addition to the retroflex, whereas this pattern is far less common in the major places of articulation, such as the bilabial, alveolar, and velar.

A peculiar entity in Table 4-25 is /^{ɳʔ}ʈ^{h}/, which is accompanied by three secondary articulations, giving it a high degree of articulatory complexity. Therefore, it is doubtful that /^{ɳʔ}ʈ^{h}/ will appear in a language with only one retroflex plosive. In Luopohe Hmong, which has /^{ɳʔ}ʈ^{h}/, there are as many as 23 plosives, but only one retroflex plosive. Luopohe Hmong also has /^{mʔ}p^{h}/ and /^{nʔ}t^{h}/ which are phonologically similar to /^{ɳʔ}ʈ^{h}/.

There are 122 languages with two retroflex plosives. Table 4-26 provides a list of inventories of two-way plosives that appear in two or more languages. The types in Table 4-26 are rather simple. A variety of types is not expected because the retroflex plosives, except for plain plosives, are infrequent. The overwhelming majority of /ʈ, ɖ/ followed by /ʈ, ʈ^{h}/ can be predicted from other places of articulation. The type containing the voiceless nasalized plosive is noticeable, but is still infrequent, making it difficult to ascribe this occurrence any significance. /ʈ, ʈ^{h}/ is mainly found in the Sino-Tibetan language family.

There are 69 languages with three retroflex plosives. Only two inventories appear in two or more languages, as shown in Table 4-27. Type-(a), in which /ʈ^{h}/ is added to the high-frequency inventory /ʈ, ɖ/ in Table 4-26, constitutes the dominant majority. In type-(b), /^{n}ɖ/ is added instead of /ʈ^{h}/. Type-(a) is mainly found in Asian languages such as the Sino-Tibetan language family and its distribution does not overlap with that of type-(b).

Finally, I will examine high-frequency inventories in languages that have four retroflex plosives. Table 4-28 provides the four inventories that appear in two or more languages. Considering the phonetic similarity of /ɖ̤/ and /ɖ^{h}/, types-(a) and (b) can be grouped together, reducing the actual number of types to three. Inventories with the same properties as type-(a) are frequent at any place of articulation, but especially in the retroflex. When types-(a) and (b) are combined, approximately 88% of

Table 4-27. Types and frequency of three-way retroflex plosive inventories

Inventory	Type-(a)	Type-(b)
	ʈ, ɖ, ʈʰ	ʈ, ɖ, ⁿɖ
Number of languages	57	7

Table 4-28. Types and frequency of four-way retroflex plosive inventories

Inventory	Type-(a)	Type-(b)	Type-(c)	Type-(d)
	ʈ, ɖ, ʈʰ, ɖʰ	ʈ, ɖ, ʈʰ, ɖ̤	ʈ, ʈʰ, ⁿʈ, ⁿʈʰ	ʈ, ɖ, ʈʲ, ɖʲ
Number of languages	74	6	4	2

the 91 languages with four retroflex plosives have this type. Type-(a) appears mainly in the Indo-European and Sino-Tibetan language families. Thus, it is found in India or the regions of Western Asia near India. This distribution is similar to that of plosives at other places of articulation.

All the types in Table 4-28 share the characteristic that they are systems in which phonological opposition is optimized by two distinctive features. Type-(a) has a contrast by [±voiced] and [±aspirated]. Type-(b) is similar to type-(a). In type-(c), four retroflex plosives are opposed by [±aspirated] and [±nasalized], and in type-(d) by [±voiced] and [±palatalized]. In particular, type-(c) can be said to be characteristic in that it consists only of four voiceless plosives. In other words, [±voiced] does not function as a distinctive feature in type-(c). When four plosives appear at one place of articulation, it is common for the inventory to include at least one voiced plosive.

4.5.2. Description of the retroflex plosives

/ʈ/

Voiceless, plain. This plosive appears in 379 languages, making it less frequent compared to other major voiceless plain plosives. /ʈ/ is common in languages of the Dravidian, Indo-European, Pama-Nyungan, and Sino-Tibetan language families. Except for the Pama-Nyungan, the rest are regionally distributed in Asia of the Northern Hemisphere. On the other hand, in the two largest language families, Atlantic-Congo and Austronesian, only a small number of languages have /ʈ/. This distribution is similar to other retroflex plosives. /ʈ/ is unaspirated plosive, but it is sometimes accompanied by light aspiration. If the aspiration accompanying /ʈ/ is slightly stronger, even if there is only one retroflex plosive, it is analyzed as /ʈʰ/ instead of /ʈ/, like in Tolowa-Chetco, a language spoken in North America.[26]

/ɖ/

Voiced, plain. This plosive appears in 323 languages, 245 of which have the contrastive pair 'ʈ : ɖ'. In other words, voiced /ɖ/ implies the presence of voiceless /ʈ/ in 75.9% of languages (245/323), which is low compared to other voiced plain plosives.

/ʈʰ/

Voiceless, postaspirated. This plosive appears in 173 languages, the majority of which appear in the Indo-European and Sino-Tibetan language families. All these languages, except for Tolowa-Chetco, have a plain plosive /ʈ/.

/ɖʰ/

Voiced, postaspirated. This plosive is a voiced opposite of /ʈʰ/. /ɖʰ/ appears in 75 languages, especially within the Indo-Iranian language family, a subfamily of Indo-European. All of the languages with /ɖʰ/, except for Kachi Koli, have four-way opposition, that is, they have /ʈ, ɖ, ʈʰ, ɖʰ/ as retroflex plosives.[27] The presence of voiced aspirated plosive is very likely to imply the existence of a four-way opposition by [±voiced] and [±aspirated].

/ⁿʈ/

Voiceless, prenasalized. This plosive appears in 10 languages, six of which belong to the Hmong-Mien language family. In general, the voiceless nasalized plosive is likely to imply the presence of voiced

26 According to Bommelyn (1997: 9), Tolowa-Chetco has two plosives each for the bilabial, dental, and velar. One is a voiceless plain plosive and the other an aspirated plosive. In the retroflex, however, there is no voiceless plain plosive, only the aspirated plosive. Looking at this, it is possible that a retroflex plain plosive once existed but then disappeared over time.

27 Kachi Koli does not have /ɖ/.

nasalized plosive. For example, 83 of 117 languages with /^{m}p/ have /^{m}b/, and 84 of 114 languages with /^{n}t/ have /^{n}d/. However, of the 10 languages that have /^{ɳ}ʈ/, only Diandongbei-Large Flowery Miao has /^{ɳ}ɖ/. It is unclear where these differences originate.

/^{ɳ}ɖ/

Voiced, prenasalized. This plosive appears in 17 languages, of which only two belong to the Hmong-Mien language family. While the voiceless /^{ɳ}ʈ/ is mainly found in the Hmong-Mien, /^{ɳ}ɖ/ does not show such bias toward a specific language family.

/ʈ^{w}/

Voiceless, labialized. This plosive appears only in Eastern Arrernte. Moreover, its voiced opposite, /ɖ^{w}/, is not found in any language. Considering that the frequency of labialization is relatively high among secondary articulations, there seems to be a phonetic reason for the extremely small number of retroflex labialized plosives.

/ʈ^{j}/

Voiceless, palatalized. This plosive appears in Kamviri and Kati, both of which belong to the Indo-Iranian language family, a subbranch of Indo-European. As with labialization, palatalization is also very infrequently accompanied by retroflex plosives.

/ɖ^{j}/

Voiced, palatalized. This plosive appears in two languages, both of which have the contrastive pair 'ʈ^{j} : ɖ^{j}'.

/ʈ^{ʔ}/

Voiceless, postlaryngealized. Ths plosive appears only in Eastern Tamang. This language has three retroflex plosives /ʈ, ʈ^{h}, ʈ^{ʔ}/, and such an inventory is not found in other languages. The three-way opposition among the voiceless plain, voiceless aspirated, and voiceless laryngealized plosives is found only in a very few languages, including Korean.[28]

---

28 Korean has such a three-way opposition not in the retroflex but in the bilabial,

/ᶯʈʰ/

Voiceless, postaspirated, prenasalized. This plosive appears in six languages, five of which belong to the Hmong-Mien language family and one to the Sino-Tibetan language family. Therefore, /ᶯʈʰ/ is distributed within a limited area of Asia. All languages with /ᶯʈʰ/ have /ʈ, ʈʰ/, which have a simpler articulatory mechanism.

/ᶯɖʰ/

Voiced, postaspirated, prenasalized. This plosive is a voiced opposite of /ᶯʈʰ/ and appears in two languages, neither of which has /ᶯʈʰ/. In other words, there is no language that has both /ᶯʈʰ/ and /ᶯɖʰ/.

/ᶯˀʈʰ/

Voiced, postaspirated, prenasalized, prelaryngealized. This consonant is a voiceless plosive that is combined with three secondary articulations. It appears only in Luopohe Hmong, a language spoken in Southwestern China. Its voiced opposite, /ᶯˀɖʰ/, is not found in any language.

/ɖ̤/

voiced, breathy-voice. This plosive appears in seven languages that are spoken in Western Asia. All of these languages have /ʈ, ɖ, ʈʰ/ in addition to /ɖ̤/ as retroflex plosives, meaning that they share type-(b) of Table 4-28 in common.

/ɖʳ/

Voiced, trill-released (or flap-released). This plosive is found only in Yandruwandha, an Australian language. For this type of plosive, refer to the description of /pʳ/ in 4.1.2.

/ʈʈ/

Voiceless, fortis. For this type of plosive, refer to the description of /pp/ in 4.1.2. /ʈʈ/ appears only in Koalib-Rere, a language spoken in Sudan.

---

alveolar, and velar.

4.6. Alveopalatal plosives

4.6.1. Overview

The alveopalatal plosive is articulated between the alveolar and the palatal regions but is positioned slightly closer to the palatal. In contrast, the class closer to the alveolar is the palatoalveolar. Alveopalatal plosives are generally very infrequent and of limited types. Therefore, I will briefly mention only a few properties.

First, the list of alveopalatal plosives is summarized in Table 4-29. Remarkablely, as shown in Table 4-29, in the alveopalatal, only plain or complex plosives accompanied by secondary articulation exist. Complex plosives with special glottal action or release do not appear. In addition, only three alveopalatal plosives appear in more than 10 languages: /ȶ, ȡ, ȶ/. All others are reported to appear only in two languages.

The number of alveopalatal plosives is summarized in Table 4-30. As shown in Table 4-30, only 25 of the 4,356 languages have alveopalatal plosives. Of these languages, 14 have one alveopalatal plosive, with eight having /ȶ/ and five having /ȡ/. There are seven languages with two alveopalatal plosives, of which five have an opposition by [±aspirated], such as /ȶ, ȶ^{h}/, and two have an opposition by [±voiced], such as /ȶ, ȡ/.

Table 4-29. List of alveopalatal plosives

a.	Plain	ȶ, ȡ
b.	Single secondary articulation	ȶ^{h}, ^{n}ȡ, ȶ^{w}, ^{ʔ}ȡ
c.	Multiple secondary articulation	ȶ^{hw}

Table 4-30. Number of alveopalatal plosives in languages

Number of alveopalatal plosives	Number of languages	Percentage
0	4,331	99.4%
1	14	0.3%
2	7	0.2%
3	2	0%
4	1	0%
6	1	0%

Given the universal tendency, there should be more languages with /ȶ, ȡ/ than languages with /ȶ, ȶʰ/, but this is not the case. The language with the most alveopalatal plosives is Ai-Cham, a language of the Tai-Kadai language family. Ai-Cham has six of the seven alveopalatal plosives in Table 4-29, except for /ⁿȡ/.

4.6.2. Description of the alveopalatal plosives

/ȶ/

Voiceless, plain. This plosive appears in 19 languages and is the most frequent among the alveopalatal plosives. It is found in many Asian languages belonging to the Tai-Kadai and Hmong-Mien language families.

/ȡ/

Voiced, plain. This plosive appears in eight languages. Of these, only two belong to the Tai-Kadai or Hmong-Mien language families, so its distribution is slightly different from that of /ȶ/. Among the eight languages with /ȡ/, only three have a voiceless /ȶ/, so the rate at which /ȡ/ implies the presence of /ȶ/ is very low.

/ȶʰ/

Voiceless, postaspirated. This plosive appears in nine languages that are spoken in Asia. All languages with /ȶʰ/ also have /ȶ/. Its voiced opposite, /ȡʰ/, is not found in any language.

/ⁿȡ/

Voiced, prenasalized. This plosive appears in Tangut and Maonan, both of which are Asian languages. In Maonan, /ⁿȡ/ is the only alveopalatal plosive. Its voiceless opposite, /ⁿȶ/, is not found in any language.

/ȶʷ/

Voiceless, labialized. This plosive appears in the Ai-Cham and T'en, members of the Tai-Kadai language family. These two languages have at least four alveopalatal plosives. Its voiced opposite, /ȡʷ/, is not found in any language.

/ˀȡ/

Voiced, prelaryngealized. This plosive is the only alveopalatal plosive with laryngealization. It appears in Ai-Cham and Mak (China), languages of the Tai-Kadai language family.

/ȶʰʷ/

Voiceless, aspirated, labialized. This plosive is the only alveopalatal plosive accompanied by two secondary articulations. Its distribution is the same as /ȶʷ/, that is, it appears in Ai-Cham and T'en.

4.7. Palatal plosives

4.7.1. Overview

The palatal plosive is one of the minor classes in the plosive, so it is infrequent and has relatively simple type. The list of palatal plosives is summarized in Table 4-31. As shown in Table 4-31, no palatal plosive exists with special glottal action or liquid-colored release.

Palatal plosives appearing in more than 10 languages are given in Table 4-32. Six high-frequency palatal plosives in Table 4-32 consist of two plain, two aspirated, and two nasalized plosives. In other words, they are composed of three contrastive pairs by [±voiced], [±aspirated], and

Table 4-31. List of palatal plosives

a.	Plain	c, ɟ
b.	Single secondary articulation	cʰ, ɟʰ, ˀɟ, cʷ, ɟʷ, cʲ, ɟʲ, ᶮc, ᶮɟ, cᶮ
c.	Multiple secondary articulation	cʰʷ, ᶮcʰ, ᶮɟʰ
d.	Tenseness	cc

Table 4-32. High-frequency palatal plosives

Ranking	Plosive	Frequency	Ranking	Plosive	Frequency
1	c	582	4	ᶮɟ	84
2	ɟ	520	5	ᶮc	19
3	cʰ	104	6	ɟʰ	18

Table 4-33. Number of palatal plosives in languages

Number of palatal plosives	Number of languages	Percentage
0	3,654	83.9%
1	238	5.5%
2	332	7.6%
3	90	2.1%
4	38	0.9%
5	2	0%
6	2	0%

[±nasalized].

The number of palatal plosives is given in Table 4-33. The average number of palatal plosives in all languages is very small, approximately 0.3. This is because many languages have no palatal plosives. However, among only those languages containing palatal plosives, the average number 1.9, which is slightly less than other places of articulation. Many such languages have one or two palatal plosives. Languages with more than five palatal plosives are very rare. Irigwe and Uduk have the most palatal plosives, with six. The palatal plosives in these languages are given in (7).

(7) Palatal plosives in Irigwe and Uduk
  a. Irigwe: /c, ɟ, c^w, $ɟ^w$, c^j, $ɟ^j$/
  b. Uduk: /c, ɟ, c^h, c^w, $ɟ^w$, c^{hw}/

The palatal plosives in Irigwe are based on a phonemic analysis by Daniel & Blench (2008) and Uduk on an analysis by Killian (2015). Irigwe and Uduk share four of the six palatal plosives in common: /c, ɟ, c^w, $ɟ^w$/. The inclusion of /c^w, $ɟ^w$/, which are labialized plosives, instead of aspirated plosives, is contrary to expectations. The frequency of the aspirated plosives 'c^h (104), $ɟ^h$ (18)' is much higher than that of the labialized plosives 'c^w (3), $ɟ^w$ (3)'.[29]

29 The numbers in parentheses indicate the number of languages in which the plosive appears.

Table 4-34. Types and frequency of single palatal plosive inventories

Plosive	c	ɟ	ᶮɟ
Number of languages	129	105	4

Table 4-35. Types and frequency of two-way palatal plosive inventories

Inventory	c, ɟ	c, c^h	c, ᶮɟ	ɟ, ᶮɟ
Number of languages	278	25	13	8

The common inventories in languages with one palatal plosive are given in Table 4-34. Only three palatal plosives appear in languages that include a single palatal plosive. Compared to the voiceless plosive /c/, the frequency of the voiced plosive /ɟ/ is very high. As already noted, this unusual result is found only for the retroflex and palatal plosives.

Table 4-35 above is a list of inventories that are found in many languages with two palatal plosives. The inventories in Table 4-35 are found in more than five languages. The inventory /c, ɟ/, which consists of two plain plosives, constitutes the overwhelming majority. It is followed by /c, c^h/, which is found mainly in Asian languages including languages of the Sino-Tibetan language family. This pattern does not deviate from the general trend.

The common inventories in languages with three palatal plosives are given in Table 4-36. Three-way inventories appearing in two or more languages occur only in the three types shown in Table 4-36. Types-(a) and (b) are the most frequent. These two types consist of two plain plosives (c, ɟ) and one complex plosive accompanied by a high-frequency secondary articulation (/c^h/ or /ᶮɟ/). Type-(a) appears most commonly in Asian languages centered on the Sino-Tibetan language family, while type-(b) is found mainly in African languages centered on the Atlantic-Congo language family. In general, these two types are mutually exclusive in their distribution within language families.

Finally, high-frequency inventories in the languages with four palatal plosives are given in Table 4-37, which demonstrates familiar trends. The characteristics of the high-frequency inventories and the exclusive distribution of the types are all the same as other places of articulation. Therefore, a detailed description is omitted.

Table 4-36. Types and frequency of three-way palatal plosive inventories

Inventory	Type-(a)	Type-(b)	Type-(c)
	c, ɟ, c^{h}	c, ɟ, ^{ɲ}ɟ	c, c^{h}, ^{ɲ}ɟ
Number of languages	46	39	2

Table 4-37. Types and frequency of four-way palatal plosive inventories

Inventory	Type-(a)	Type-(b)	Type-(c)
	c, ɟ, c^{h}, ɟ^{h}	c, ɟ, ^{ɲ}c, ^{ɲ}ɟ	c, ɟ, c^{h}, ^{ɲ}ɟ
Number of languages	18	10	4

4.7.2. Description of the palatal plosives

/c/

Voiceless, plain. This plosive appears in 582 languages and shows no bias regarding region or language family. Since /c/ is similar to the affricate /ʧ/, it is possible that the affricate is incorrectly analyzed as a plosive, or vice versa. Therefore, it is difficult to determine the exact frequency of this plosive.

/ɟ/

Voiced, plain. 'ɟ' appears in 520 languages. Its absolute frequency is much lower than that of other major voiced plain plosives, such as /b, d, g/. However, compared to the frequency of the voiceless plain plosive /c/, as shown in Figure 3-3, the value of /ɟ/ is rather higher than that of /b, d, g/. Of the 520 languages with /ɟ/, 404 have the contrastive pair by [±voiced] such as 'c : ɟ'.

/c^{h}/

Voiceless, postaspirated. This plosive appears in 104 languages, of which approximately 40% belong to the Sino-Tibetan language family. Without exception, languages with /c^{h}/ have other palatal plosives. There are 46 languages with three series such as /c, ɟ, c^{h}/, and 18 languages with four series such as /c, ɟ, c^{h}, ɟ^{h}/, as well as other languages with at least two series.

/$ɟ^h$/

Voiced, aspirated. This plosive appears in 18 languages that, with the exception of Kharia, belong to the Indo-European or Sino-Tibetan language families.[30] In particular, /$ɟ^h$/ is found mainly in the Indo-European language family. All languages with /$ɟ^h$/ have four-way oppositions such as /c, ɟ, c^h, $ɟ^h$/. In other words, /$ɟ^h$/ implies the existence of specific phonological opposition, which goes beyond the phoneme level. Most languages with the voiced aspirated plosive in other places of articulation also have the same phonological opposition.

/^ɲc/

Voiceless, prenasalized. This plosive appears in 19 languages, of which 10 belong to the Atlantic-Congo language family. Although the Austronesian language family is one of the two largest (along with the Atlantic-Congo), only Western Lawa in this language family has /^ɲc/. All languages with /^ɲc/ have /c/.

/$^ɲɟ$/

Voiced, prenasalized. This plosive appears in 84 languages, and, as with /^ɲc/, many of these languages belong to the Atlantic-Congo language family.

/$c^ɲ$/

Voiceless, postnasalized. This plosive appears only in Nemi. In this language, plosives with the same character as /$c^ɲ$/ exist in the bilabial, alveolar, and velar. /$c^ɲ$/ is distinguished from /^ɲc/ by the position of nasalization. However, no language has not been reported to have both /$c^ɲ$/ and /^ɲc/ as separate phonemes.

/c^w/

Voiceless, labialized. This plosive appears only in three languages, all of which have four or more palatal plosives.

/$ɟ^w$/

Voiced, labialized. This plosive occurs in three languages, which

30 Kharia is spoken in India, so it is regionally close to other languages with /$ɟ^h$/.

exactly match the languages with /c^{w}/, i.e., they have a contrastive pair by [± voiced] such as 'c^{w} : ɟ^{w}'.

/c^{j}/

Voiceless, palatalized. This plosive only appears in Irigwe. Palatalization as a secondary articulation rarely accompanies palatal plosives because palatalization overlaps with the palatal plosive in the place of articulation, making it difficult to properly reveal the phonetic effect of palatalization as secondary articulation.

/ɟ^{j}/

Voiced, palatalized. This plosive, like /c^{j}/, appears only in Irigwe. As a result, Irigwe is the only language that has an opposition by [± voiced] in the palatalized palatal plosive.

/^{ʔ}ɟ/

Voiced, prelaryngealized. This plosive appears in Nyaheun, Western Lawa, and Brao, which are spoken in the Indochina Peninsula. /^{ʔ}ɟ/ is the only consonant among the palatal plosives that is accompanied by laryngealization. There is no known language with /^{ʔ}c/, which is a voiceless opposite of /^{ʔ}ɟ/.

/^{ɲ}c^{h}/

Voiceless, postaspirated, prenasalized. This plosive appears in three languages, all of which also have the plain plosive /c/.

/^{ɲ}ɟ^{h}/

Voiced, postaspirated, prenasalized. This plosive is the voiced opposite of /^{ɲ}c^{h}/. /^{ɲ}ɟ^{h}/ appears in Hmong Daw and South Wa, both of which have the same inventory of palatal plosives: /c, c^{h}, ^{ɲ}ɟ, ^{ɲ}ɟ^{h}/. No language has the contrastive pair '^{ɲ}c^{h} : ^{ɲ}ɟ^{h}'.

/c^{hw}/

Voiceless, postaspirated, labialized. This plosive appears only in Uduk which has five other palatal plosives, /c, ɟ, c^{h}, c^{w}, ɟ^{w}/, which are simpler than /c^{hw}/ in terms of articulatory complexity.[31]

31 In Uduk, there are also two palatal ejectives.

/cc/

Voiceless, fortis. For this type of plosive, refer to the description of /pp/ in 4.1.2. /cc/ appears only in Koalib-Rere, which has five voiceless fortis plosives in five places of articulation.

4.8. Velar plosives

4.8.1. Overview

The velar plosive is the most frequent among the plosives and, like the alveolar plosive, has highly diverse types. In other words, the velar plosive is one of the major classes. The list of velar plosives is summarized in Table 4-38.

As shown in Table 4-38, various types of the velar plosives appear across all categories. In addition, there are numerous high-frequency velar plosives. Eighteen types of velar plosives appear in more than 10 languages. The top 10 high-frequency velar plosives are given in Table 4-39.

There is no significant difference in the characteristics of the plosives in Table 4-39, compared to those in other places of articulation. Plain plosives and most of the complex plosives accompanied by major secondary articulations are seen here. Notably, /^{ŋ}g^{w}/, which is accompanied by nasalization and labialization, appears in the top 10. The complex plosives with two secondary articulations are usually less frequent, but /^{ŋ}g^{w}/ is an exception. This higher frequency seems to be possible because labialization is a frequent accompaniment, especially for

Table 4-38. List of velar plosives

a.	Plain	k, g
b.	Single secondary articulation	k^{h}, g^{h}, ^{h}k, ^{ŋ}k, ^{ŋ}g, k^{ŋ}, g^{ŋ}, k^{ʔ}, g^{ʔ}, ^{ʔ}g, k^{w}, g^{w}, k^{j}, g^{j}, k^{ʕ}, g^{ʕ}
c.	Multiple secondary articulations	k^{hw}, k^{ʔw}, k^{hj}, k^{wj}, g^{wj}, k^{hwj}, ^{ŋ}k^{h}, ^{ŋ}g^{h}, ^{ŋʔ}k, ^{ŋʔ}g, ^{ŋ}k^{w}, ^{ŋ}g^{w}, ^{ŋ}k^{j}, ^{ŋ}g^{j}, ^{ŋ}k^{hw}, ^{ŋ}k^{hj}, ^{ŋ}g^{wj}, k^{wʕ}
d.	Glottal action	k̰, g̃, k̤, g̈, k̤^{h}, k̤^{w}, g̈^{w}, ^{ŋ}g̈
e.	Liquid-colored release	k^{r}, g^{r}, k^{l}, g^{l}, k^{hr}, k^{hl}, k^{lw}, ^{ŋ}g^{r}
f.	Tenseness	kk, gg, g̊, kk^{w}, gg^{w}

Table 4-39. Top 10 velar plosives

Ranking	Plosive	Frequency	Ranking	Plosive	Frequency
1	k	4,205	6	g^{w}	256
2	g	2,750	7	^{ŋ}k	122
3	k^{h}	831	8	k^{j}	111
4	^{ŋ}g	592	9	g^{h}	104
5	k^{w}	562	10	$^{ŋ}g^{w}$	96

the velar plosives.[32]

The number of velar plosives is given in Table 4-40 below. Only 15 languages have no velar plosive. Approximately 99.7% of all languages have at least one velar plosive. These figures are so overwhelming that it is very difficult to observe this pattern in other places of articulation. Six of the languages without a velar plosive are found in the Austronesian language family. In sharp contrast, the Atlantic-Congo, which is one of the two largest language families along with the Austronesian, has no languages without a velar plosive.

The average number of velar plosives in all languages is 2.3. In Table 4-40, languages with two velar plosives are the most common, constituting approximately half of the total. The language with the most velar plosives is Maonan, which has 13. Below is an inventory of the velar plosives in Maonan.[33]

(8) Velar plosives in Maonan

k, g, k^{h}, ^{ŋ}g, k^{w}, g^{w}, k^{j}, g^{j}, k^{hw}, k^{hj}, $^{ŋ}g^{w}$, k^{wj}, k^{hwj}

Maonan has a large inventory consisting of 37 plosives, approximately one-third (35.1%) of which are articulated in the velar. In (8), in addition to plain plosives, most of the complex plosives accompanied by major secondary articulations, such as aspiration, nasalization, labialization, and palatalization, are included. There are also plosives in which multiple secondary articulations are combined.

32 For this, see Figure 3-9.

33 The phonemic analysis of Maonan is based on Lu (2008: 79).

Table 4-40. Number of velar plosives in languages

Number of velar plosives	Number of languages	Percentage
0	15	0.3%
1	895	20.5%
2	2,232	51.2%
3	625	14.3%
4	431	9.9%
5	45	1.0%
6	85	2.0%
7	2	0%
8	12	0.3%
9	9	0.2%
10~	5	0.1%

The 13 velar plosives of Maonan shown in (8) represent the maximum number of plosives appearing at one place of articulation.

The common plosives in languages with one velar plosive are given in Table 4-41. The velar plosives in Table 4-41 appear in two or more languages. As expected, the voiceless plain plosive /k/ is the most frequent, followed by voiced plain /g/. In other places of articulation, aspirated or nasalized plosives are frequent, but in the velar, the labialized plosives are more common. As pointed out earlier, velar plosives are quite frequently accompanied by labialization.

There are 2,232 languages with two velar plosives. Table 4-42 lists the common inventories in these languages. Each inventory in Table 4-42 is found in more than 10 languages. As expected, /k, g/, comprising two plain plosives, is dominant, followed by /k, k^h/, including the voiceless plain and aspirated plosives. Thus far, these trends are no different from the plosives in other major places of articulation. However, in Table 4-42, /k, k^w/ is more frequent than /k, ^ŋg/, which is distinct from other places of articulation. As pointed out several times above, the velar labialized

Table 4-41. Types and frequency of single velar plosive inventories

Plosive	k	g	k^w	k^h
Number of languages	803	74	14	2

Table 4-42. Types and frequency of two-way velar plosive inventories

Inventory	k, g	k, k^h	k, k^w	k, $^{\text{ŋ}}g$	g, k^h	k, $^{\text{ŋ}}k$	k, k^j
Number of languages	1,617	246	156	137	22	12	12

plosive is fairly common.

The most frequent inventory /k, g/, is evenly distributed across several languages without bias by language family or region, whereas, the other inventories do reflect such biases. For example, /k, k^h/ appears in more than 100 languages, mainly in Asian languages of the Sino-Tibetan language family, but in very few languages of the Atlantic-Congo and Austronesian language families, i.e., the first and second largest language families, respectively. /k, k^w/ appears frequently in North American languages centered on the Otomanguean language family. Moreover, /k, $^{\text{ŋ}}g$/ appears in many African languages of the Atlantic-Congo and Papunesian languages of the Austronesian.

The common inventories in languages with three velar plosives are given in Table 4-43. A total of 625 languages have three velar plosives. The inventories in Table 4-43 are each found in more than 10 languages. The characteristics of these high-frequency inventories and the exclusive distribution of types are the same as for other major places of articulation. The only difference is that the labialized plosive /k^w/ is seen in two types. /k^w/ is common and is often included within the high-frequency inventories. This trend is the same in languages with three velar plosives. Type-(c) with /k^w/ is found in many language families, including the Uto-Aztecan and Tupian language families, which are spoken in North and South America.

Finally, I will consider inventories that are often found in languages with four velar plosives. There are 431 languages that have four velar plosives. The inventories in Table 4-44 each appear in more than 10 languages. Contrary to expectations, as many as eight different types are given, making this group more diverse than the bilabial or alveolar

Table 4-43. Types and frequency of three-way velar plosive inventories

Plosive inventory	Type-(a)	Type-(b)	Type-(c)	Type-(d)	Type-(e)	Type-(f)
	k, g, k^h	k, g, $^{\text{ŋ}}g$	k, g, k^w	k, $^{\text{ŋ}}k$, $^{\text{ŋ}}g$	k, k^h, $^{\text{ŋ}}g$	k, k^w, $^{\text{ŋ}}g$
Number of languages	279	191	35	24	15	14

Table 4-44. Types and frequency of four-way velar plosive inventories

Plosive inventory	Type-(a)	Type-(b)	Type-(c)	Type-(d)	Type-(e)	Type-(f)	Type-(g)	Type-(h)
	k, g, k^w, g^w	k, g, k^h, g^h	k, g, ᵑk, ᵑg	k, k^h, k^w, k^{hw}	k, g, k^h, ᵑg	k, ᵑg, k^w, $ᵑg^w$	k, g, k^j, g^j	k, g, k^h, g̈
Number of languages	125	102	50	30	24	23	20	12

plosive inventories. These results are unexpected because the more opposed members within an inventory, the more difficult it is for high-frequency types to appear.

The characteristic inventory in Table 4-44 is type-(a), consisting of two plain plosives and two labialized plosives. Type-(a) is the most frequent, which is only observed for the velar plosive due to the high frequency of velar labialized plosives. Approximately 60% of the languages in which type-(a) appears belong to three language families: Afro-Asiatic, Atlantic-Congo, and Austronesian. In Tables 4-42 and 4-43, inventories with labialized plosive are frequently found in languages of South or North America, but in Table 4-44, such a tendency is weak. The Afro-Asiatic and Austronesian language families are geographically distant from the Americas.

Other aspects are not significantly different compared to the plosive at other places of articulation. Contrast by [±voiced] plays a crucial role in four-way opposition, and the inventories in which phonological contrast is maximized by two distinctive features are frequent. Inventories that include aspirated plosives are found mainly in Asian languages centered on the Indo-European language family, and inventories that include prenasalized plosives are primarily found in African languages centered on the Atlantic-Congo language family.

The activeness hierarchy of distinctive features has been discussed through high-frequency inventories. It is also possible to examine the activeness hierarchy of the distinctive features involved in the contrast of the velar plosives. In the bilabial and alveolar plosives, [±voiced], [±aspirated], and [±nasalized] are actively involved in phonological contrast. These three features are also important in the velar plosive, but [±labialized] for the labialized plosives must be added. Of these, the [±voiced] works most actively in contrast of the velar plosive. Contrastive pairs by [±voiced] are the most common, regardless of the number of velar plosives. The activeness hierarchy of the remaining three features is inconsistent. When the opposing member of velar plosives is two or three, [±aspirated] is more actively involved in the contrast, whereas with four velar plosives, [±labialized] is more active. Except for [±voiced], the activeness hierarchy of the features is not fixed but inconsistent depending on the opposing number of plosives.

4.8.2. Description of the velar plosives

/k/

Voiceless, plain. This plosive appears in 4,205 languages, making it by far the most common (96.5%, 4,205/4,356) among all plosives.[34] The frequency of /k/ in this study not only exceeds 90%, which is the frequency given in PHOIBLE (https://phoible.org/), but is higher than that of /m/ (96%) which is the most common consonant in PHOIBLE.[35] The 151 languages without /k/ do not show a distinct bias toward a specific language family. Among the large-scale language families, the Indo-European language family almost always includes /k/ because, of 263 languages to be discussed, only Dalecarlian does not. In contrast, in the Pama-Nyungan language family, 32 of 127 languages do not have /k/, and in the Salishan language family, 11 of 24 languages do not. /k/ is unaspirated, but is sometimes accompanied by light aspiration. If the aspiration accompanying /k/ is slightly stronger, even if there is only one velar plosive, it is analyzed as /kʰ/ instead of /k/, like in Southern Sotho and Tojolabal.

/g/

Voiced, plain. Since /k/ is the most frequent plosive, its voiced opposite, /g/, is expected to be the most frequent among the voiced plosives. Contrary to expectations, however, /g/ appears in only 2,750 languages, which is considerably fewer than /b/ (3,105). Of the languages with /g/, 2,644 (96.1%) have a contrastive pair by [±voiced],

34 The frequency of the major plosives is given in Table 5-1.

35 The high-frequency consonants of PHOIBLE are presented in Table 1-2. The differences in frequency between PHOIBLE and this book stems from the different number of target languages and the different phoneme analysis referenced.

such as ‘k : g’. Among the voiced plosives at the major places of articulation, /g/ has very high rate implying the presence of a voiceless opposite.[36]

/kʰ/

Voiceless, postaspirated. This plosive appears in 831 languages, making it the most frequent of the voiceless aspirated plosives. In the Sino-Tibetan language family, 339 of 363 languages have /kʰ/, which is the largest number of languages and highest percentage within any language family. Languages in this language family also have many other voiceless aspirated plosives. A high frequency of /kʰ/ is also seen in the Athabaskan-Eyak-Tlingit language family, in which 30 of 33 languages have /kʰ/. Interestingly, very few languages belonging to the Athabaskan-Eyak-Tlingit language family have /pʰ/ or /tʰ/. That is, rather than having a system of voiceless aspirated plosives, they have an isolated /kʰ/.

/gʰ/

Voiced, postaspirated. This plosive appears in 104 languages, most of which are Asian. Among the voiced aspirated plosives, only /bʰ/ (112) is more frequent than /gʰ/. Of the 104 languages with /gʰ/, 102 have /k, g, kʰ, gʰ/, a four-way opposition inventory. In other words, the presence of /gʰ/ is highly likely to imply the existence of a specific four-way opposition, as is the case for voiced aspirated plosives at other places of articulation.

/ʰk/

Voiceless, preaspirated. Unlike /kʰ/, the aspiration of /ʰk/ is in front of the primary articulation. /ʰk/ appears in six languages, of which three (Osage, Bonan, and Zhongu) have /kʰ/ and /ʰk/ as separate phonemes, that is, they have a phonological contrast by the position of aspiration. There is no known language with its voiced opposite, /ʰg/.

36 The implicational relationship between the voiced and voiceless plosives will be discussed in 5.2.

/^{ŋ}k/

Voiceless, prenasalized. This plosive appears in 112 languages and is widely distributed in the Atlantic-Congo or Austronesian language families, similar to other voiceless prenasalized plosives. Except for Samberigi, a language of Papua New Guinea, all languages with /^{ŋ}k/ have the plain plosive /k/.

/^{ŋ}g/

Voiced, prenasalized. This plosive appears in 592 languages, making it the second most frequent after /^{m}b/ (608) among the voiced prenasalized plosives. While the ratio of /^{ŋ}k/ implying the existence of /k/ is very high, that of /^{ŋ}g/ is not. Of the 592 languages with /^{ŋ}g/, 355 languages have /g/, so the ratio of implication is 60.0%, which is very low compared to 99.2% (111/112), the ratio of /^{ŋ}k/ implying the presence of /k/.

/k^{ŋ}/

Voiceless, postnasalized. This plosive is distinguished from /^{ŋ}k/ by the position of nasalization. It appears in three languages, none of which have /^{ŋ}k/, that is, there is no language that has a contrastive pair by the position of nasalization.

/g^{ŋ}/

Voiced, postnasalized. This plosive is a voiced opposite of /k^{ŋ}/. As with /^{ŋ}k/, there is no language that has a contrastive pair by the position of nasalization. Gaa, the only language in which /g^{ŋ}/ appears, has both /g^{ŋ}/ and /k^{ŋ}/, so the postnasalized plosive shows a contrast by [±voiced].

/k^{w}/

Voiceless, labialized. This plosive appears in 562 languages. Its frequency is so overwhelming that it is more frequent than all other voiceless labialized plosives combined. /k^{w}/ is distributed in many language families of various regions. The Otomanguean, Tupian, and Uto-Aztecan language families of the Americas are home to comparatively numerous languages containing /k^{w}/, considering the size of these language families.

/g^w/

Voiced, labialized. This plosive appears in 256 languages, of which 164 belong to three language families: Afro-Asiatic, Atlantic-Congo, and Austronesian. Therefore, unlike /k^w/, /g^w/ is not widely distributed in the languages of the Americas. Among the 256 languages with /g^w/, 241 have the plain /g/ and the voiceless /k^w/ as separate phonemes. In other words, the ratio of /g^w/ implying the presence of /g/ and /k^w/ is as high as 94%.

/k^j/

Voiceless, palatalized. This plosive appears in 111 languages, making it the second most frequent after /t^j/ among the palatalized plosives. No language of the Austronesian language family, which is the second largest, has /k^j/ as a phoneme. Of the 111 languages with /k^j/, 107 languages have /k/, so the rate of implication between /k^j/ and /k/ is very high.

/g^j/

Voiced, palatalized. This plosive appears in 72 languages, making it the most frequent of the voiced palatalized plosives. As with /k^j/, none of the languages belonging to the Austronesian language family have /g^j/. Of the 72 languages with /g^j/, 55 have the contrastive pair by [±voiced], such as 'k^j : g^j'. In addition, of these 72 languages, 68 have /g/. Considering /g^j/ in conjunction with /k^j/, the rate at which the palatalized velar plosives imply the existence of the plain plosives is very high.

/$k^ʕ$/

Voiceless, pharyngealized. This plosive appears in six languages, which are spoken in Arab and near Arabic regions.

/$g^ʕ$/

Voiced, pharyngealized. This plosive appears only in Khwarshi-Inkhoqwari, which has the contrastive pair by [±voiced], such as '$k^ʕ$: $g^ʕ$'.

/$k^ʔ$/

Voiceless, postlaryngealized. This plosive appears in 13 languages and is common in North or South American languages. It is also found in

Far Eastern languages such as Korean and Kunigami. By contrast, it is not distributed in the African or oceanic languages.

/$g^{ʔ}$/

Voiced, postlaryngealized. This plosive appears in Kakua, a language spoken in Columbia, which does not have /$k^{ʔ}$/. No language with both /$k^{ʔ}$/ and /$g^{ʔ}$/ is known to exist. Regardless of the place of articulation, there is no language that has a contrastive pair by [±voiced] in the postlaryngealized plosives.

/^{ʔ}g/

Voiced, prelaryngealized. This plosive is distinguished from /$g^{ʔ}$/ by the position of laryngealization. /^{ʔ}g/ appears in three languages, whereas /$g^{ʔ}$/ appears in only one. None of the languages with /^{ʔ}g/ have /$g^{ʔ}$/. In other words, there is no language that has a contrastive pair by the position of laryngealization. Its voiceless opposite, /^{ʔ}k/, is not found in any language.

/$^{ŋ}k^{h}$/

Voiceless, postaspirated, prenasalized. This plosive appears in 23 languages. These languages have at least three velar plosives and are mostly distributed in Asia. The presence of /$^{n}k^{h}$/ implies the existence of /k^{h}/ in 18 of 23 languages (78.3%), but /$^{n}k^{h}$/ implies the existence of /^{ŋ}k/ in only 12 (52.2%). Therefore, the ratio at which the plosive accompanied by two secondary articulations implies the presence of phonetically simpler plosives varies depending on the types of secondary articulation. The same pattern is also found in the bilabial or alveolar plosives.

/$^{ŋ}g^{h}$/

Voiced, postaspirated, prenasalized. This plosive is a voiced opposite of /$^{n}k^{h}$/. It appears in four languages, which share several common features. They are geographically closely distributed, that is, in Southwestern China or around Vietnam, and the plosives of the same character as /$^{n}g^{h}$/ exist in other places of articulation. In addition, these languages do not have its voiceless opposite, /$^{ŋ}k^{h}$/. There is no language that has both voiceless and voiced aspirated nasalized plosives.

/k^{hw}/

Voiceless, postaspirated, labialized. This plosive appears in 57 languages. Among the voiceless aspirated labialized plosives, the frequency of /k^{hw}/ is overwhelming. It is common in the Sino-Tibetan and Tai-Kadai language families, which have many other voiceless aspirated plosives. However, eight languages belonging to the Athabaskan-Eyak-Tlingit language family in North America also have /k^{hw}/. There is no language with its voiced opposite, /g^{hw}/.

/k^{hj}/

Voiceless, postaspirated, palatalized. This plosive is found in 23 languages, mainly in Asia. There is no language with its voiced opposite, /g^{hj}/.

/$^{ŋ}k^{w}$/

Voiceless, prenasalized, labialized. This plosive appears in 11 languages. It has a high ratio of implying the presence of phonetically simple plosives. For example, all languages with /$^{ŋ}k^{w}$/ have /k/ and /k^{w}/, and nine of 11 languages have /^{ŋ}k/. In addition, seven of those have the contrastive pair by [±voiced], such as '$^{ŋ}k^{w}$: $^{ŋ}g^{w}$'.

/$^{ŋ}g^{w}$/

Voiced, prenasalized, labialized. This plosive is found in 96 languages and is the most frequent among the plosives that are combined with two secondary articulations. Approximately one-third of languages with /$^{ŋ}g^{w}$/ belong to the Chadic language family, a subbranch of the Afro-Asiatic.

/$^{ŋ}k^{j}$/

Voiceless, prenasalized, palatalized. This plosive appears only in Western Xiangxi Miao, which is characterized by as many as eight velar plosives.

/$^{ŋ}g^{j}$/

Voiced, prenasalized, palatalized. This plosive is a voiced opposite of /$^{ŋ}k^{j}$/. It appears in 12 languages. Ten of these 12 languages are spoken in Africa, and the other two are spoken in Mexico. There is no language that has both /$^{ŋ}k^{j}$/ and /$^{ŋ}g^{j}$/.

/ᵑˀk/

Voiceless, prenasalized, prelaryngealized. This plosive appears only in Luopohe Hmong, which has some similar plosives in other places of articulation.

/ᵑˀg/

Voiced, prenasalized, prelaryngealized. This plosive is found only in San Martín Itunyoso Triqui. This language has no relationship with Luopohe Hmong, which has /ᵑˀk/, a voiceless opposite of /ᵑˀg/, in terms of region or language family.

/k^{wj}/

Voiceless, labialized, palatalized. This plosive appears in seven languages, which all have at least four velar plosives.

/g^{wj}/

Voiced, labialized, palatalized. This plosive is a voiced opposite of /k^{wj}/. It appears in three languages, which all have the contrastive pair by [±voiced], such as 'k^{wj} : g^{wj}'.

/$k^{wʕ}$/

Voiceless, labialized, pharyngealized. This consonant is a voiceless plosive that is combined with labialization and pharyngealization. Combination types such as this one are rare and appear only with /$k^{wʕ}$/ and /$q^{wʕ}$/. Both plosives share a dorsal articulator. /$k^{wʕ}$/ appears only in Geez, which also has /$k^{ʕ}$/ without labialization. Its voiced opposite, /$g^{wʕ}$/, is not found in any language.

/$k^{ʔw}$/

Voiceless, labialized, postlaryngealized. This plosive appears in Central Mazahua and Central Kalapuya, languages of the North America. '$k^{ʔw}$' is the only voiceless plosive that is accompanied by labialization and laryngealization.[37] Its voiced opposite, '$g^{ʔw}$', is not found in any language.

37 There are voiced plosives that are combined with labialization and laryngealization, such as /$^{ʔ}b^{w}$/ and /$^{ʔ}d^{w}$/. However, they are extremely infrequent, with each being found in only one language.

/k^{hwj}/

Voiceless, postaspirated, labialized, palatalized. This plosive has a complicated articulatory mechanism accompanied by three secondary articulations. It appears only in Maonan, which has as many as 13 velar plosives. Its voiced opposite, /g^{hwj}/, is not found in any language. Voiced plosives combined with two or three secondary articulations, one of which is aspiration, are very rare.

/$^{ŋ}k^{hw}$/

Voiceless, postaspirated, prenasalized, labialized. This plosive is found only in Wuding-Luquan Yi, which has seven velar plosives. Its voiced opposite, /$^{ŋ}g^{hw}$/, is not found in any language.

/$^{ŋ}k^{hj}$/

Voiceless, postaspirated, prenasalized, palatalized. This plosive appears only in Western Xiangxi Miao, which has eight velar plosives. Its voiced opposite, /$^{ŋ}g^{hj}$/, is not found in any language.

/$^{ŋ}g^{wj}$/

Voiced, prenasalized, labialized, palatalized. This consonant is a voiced plosive combined with three secondary articulations, making it very rare. /$^{ŋ}g^{wj}$/ appears in San Francisco del Mar Huave and San Mateo del Mar Huave, both of which belong to the Huavean language family in the North America. These languages have eight and ten velar plosives, respectively. The existence of its voiceless opposite, /$^{ŋ}k^{wj}$/, has not yet been found.

/k̤/

Voiceless, breathy-voice. This plosive appears only in Chantyal, a language spoken in Nepal. Regarding the specificity of the voiceless breathy-voice plosive, refer to the description of /p̈/ in 4.1.2.

/g̈/

Voiced, breathy-voice. This plosive appears in 18 languages, many of which belong to the Sino-Tibetan and Atlantic-Congo language families. Sino-Tibetan languages with /g̈/ have /k, g, k^{h}/ without exception. Given the phonetic similarity between /g̈/ and /g^{h}/, it is no exaggeration to say that Sino-Tibetan languages with /g̈/ are the same as other languages with a four-way opposition like /k, g, kʰ, gʰ/. Chantyal in the Sino-Tibetan is the only language to have both /k̤/ and /g̈/, which form a contrastive pair by [±voiced].

/k̰/

Voiceless, creaky-voice. This plosive appears only in Siona-Tetete, a language of the South America. Siona-Tetete has several voiceless creaky-voice plosives. For the voiceless creaky-voice plosive, refer to the description of /p̃/ in 4.1.2.

/g̃/

Voiced, creaky-voice. This plosive is found only in Fyer, which also has voiced creaky-voice plosives in other places of articulation. There is no known language that has both /k̰/ and /g̃/. Siona-Tetete, which has voiceless /k̰/, and Fyer, which has voiced /g̃/, are geographically distant, as they are spoken on different continents.

/k̤ʰ/

Voiceless, postaspirated, breathy-voice. This plosive appears only in Chantyal. For the voiceless aspirated breathy-voice plosive, refer to the description of /t̤ʰ/ in 4.4.2.

/g̈ʷ/

Voiced, labialized, breathy-voice. This plosive is the only breathy-voice plosive that is accompanied by labialization. It appears only in Kalanga, a language spoken in Southern Africa. Interestingly, Kalanga does not have /g̈/, which is not accompanied by labialization.

/ᵑg̈/

Voiced, prenasalized, breathy-voice. This plosive appears only in Chopi, a language spoken in Mozambique. Chopi also has voiced breathy-voice plosives in other places of articulation.

/k̰ʷ/

Voiceless, labialized, creaky-voice. This plosive is the only creaky-voice plosive that is accompanied by labialization. It is found only in Siona-Tetete, which also has /k̰/ without labialization.

/k^r/

Voiceless, trill-released (or flap-released). For this type of plosive, refer to the description of /p^r/ in 4.1.2. /k^r/ appears in Peve and Pochuri Naga. Peve has many liquid-colored plosives, such as trill-released or lateral-released plosives.

/g^r/

Voiced, trill-released (or flap-released). This plosive is found only in Peve which has a contrastive pair by [±voiced], such as 'k^r : g^r'.

/k^l/

Voiceless, lateral-released. For this type of plosive, refer to the description of /p^l/ in 4.1.2. /k^l/ appears in three languages, that are unrelated by region or language family.

/g^l/

Voiced, lateral-released. This plosive is a voiced opposite of /k^l/. It appears only in Thou-Kathu, a language of the Sino-Tibetan language family. Thou-Kathus has unique three-way opposition within the lateral-released velar plosive: /k^l, g^l, k^{hl}/. Moreover, Thou-Kathus also has /k, g, k^h/, which are not laterally released. As a result, these two three-way opposition systems are distinguished by the presence or absence of lateral-release.

/k^{hr}/

Voiceless, postaspirated, trill-released (or flap-released). This plosive is found only in Pochuri Naga, which also has /k^r/. There is no known language that has its voiced opposite, /g^{hr}/.

/k^{hl}/

Voiceless, postaspirated, lateral-released. This plosive appears in Thou-Kathu and //Xegwi, which are unrelated but have similar velar plosive inventories. Thou-Kathu has /k, g, k^h, k^l, g^l, k^{hl}/ and //Xegwi has /k, g, k^h, k^l, k^{hl}/, so the only difference between two languages is the presence or absence of /g^l/. The existence of /g^{hl}/, a voiced opposite of /k^{hl}/, is unknown.

/k^{lw}/

Voiceless, labialized, lateral-released. This consonant appears only in Idoma, an African language. /k^{lw}/ is the only lateral-released plosive that is accompanied by labialization.

/$^{ŋ}g^{r}$/

Voiced, prenasalized, trill-released (or flap-released). This plosive appears only in Peve, which has three-way trill-released plosives: /k^{r}, g^{r}, $^{ŋ}g^{r}$/.[38] Its voiceless opposite, /$^{ŋ}k^{r}$/, is not found in any language.

/kk/

Voiceless, fortis. For the fortis plosive, refer to the description of /pp/ in 4.1.2. /kk/ appears in eight languages with scattered distribution.

/gg/

Voiced, fortis. This plosive appears in Tyap and Northern Paiute. Tyap, a language spoken in Nigeria, has a contrastive pair by [±voiced], such as 'kk : gg'. In Tyap, there are the four-way velar plosives /k, g, kk, gg/.

/g̊/

Devoiced. This plosive is distinguished from the voiceless /k/. For the devoiced plosive, refer to the description of /b̥/ in 4.1.2. /g̊/ appears in three languages.

/kk^{w}/

Voiceless, labialized, fortis. Fortis plosives combined with secondary articulation are so rare that no example other than /kk^{w}/ and /gg^{w}/ exist. In other places of articulation, such fortis plosives are not found, and the type of secondary articulation is limited to labialization. /kk^{w}/ appears only in Koalib-Rere, an African language.

/gg^{w}/

Voiced, labialized, fortis. This plosive is a voiced opposite of /kk^{w}/. It appears only in Northern Paiute. There are no known languages with

38 In addition to /k^{r}, g^{r}, $^{ŋ}g^{r}$/, Peve has /k, g, k^{w}, g^{w}, ^{ŋ}g/ as velar plosives.

both /kkʷ/ and /ggʷ/. Koalib-Rere, with /kkʷ/, and the Northern Paiute, with /ggʷ/, are distinct in terms of both region and language family.

4.9. Uvular plosives

4.9.1. Overview

The uvular plosive is a minor plosive class as shown by its lower frequency than that of the retroflex plosive in Figure 2-1. The types of uvular plosives are also less diverse than the other major classes. The list of uvular plosives is summarized in Table 4-45. As shown in Table 4-45, breathy-voice or creaky-voice plosives are not found in the uvular. Plosives that are articulated close to the larynx show a similar pattern.

The uvular plosives appearing in more than 10 languages are given in Table 4-46. Of the seven uvular plosives in Table 4-46, the bottom three each appear in approximately 10 languages. This clearly shows that uvular plosives are not common. Moreover, the frequency of voiced plain /ɢ/ is considerably lower than that of voiceless plain /q/. Without exception, the frequency of the voiced plain plosive is lower than that of voiceless plain plosive, but the difference is not as considerable as with the uvular plosive. The frequency of /ɢ/ is only approximately one-ninth that of /q/. As a result, the fourth-place ranking of /ɢ/ in Table 4-46 deviates from the general tendency of other voiced plain plosives to occupy second place after the voiceless plain plosive. The decrease in the relative frequency of the voiced plain plosive compared to the voiceless plain plosive becomes evident in the velar plosives, and there is no voiced plain plosive in the glottal. It has been pointed out earlier that this is related to the distance between the larynx and the place of

Table 4-45. List of uvular plosives

a.	Plain	q, ɢ
b.	Single secondary articulation	qʰ, ɢʰ, ᴺq, ᴺɢ, qˀ, qʷ, ɢʷ, qʲ, qˤ, ɢˤ
c.	Multiple secondary articulation	qʰʷ, qʰʲ, ᴺqʰ, ᴺɢʰ, ᴺqʷ, ᴺqʰʷ, qʷˤ
d.	Liquid-colored release	qˡ
e.	Tenseness	qq

Table 4-46. High-frequency uvular plosives

Ranking	Plosive	Frequency	Ranking	Plosive	Frequency
1	q	373	5	ᴺq	11
2	q^h	106	6	q^{hw}	10
3	q^w	67	6	ᴺɢ	10
4	ɢ	42			

articulation. The closer the distance is between the two, the lower the frequency of the voiced plosive compared to the voiceless plosive.

Table 4-47 gives the number of uvular plosives in languages. The average number of uvular plosives across all languages is very small, approximately 0.2, because 91% of all languages have no uvular plosive. The average number of uvular plosives in languages that include them is to 1.7. However, compared to other places of articulation, this average number is still not high.

Many languages with the uvular plosive have one or two. There are more languages with one uvular plosive than languages with two, which is the same as for the retroflex plosive. The languages with the most uvular plosives are found mainly in East Asia. Five of the eight languages with five or more uvular plosives belong to the Sino-Tibetan and Hmong-Mien language families. Western Xiangxi Miao is the language with the most uvular plosives.

Table 4-47. Number of uvular plosives in languages

Number of uvular plosives	Number of languages	Percentage
0	3,965	91.0%
1	210	4.8%
2	139	3.2%
3	15	0.3%
4	19	0.4%
5	5	0.1%
6	2	0%
7	0	0%
8	1	0%

(9) Uvular plosives in Western Xiangxi Miao

$q, q^h, q^w, q^{hw}, {}^Nq, {}^Nq^h, {}^Nq^w, {}^Nq^{hw}$

According to Sposato (2015: 59), Western Xiangxi Miao, which belong to the Hmong-Mien language family, has eight uvular plosives, all of which are voiceless. In other words, there is no phonological contrast by [±voiced], and thus, the eight plosives are opposed by three secondary articulations: aspiration, nasalization, and labialization. The presence of eight plosives at one place of articulation, with none of them voiced, is unique.

Now, it is time to determine the general pattern according to the number of uvular plosives. The common plosives in languages with one uvular plosive are given in Table 4-48. There are three uvular plosives in table 4-48, and /q/ is overwhelmingly the most frequent. By comparison, the frequency of voiced /ɢ/ is relatively very low. As seen in Table 4-46, /ɢ/ itself is very rare.

The common inventories in languages with two uvular plosives are given in Table 4-49. The phonological characteristics of the inventories in Table 4-49 are quite different from other places of articulation. In general, the highest-frequency inventory should consist of two plain plosives. However, contrary to expectations, the frequency of /q, q^h/, which is opposed by [±aspirated], is ranked first. Moreover, /q, q^w/, which is opposed by [±labialized], has a slightly less frequent than / q, q^h/ and takes second place. By contrast, /q, ɢ/, which comprises two plain plosives, is not only ranked third in frequency, but also far less common than the first and second inventories. This result is due to two reasons that have already been identified. One is that the frequency of /

Table 4-48. Types and frequency of single uvular plosive inventories

Plosive	q	ɢ	q^h
Number of languages	196	10	4

Table 4-49. Types and frequency of two-way uvular plosive inventories

Plosive inventory	q, q^h	q, q^w	q, ɢ	q, ${}^Nq$	q, ${}^Nɢ$
Number of languages	64	50	12	3	3

Table 4-50. Types and frequency of three-way uvular plosive inventories

Plosive inventory	Type-(a)	Type-(b)
	q, ɢ, qʰ	q, qʰ, ᴺɢ
Number of languages	8	4

Table 4-51. Types and frequency of four-way uvular plosive inventories

Plosive inventory	Type-(a)	Type-(b)	Type-(c)	Type-(d)
	q, qʰ, qʷ, qʰʷ	q, qʰ, ᴺq, ᴺqʰ	q, ɢ, qʷ, ɢʷ	q, ɢ, qʰ, ɢʰ
Number of languages	7	5	4	2

ɢ/ itself is low, and the other is that the frequency of /qʷ/ is relatively high. The low ranking of /q, ɢ/ in Table 4-49 clearly indicates once again the inferior status of the voiced /ɢ/.

There are few languages with three or more uvular plosives, so discussing the preferred type or phonological contrast in such languages is largely unnecessary. Therefore, I end the discussion here with a brief reference along with inventories that appear in two or more languages.

It is not unusual for type-(a) to be included in Table 4-50 because it is also frequent in other places of articulation. However, the inclusion of type-(b) is unexpected. In Table 4-51, the frequency of type-(d) would have been the highest for other places of articulation. It is relatively uncommon to find both /q/ and /g/ included in the high-frequency inventories.

4.9.2. Description of the uvular plosives

/q/

Voiceless, plain. This plosive appears in 303 languages. /q/ is found in several language families distributed in various regions, although a slight bias regarding language family exists. For example, relatively few languages belonging to the Atlantic-Congo and Austronesian language families have /q/ as a phoneme. The number of languages covered in this book is high enough to exceed 700 for each language family, but /q/ appears in only five Atlantic-Congo languages and 14 Austronesian languages. In contrast, 43 of 219 languages in the Afro-Asiatic language family have /q/. The concentration is particularly high in the Mayan and Hmong-Mien language families, where over half of the languages have /q/.[39] /q/ is unaspirated, but is sometimes accompanied by light aspiration depending on the language. If the aspiration accompanying /q/ is slightly stronger, even if there is only one uvular plosive, it is analyzed as /q^{h}/ instead of /q/, like in Hunzib, Northern Haida, Svan, and Udi.

/ɢ/

Voiced, plain. This plosive is found in 42 languages and its frequency is very low compared to voiceless /q/ (373). This relatively low figure within the list of high-frequency uvular plosives deviates from the general trend. Only thirty-one of the 42 languages with /ɢ/ have a contrastive pair by [±voiced] such as 'q : ɢ'.

/q^{h}/

Voiceless, postaspirated. This plosive appears in 106 languages and is the second most frequent of the uvular plosives after /q/. Ninety-eight of the languages with /q^{h}/ have /q/, so the ratio at which the aspirated /q^{h}/ implies the existence of the plain /q/ is quite high. Many languages in which /q^{h}/ appears are concentrated in Asia, with more than half belonging to the Sino-Tibetan and Hmong-Mien language families. By contrast, it is found rarely in the two largest language families, appearing only in Kgalagadi within the Atlantic-Congo family and in no language within the Austronesian family. This distribution of voiceless aspirated plosive is similar to that for other places of articulation.

/ɢ^{h}/

Voiced, postaspirated. This plosive appears in East Taa and West !Xoon, both of which belong to the Tuu language family in Africa. Compared to voiced aspirated plosives at other places of articulation, /ɢ^{h}/ is quite rare. East Taa and West !Xoon have the four-way plosive /q, ɢ, q^{h}, ɢ^{h}/. It is a common trend for the voiced aspirated plosive to imply the existence of such a four-way opposition. The distribution of /ɢ^{h}/ is

39 The plosive /q/ appears in 13 of 21 languages in the Mayan and 16 of 32 languages in the Hmong-Mien language families.

different from that of other voiced aspirated plosives. In general, voiced aspirated plosives are found in many Asian languages, but the /ɢʰ/ is found in African languages.

/ᴺq/

Voiceless, prenasalized. This plosive is found in 11 languages, of which seven belong to the Hmong-Mien language family, reflecting a bias toward a specific language family. All languages with /ᴺq/ have /q/, which is not accompanied by nasalization. However, of the 11 languages with /ᴺq/, only Diandongbei-Large Flowery Miao have its voiced opposite, /ᴺɢ/. In other places of articulation, the voiceless prenasalized plosive often implies the presence of voiced opposite, but the uvular plosive is exception to this trend.

/ᴺɢ/

Voiced, prenasalized. This plosive appears in 10 languages, of which five belong to the Sino-Tibetan and two to the Hmong-Mien language families, limiting its distribution to Asian languages. Among the nasalized plosives, /ᴺɢ/ is the only one whose frequency is lower than that of its voiceless opposite. It is not advantageous the uvular plosive to accompany the vibration of the vocal folds, so the voiced uvular plosives are infrequent.

/qʷ/

Voiceless, labialized. This plosive appears in 67 languages and is common in languages spoken in North America, especially in the Salishan language family. Of the large language families, the Atlantic-Congo has no language with /qʷ/, and only one language, Keapara, in the Austronesian, has this phoneme. The frequency of /qʷ/ is lower than that of /pʷ/ or /kʷ/, but higher than that of /tʷ/. Considering that uvular plosives occur at a rate less than a tenth that of alveolar plosives, as shown in Figure 2-1, it is unexpected for /qʷ/ to be more frequent than /tʷ/. Of the languages with /qʷ/, all except Kabardian also have /q/, which is not accompanied by labialization.

/ɢʷ/

Voiced, labialized. This plosive appears in five languages, which all also have /ɢ/. Four of these languages have a contrastive pair by

[±voiced], such as 'q^w : G^w'.

/q^j/

Voiceless, palatalized. This plosive appears in Maang and Ubykh, and less frequent among the palatalized plosives. Its voiced opposite, /G^j/, is not found in any language.

/$q^ʕ$/

Voiceless, pharyngealized. This plosive appears in five languages, four of which belong to the Nakh-Daghestanian language family. Pharyngealized plosives are common in languages of the Semitic language family, a subbranch of the Afro-Asiatic, but there is no Semitic language with /$q^ʕ$/.

/$\text{G}^ʕ$/

Voiced, pharyngealized. This plosive is found in Rutul and Tsakhur, which are languages of the Nakh-Daghestanian language family. Rutul and Tsakhur have a contrastive pair by [±voiced], such as '$q^ʕ$: $\text{G}^ʕ$'. Both languages have numerous uvular plosives, with Rutul having six and Tsakhur having five.

/$q^ʔ$/

Voiceless, postlaryngealized. This plosive appears in Achumawi and Selk'nam. Achumawi has the unique three-way opposition /q, q^h, $q^ʔ$/. In Achumawi, the same three-way opposition appears at four places of articulation.

/$^{\text{N}}q^h$/

Voiceless, postaspirated, prenasalized. This plosive appears in nine languages, seven of which belong to the Hmong-Mien language family. It has a high ratio of implying the presence of phonetically simple plosives. For example, all languages with /$^{\text{N}}q^h$/ have /q^h/, eight of the nine languages have /q/, and seven have /$^{\text{N}}q$/.

/$^{\text{N}}\text{G}^h$/

Voiced, postaspirated, prenasalized. This plosive is a voiced opposite of /$^{\text{N}}q^h$/. It appears only in Hmong Daw. This langue has balanced and systematic oppositions such as /q, q^h, $^{\text{N}}\text{G}$, $^{\text{N}}\text{G}^h$/. No language has both

/ᴺqʰ/ and /ᴺɢʰ/ as separate phonemes.

/qʰʷ/

Voiceless, postaspirated, labialized. This plosive appears in 10 languages, seven of which have the same inventory for the uvular plosive: /q, qʰ, qʷ, qʰʷ/.[40] No known language has /ɢʰʷ/, the voiced opposite of /qʰʷ/. Even in other places of articulation, all plosives combined with aspiration and labialization are voiceless without exception.

/qʰʲ/

Voiceless, postaspirated, palatalized. This plosive appears only in Maang, which also has /qʲ/. There is no known language that has its voiced opposite, /ɢʰʲ/.

/ᴺqʷ/

Voiceless, prenasalized, labialized. This plosive appears only in Western Xiangxi Miao. Its voiced opposite, /ᴺɢʷ/, is not found in any language.

/qʷˤ/

Voiceless, labialized, pharyngealized. This plosive appears only in Rutul and Ubykh. These two languages belong to different language families but are close regionally. The existence of its voiced opposite, /ɢʷˤ/, has not been reported.

/ᴺqʰʷ/

Voiceless, postaspirated, prenasalized, labialized. This consonant is the only uvular plosive accompanied by three secondary articulations. Like /ᴺqʷ/, /ᴺqʰʷ/ appears only in Western Xiangxi Miao, and its voiced opposite, /ᴺɢʰʷ/, has not been found.

40 In addition to these seven languages, two languages, Luopohe Hmong and Western Xiangxi Miao, also include these four consonants in the inventory, but they have more uvular plosives. Interestingly, these nine languages have similar inventories even though they are unrelated in terms of region and language family.

/q^l/

Voiceless, lateral-released. For this type of plosive, refer to the description of /p^l/ in 4.1.2. /q^l/ is found only in Luopohe Hmong. The existence of its voiced opposite, /ɢˡ/, has not been reported.

/qq/

Voiceless, fortis. For the fortis plosive, refer to the description of /pp/ in 4.1.2. /qq/ appears only in Akhvakh, which also has the plain plosive /q/.

4.10. Pharyngeal plosive

The only consonant known as a pharyngeal plosive is /ʕ/. There is no voiced plosive and no complex plosive accompanying secondary articulation in the pharyngeal.

/ʕ/

Voiceless, plain. This plosive appears in 19 languages, many of which belong to the Afro-Asiatic and Nakh-Daghestanian language families. There is little correlation between languages with the pharyngeal plosive and languages with the pharyngealized plosive. Among the Semitic languages, where pharyngealized plosives are common, only four have /ʕ/. Of 19 languages with /ʕ/, only five have the pharyngealzied plosives. The distribution of /ʕ/ and the plosives with pharyngealization as a secondary articulation has very few overlaps.

4.11. Epiglottal plosive

Like the pharyngeal plosive, there is only one voiceless plain plosive in the epiglottal.

/ʡ/

Voiceless, plain. The phoneme appears in Aghul, a language of the Nakh-Daghestanian language family, and Dahalo, a language of the Afro-Asiatic language family. As mentioned in 2.1, differences in the place of articulation between the pharyngeal /ʕ/ and epiglottal /ʡ/ may not be recognized. These two plosives, which are very rare and close to each other, have something in common. Languages in which /ʕ/ and /ʡ/ appear are not regionally distant. Moreover, no language has both /ʕ/ and /ʡ/ as separate phonemes. This mutual exclusivity demonstrates the similarity between /ʕ/ and /ʡ/.

4.12. Glottal plosives

4.12.1. Overview

The glottal consonant has several characteristics that distinguish it from consonants in other places of articulation. First, the articulator and the point of articulation are not clearly distinguished. Additionally, it is not easy for an articulator to move actively. Moreover, there is no voiced consonant among the glottal plosives. Due to these various articulatory restrictions, the types of glottal plosive are very limited. The list of glottal plosives is summarized in Table 4-52.

As already seen in Figure 2-1 and 2-2, the glottal plosive itself is neither infrequent nor uncommon among the plosives, but it has very few types, with only eight. Moreover, there are no complex plosives combined with glottal action or tenseness due to the glottal characteristics. Except for the plain /ʔ/ and the complex /ʔ^{w}, ʔ^{j}/, the glottal plosives are rare and appear in only three or fewer languages.

The number of glottal plosives is given in Table 4-53. Although there are few types of glottal plosives, the proportion of languages with them is higher than expected. Approximately 40% of all languages have one or more glottal plosives. The reason for this is that /ʔ/ appears in 1,754 languages, making its frequency the seventh most frequent after /k, p, t, b, g, d/, which belong to the major plosive.[41]

Table 4-52. List of glottal plosives

a.	Plain	ʔ
b.	Single secondary articulation	ʔ^{h}, ^{N}ʔ, ʔ^{w}, ʔ^{j}, ʔ^{ʕ}
c.	Multiple secondary articulations	^{N}ʔ^{w}
d.	Liquid-colored release	ʔ^{l}

41 For this, refer to Table 5.1.

Table 4-53. Number of glottal plosives in languages

Number of glottal plosives	Number of languages	Percentage
0	2,601	59.7%
1	1,722	39.5%
2	26	0.6%
3	7	0.2%

The average number of glottal plosives in all languages is 0.4, but among language that include these plosives, the average is 1.0. In other words, if a language has a glottal plosive, it is most likely to have only one. As shown in Table 4-53, languages with two or more glottal plosives account for less than 1% of all languages. Languages with only one glottal plosive have /ʔ/ without exception. Among the languages with two glottal plosives, 16 of 26 have /ʔ, ʔʷ/. In addition, there are three languages each with /ʔ, ʔʲ/ and /ʔ, ᴺʔ/. Hlai, a member of the Tai-Kadai language family, is unique in that it does not have a /ʔ/, a plain plosive, even though it has two glottal plosives. Hlai is the only language with two or more glottal plosives that does not include /ʔ/.

The maximum number of glottal plosives in a language is three. There are seven languages with three glottal plosives, all of which are spoken in Africa. Of these, six share a common inventory of the glottal plosives: /ʔ, ʔʷ, ʔʲ/. As noted earlier in Table 4-52, five of the eight glottal plosives appear in three or fewer languages. The remaining three glottal plosives, /ʔ, ʔʷ, ʔʲ/, appear in more than 10 languages and are found in the shared inventory. The only exception is Psikye, which has /ᴺʔʷ/ instead of /ʔʲ/.

4.12.2. Description of the glottal plosives

/ʔ/

Voiceless, plain. This plosive is found in 1,754 languages and is the seventh most frequent of the plosives. None of the complex positives is more frequent than /ʔ/. Only six plain plosives at the major places of articulation, namely /p, b, t, d, k, g/, have a higher frequency than /ʔ/. The plosive /ʔ/ is often classified as an ejective rather than plain plosive in the description of individual languages, and in languages that include implosives, /ʔ/ is sometimes grouped with that category. However, it seems reasonable to analyze it as having the same characteristics as other plain plosives. In some languages, /ʔ/ has a demarcative function between two vowels, or words, and thus is not involved in discriminating the word meaning. In this case, /ʔ/ is difficult to establish as a phoneme, but, depending on the discussion, it is nonetheless included in the phoneme inventory. Therefore, it is possible that /ʔ/ may be less frequent than asserted here. However, this difference is insufficient to affect the overall frequency of /ʔ/.

/$ʔ^h$/

Voiceless, postaspirated. This plosive has been reported to appear only in Wuding-Luquan Yi, a member of the Sino-Tibetan language family. It is spoken in Southwestern China. Little is known about whether glottal plosives can be accompanied by aspiration. Aspiration and laryngealization as secondary articulations are not combined in one plosive. Considering this restriction, /$ʔ^h$/ is a very unusual consonant. The phoneme inventory of Wuding-Luquan Yi presented in Namkung (1996) is recited by normalizing other primary data, so it is difficult to rule out an error.[42]

/$^Nʔ$/

Voiceless, prenasalized. This plosive is found in three languages of the Austronesian language family, in which nasalized plosives are frequent. Languages with /$^Nʔ$/ share a common inventory of the glottal plosive, /ʔ, $^Nʔ$/.

/$ʔ^w$/

Voiceless, labialized. It is not easy to imagine that the glottal plosive can be accompanied by labialization, but it is not so rare that it appears in 24 languages. Its frequency is the second highest among the glottal plosives. /$ʔ^w$/ is found in many African languages, particularly those in the Chadic language family, a subbranch of the Afro-Asiatic. Eight of the 24 languages in this language family, equivalent to one-third, have /$ʔ^w$/.

42 In Namkung (1996: 231), /$ʔ^h$/ is transcribed as /ʔh/. Its place of articulation is the same as /ʔ/, and its manner of articulation is the same as the aspirated plosive. Therefore, it is interpreted as a glottal aspirated plosive.

All languages with /ʔ^{w}/ have two or more glottal plosives, and all others except Hlai have /ʔ/.

/ʔ^{j}/

Voiceless, palatalized. This plosive appears in 10 languages. Like /ʔ^{w}/, it is found mainly in African languages.

/ʔ^{ʕ}/

Voiceless, pharyngealized. This plosive appears only in Rutul, a language of the Nakh-Daghestanian language family. Considering the close distance between the larynx and pharynx, /ʔ^{ʕ}/ is expected to have considerable articulatory difficulties, which is the likely reason why it is so infrequent.

/^{N}ʔ^{w}/

Voiceless, prenasalized, labialized. This plosive is the only glottal plosive that is accompanied by two secondary articulations. It appears only in Psikye which has /ʔ, ʔ^{w}, ^{N}ʔ^{w}/ as glottal plosives.

/ʔ^{l}/

Voiceless, lateral-released. According to Niedere (1998: 125), /ʔ^{l}/ appears only in Northern Guiyang Hmong. To date, few studies have reported that a lateral release combines with glottal plosives. Thus, /ʔ^{l}/ is a highly unusual consonant. In Northern Guiyang Hmong, lateral-released plosives appear in the bilabial and glottal, but not in other places of articulation.[43]

4.13. Labiovelar plosives

4.13.1. Overview

Labiovelar plosives are double-articulated consonants whose primary articulation is created almost simultaneously in the labial and

43 In Northern Guiyang Hmong, the phonological opposition of the plosive differs depending on the place of articulation.

Table 4-54. List of labiovelar plosives

a.	Plain	kp, gb
b.	Single secondary articulation	kp^{h}, gb^{h}, ^{ŋm}kp, ^{ŋm}gb, gb^{ŋm}, kp^{w}, gb^{w}, kp^{j}, gb^{j}
c.	Liquid-colored release	kp^{r}, gb^{r}, ^{ŋm}gb^{r}
d.	Tenseness	kkpp

velar. Labiovelar plosives are the only double-articulated plosives that have a certain frequency and various types. The proportion of languages with labiovelar plosives is slightly higher than that of retroflex plosives, and there are more than 10 types. The list of labiovelar plosives is summarized in Table 4-54.

Table 4-54 shows that there is no plosive accompanied by two secondary articulations. Plosives with two secondary articulations are often found among single-articulated plosives whose primary articulation is created in one point, but are not in the labiovelar plosives. Since the labiovelar itself has two primary articulation points, it is very difficult to accompany two secondary articulations. In addition, among labiovelar plosives, neither breathy-voice nor creaky-voice exists. Of the various plosives in Table 4-54, /kp, gb, ^{ŋm}gb/ appear in more than 10 languages.[44]

The number of labiovelar plosives is given in Table 4-55. The average number of labiovelar plosives in all languages is 0.2, but is

Table 4-55. Number of labiovelar plosives in languages

Number of labiovelar plosives	Number of languages	Percentage
0	3,862	88.7%
1	75	1.7%
2	318	7.3%
3	89	2.0%
4	10	0.2%
5	1	0%
6	1	0%

44 The frequency of plosives in Table 4-54 is given in 4.13.2.

2.1 among only those languages with the labiovelar plosive, which is similar to other major places of articulation. Among languages with the labiovelar plosive, the ratio of languages with two is relatively high, which accords with the average number. The language with the most labiovelar plosives is Baka (Sudan). According to Sampson (1997: 115), the labiovelar plosives of Baka (Sudan) are as follows.

(10) Labiovelar plosives in Baka (Sudan)

kp, gb, ^{ŋm}gb, kp^{r}, gb^{r}, ^{ŋm}gb^{r}

Baka (Sudan) has six labiovelar plosives. Among them, three are trill-released plosives, which are very rare. The inventory of (10) is phonologically systematic in that three-way opposition between voiceless plain, voiced plain, and voiced nasalized plosives is established in both the trill-release type and general release type.

Next, let us examine the general pattern according to the number of labiovelar plosives. The common plosives in languages with one labiovelar plosive are provided in Table 4-56. Languages with one labiovelar plosive are the most common in African languages, many of which belong to the Atlantic-Congo language family. There are three types of labiovelar plosives in Table 4-56. Among them, predictably, the highest-frequency plosive is a voiceless plain /kp/. The voiced plain /gb/ is quite frequent compared to the other voiced plain plosives. Similar results are demonstrated by the retroflex or palatal plosives. All of these places of articulation are minor classes, not major. In the case of major classes such as the bilabial, alveolar, and velar, if a language has only one plain plosive, the plosive is much more likely to be voiceless than voiced.

Languages with two labiovelar plosives are also common in Africa. The frequent inventories found in these languages are provided in Table 4-57. The inventories in Table 4-57 appear in more than two languages. The results reveal two distinct differences compared to other places

Table 4-56. Types and frequency of single labiovelar plosive inventories

Plosive	kp	gb	kp^{w}
Number of languages	46	26	3

Table 4-57. Types and frequency of two-way labiovelar plosive inventories

Plosive inventory	kp, gb	kp, ^{ŋm}gb	gb, ^{ŋm}gb
Number of languages	305	8	3

of articulation. First, the frequency of /kp, gb/, which consists of two plain plosives, is exceptionally high. Even in other places of articulation, similar inventories are the most frequent, but not as overwhelmingly so as in Table 4-57. This dominance is related to the relatively higher frequency of /gb/ compared to /kp/. As shown in Figure 3-3, when the frequency of /kp/ is set to '1', the frequency of /gb/ compared to /kp/ is nearly identical, at 0.95, and its value is the highest among the voiced plain plosives. Owing to this high frequency of /gb/, /kp, gb/ can also occur frequently.

Second, the inventory consisting of voiceless plain and aspirated plosives, which is the second most frequent in other places of articulation, is not found in Table 4-57. None of the languages with two labiovelar plosives have /kp, kp^h/, which is related to the very low frequency of /kp^h/. The plosive /kp^h/ appears in nine languages, which is less than 2% of the frequency of /kp/, and this percentage is only a tenth that of voiceless aspirated plosives at other places of articulation. As a result, languages having /kp, kp^h/ as two opposed members have not been reported.[45]

The common inventories in languages with three labiovelar plosives are very limited. Only one inventory appears in more than one language, /kp, gb, ^{ŋm}gb/, which is found in 84 of 89 languages. This extreme bias toward a specific inventory is unparalleled. In most places of articulation, inventories consisting of two plain plosives and one voiceless aspirated plosive are the most common, followed by inventories consisting of two plain plosives and one voiced nasalized plosive. However, among the labiovelar plosive, voiceless aspirated plosives are extremely infrequent. Therefore, the unusually high frequency of /kp, gb, ^{ŋm}gb/, including a voiced nasalized plosive instead of a voiceless aspirated plosive, is expected.

45 There seems to be another reason for this. For details, refer to the description of /kp^h/ in 4.13.2.

Table 4-58. Types and frequency of four-way labiovelar plosive inventories

Plosive inventory	Type-(a)	Type-(b)
	kp, gb, kp^h, gb^h	kp, gb, ^{ŋm}kp, ^{ŋm}gb
Number of languages	5	2

Finally, I will consider the inventories that are common in languages with four labiovelar plosives. Ten languages have four labiovelar plosives. Only two inventories appear in more than one language, as presented in Table 4-58. The plosives included in type-(a) are opposed by [±voiced] and [±aspirated], whereas in type-(b) are opposed by [±voiced] and [±nasalized]. Phonological oppositions of these two types are optimized by two distinctive features, which are also commonly found in other places of articulation. Unlike languages with two or three labiovelar plosives, the inventories that are common in languages with four labiovelar plosives follow the general trend.

4.13.2. Description of the labiovelar plosives

/kp/

Voiceless, plain. This plosive appears in 459 languages. The distribution of labiovelar plosives, including /kp/, tends to be biased by region. In general, they are commonly found in African languages, whereas they are very rare in Asian or American languages.

/gb/

Voiced, plain. This plosive appears in 435 languages, of which 404 have a contrastive pair by [±voiced] such as 'kp : gb'. In other words, /gb/ implies the existence of /kp/ in 92.9 % (404/435), which is very high.

/kp^h/

Voiceless, postaspirated. This plosive appears in nine languages and is both absolutely and relatively infrequent. In general, voiceless aspirated plosives occur at a rate of approximately 20% that of corresponding voiceless plain plosives, but the frequency of /kp^h/ is only 2% that of /kp/. Therefore, in other places of articulation, [±aspirated] is quite actively involved in phonemic opposition of the plosive, but is not in the labiovelar.

There seem to be several reasons for the low frequency of /kpʰ/. First, as pointed out regarding aspiration in 3.5, there are restriction on the combination of double-articulated plosives and secondary articulation, which limits the frequency of /kpʰ/. However, there are complex plosives that appear in more than 100 languages, such as /ᵑᵐgb/, so this restriction alone does not properly explain why /kpʰ/ is so infrequent. A more direct reason seems to be related to the distribution in language families. The labiovelar plosive is common in African languages, especially those of the Atlantic-Congo language family. Aspirated plosives, however, are mainly found in Asian languages belonging to the Sino-Tibetan and Indo-European language families. That is, labiovelar plosives and aspirated plosives are distributed mutually exclusively. Therefore, the infrequency of /kpʰ/, a labiovelar plosive accompanied by aspiration, is expected.

/gbʰ/

Voiced, postaspirated. This plosive appears in six languages, all of which have four-way opposition by [±voiced] and [±aspirated], as seen in /kp, gb, kpʰ, gbʰ/. Generally, voiced aspirated plosives implies the existence of four-way opposition. While other aspirated plosives are common in Asian languages, /gbʰ/ is only found in languages of the Atlantic-Congo language family in Africa.

/ᵑᵐkp/

Voiceless, prenasalized. This plosive is found in four languages belonging to the Atlantic-Congo language family. Three of the four languages with /ᵑᵐkp/ have a contrastive pair by [±voiced] such as 'ᵑᵐkp : ᵑᵐgb'.

/ᵑᵐgb/

Voiced, prenasalized. This plosive appears in 102 languages and is principally found in African languages. However, unlike /ᵑᵐkp/, the distribution of /ᵑᵐgb/ includes the Afro-Asiatic and Central Sudanic language families as well as the Atlantic-Congo.

/gbᵑᵐ/

Voiced, postnasalized. This plosive is opposed to /ᵑᵐgb/ by the position of nasalization. It appears only in Mumuye spoken in Nigeria. Mumuye is characterized by its several postnasalized plosives. /$kp^{ŋm}$/, the voiceless opposite of /$gb^{ŋm}$/, is not found in any language.

/kp^w/

Voiceless, labialized. This plosive is found in five languages and is distributed in two distant regions. Cori and North Mofu are African languages, while Lelepa, Mwotlap, and Vurës are spoken in Vanuatu, which is far from Africa.

/gb^w/

Voiced, labialized. This plosive is found in Cori and Mbedam, both of which are spoken in Africa. Cori, unlike Mbedam, has the contrastive pair by [±voiced], such as 'kp^w : gb^w'.

/kp^j/

Voiceless, palatalized. This plosive appears only in Gwandara. Considering that palatalization is a common secondary articulation, it is somewhat surprising that /kp^j/ appears only in one language. Moreover, its voiced opposite, /gb^j/, is also found in only one language. Thus, there seems to be a phonetic reason for the difficulty of accompanying the labiovelar plosive with palatalization.

/gb^j/

Voiced, palatalized. Like /kp^j/, /gb^j/ appears only in Gwandara. As a result, the labiovelar plosive combined with palatalization functions as a phoneme only in Gwandara.

/kp^r/

Voiceless, trill-released (or flap-released). For this type of plosive, refer to the description of /p^r/ in 4.1.2. /kp^r/ appears only in Baka (Sudan), which has /gb^r/ and /$^{ŋm}gb^r$/ in addition to /kp^r/.

/gb^r/

Voiced, trill-released (or flap-released). This plosive is a voiced opposite of /kp^r/ and, like /kp^r/, appears only in Baka (Sudan).

/^{ŋm}gb^{r}/

Voiced, prenasalized, trill-released (or flap-released). This plosive is a rare consonant in that it combines a double-articulated plosive with nasalization and trill-release. It is only found in Baka (Sudan).[46]

/kkpp/

Voiceless, fortis. For the fortis plosive, refer to the description of /pp/ in 4.1.2. /kkpp/ is found only in Cross River Mbembe, a language spoken in Nigeria. Cross River Mbembe has three-way opposition such as /kp, gb, kkpp/.

4.14. Labial alveolar plosives

Labial alveolar plosives are the double-articulated consonants whose primary articulation is created in the labial and alveolar. According to Rogers (2000: 203), the representative language with this consonant is Bura-Pabir, a language spoken in Nigeria, but the discussion referenced in this book shows that Bura-Pabir does not have this consonant. Ladefoged & Maddieson (1996: 344) argued that previous works had asserted that Margi and Bura-Pabir have the labial alveolar consonant but that, upon closer examination, labial alveolar plosive in these languages was not a single consonant, but a consonant cluster. Ladefoged & Maddieson (1996: 344) presented the labial alveolar /tp/ and the labial-postalveolar /ṭp/ in Yele as true examples of the labial alveolar plosive.[47] Henderson (1995: 7~8), which described the phonemic system of Yele in detail, presented several examples of labial alveolar consonants, claiming that the nonbilabial consonants of Yele can be combined with contrastive feature

46 As shown above, labiovelar trill-released plosives appear only in Baka (Sudan). In the GLOTTOLOG, two languages called Baka are set as a separate language. One is Baka (Sudan) and the other is Baka (Cameroon). According to the GLOTTOLOG, these languages are not close to each other, nor do they belong to the same language family. Baka (Sudan) is in the Central Sudanic, and Baka (Cameroon) in the Atlantic-Congo. The consonant inventory of Baka (Sudan) is from Sampson (1997).

47 In Ladefoged & Maddieson (1996: 344), Yele is called Yeletnye. It is spoken in Papua New Guinea.

[simultaneous bilabial closure].[48] According to this approach, various consonants in the dental, postdental, and velar can be combined with [simultaneous bilabial closure] to form double-articulated consonants. Moreover, minimal pairs are presented depending on the presence or absence of combination with [simultaneous bilabial closure]. The feature [simultaneous bilabial closure] can be accompanied by a nasal or lateral /l/ as well as a plosive. However, since the consonant inventory in Henderson (1995) is somewhat unclear, Yele is excluded from discussion in this book.

/pt/

Voiceless, plain. This plosive appears in Gavar and Nzima. Chinebuah (1973: 113) described /pt/ in Nzima as follows: "the air passage is completely blocked by an outer closure formed by bringing the lips together and by an inner closure between the front of the tongue and the hard palate in the alveolar region with the tip of the tongue down against the lower teeth. Both the outer closure at the lips and the inner closure on the alveolar ridge are made and released simultaneously." According to this explanation, /pt/ must be a double-articulated plosive. However, regarding the /pt/ in Nzima, Ladefoged & Maddieson (1996: 344) noted that some works analyze this consonant as a variant of /kp/.[49]

/bd/

Voiced, plain. This plosive appears only in Nzima. As a result, Nzima is the only language that has the contrastive pair 'pt : bd'.

4.15. Labiopalatal plosive

/bɟ/

Voiced, plain. This plosive is a double-articulated plosive whose primary articulation is created in the labial and palatal. It appears only

48 When this feature is combined with the alveolar plosive, it becomes a labial alveolar plosive.

49 Chinebuah (1973: 113) described the articulatory process of /pt/ in contrast to that of /kp/, thereby clearly distinguished the two consonants.

in Birwa, an African language. Chebanne (2000: 189) described /bɟ/ as follows: "double articulations with the labial coming first and the palatal coming next." According to these descriptions, the articulations at the lips and palate do not occur simultaneously. However, in the double-articulated plosive, the timing of the closure and release in two places of articulation do not have to completely coincide, so /bɟ/ in Birwa can be analyzed as a double-articulated plosive.

4.16. Dentovelar plosive

In pronouncing the dentovelar plosive, the coronal and dorsal are involved as articulators. Ladefoged & Maddieson (1996: 348) argued that there is no double-articulated consonant in which the labial is not involved as an articulator. Maddieson & Maddieson (1996: 345~347) reviewed previously reported alveo-velar or dental-palatal consonants and concluded that they cannot be considered double-articulated consonants. However, in the phonological description of individual languages, a double-articulated consonant, in which the labial does not participate in articulation, is sometimes recognized as a phoneme.

/t̪k/

Voiceless, plain. This plosive is found in Bribri and Cabécar, both of which belong to the Chibchan language family in North America and are regionally close. Constenla (1981: 111) cited a reference to this consonant in the 1920s. According to this explanation, the articulatory process of /t̪k/ is as follows: "/t̪/ is created interdentally and is simultaneously articulated into /k/ at the palate." In particular, this description emphasizes that /t̪/ and /k/ in /t̪k/ must never be separated. That is, it clearly states that /t̪k/ is a true double-articulated plosive.

Chapter 5

CHARACTERISTICS OF THE PLOSIVE

Thus far, the characteristics of plosives in the world's languages have been examined in detail, and the typological patterns of plosives in the place and manner of articulation has been determined. In addition, the approximate trends were captured in the frequency, distribution, and implicational relationships of individual plosives. Based on these findings, in this chapter, I will consider the overall aspects of the plosive.

Five main topics will be reviewed in this chapter. First, quantitative characteristics of the plosive will be discussed, including the list of high-frequency plosives, the average number of plosives, and the difference in the proportion of plosives depending on the size of the consonant inventory. Second, I will extract some implicational relationships between various plosives. As the approach to implicational relationships has shifted from finding absolute laws to finding relative tendencies, it is necessary to consider the rate at which the implicational relationship is valid. This book is well suited for such discussions because an unparalleled number of languages have been examined herein. Third, among the inventories of the plosive, I will examine trends that appear repeatedly across languages according to various conditions and determine their phonological characteristics. Based on the results of the examination of individual places of articulation in Chapter 4, I will expand the subject of discussion to determining the high-frequency plosive inventories. Fourth, I will review which of the major plosives are frequently omitted in many languages. There have been some previous discussions of this, but those studies examined only a small number of target languages. Therefore, I will verify whether the previous conclusions remain valid even with large-scale language data. Finally, some peculiar inventories will be introduced from languages worldwide.

A wide variety of inventories exists, including inventories with unique phonological contrasts as well as inventories with unusually large numbers of plosives.

5.1. Quantitative characteristics

This section provides an overview of several quantitative characteristics related to the plosive. First is a list of the high-frequency plosives. In

Table 5-1. High-frequency plosives[1]

	[A]		[B]	
Ranking	Plosive	Frequency	Plosive	Frequency
1	k	96.5%	k	90%
2	p	87.9%	p	86%
3	t	79.0%	t	68%
4	b	71.3%	b	63%
5	g	63.1%	g	57%
6	d	56.4%	d	46%
7	ʔ	40.3%	ʔ	37%
8	t̪	22.5%	t̪	23%
9	k^h	19.1%	k^h	20%
10	p^h	18.0%	p^h	20%
11	d̪	15.6%	ʈ	16%
12	t^h	14.8%	d̪	14%
13	^mb	14.8%	c	14%
14	^ŋg	13.6%	t^h	13%
15	c	13.4%	gb	12%
16	k^w	12.9%	kp	12%
17	nd	12.6%	k^w	12%
18	ɟ	11.9%	ɟ	12%
19	kp	10.5%	ȶ	10%
20	gb	10.0%	^mb	10%

1 In Lee (2020: 7), /ʈ/ and /ɖ/, which are retroflex plosves, were ranked 19th and 20th, respectively, but their frequency is lower than that of /kp/ and /gb/.

Chapter 4, the frequency of individual plosives was examined. Based on this result, a list of the top 20 plosives and their frequency will be created. For comparison, the list in PHOIBLE (www.https://phoible.org/parameters) is also presented. PHOIBLE's frequency rankings are based on the analysis of 3,020 languages, which include the results of multiple studies on the same language, so there are fewer than 2,000 actual target languages. Nonetheless, the PHOIBLE list is also worth referencing, as it deals with large-scale language data.

In Table 5-1, [A] presents the results of analyzing the 4,356 languages in Lee (2020), and [B] presents the results of PHOIBLE. The frequency is expressed as the proportion of the languages in which each plosive appears among the target languages. Comparing [A] and [B] reveals many similarities but also some differences. The ranking of each list's top 10 is identical, but their proportions are slightly different. The frequencies of five of the top six plosives differ by more than 5%p between [A] and [B]. In the most frequent plosive, /k/, there is a difference of 6.5%p between [A] and [B]. The difference can be considerable, for example, 11.0%p for /t/ and 10.4%p for /d/. The reason for this unusually large frequency difference among alveolar plosives is that the result can vary greatly depending on whether one plosive is classified as dental or alveolar.

There are multiple differences between the 11th and 20th percentiles, including the list, ranking, and frequency. For example, nasalized plosives are relatively common in [A] but not in [B]. The retroflex /ʈ/ is ranked 11th in [B] but is not even among the top twenty in [A].[2] Another such example is /ȶ/, which is ranked 19th in [B], whereas in [A], it is so infrequent that it appears in less than 0.5% of languages. According to PHOIBLE, /ȶ/ appears in many Australian languages.[3] However, /ȶ/ is often analyzed as /tʲ/ or /c/ instead. Because of this difference in phoneme analysis, the frequency of /ȶ/ shows extreme differences in [A] and [B].

Henceforth, the description of plosives will be based on [A]. As expected, plain plosives are more frequent than complex plosives in

2 In [A], /ʈ/ appears in 379 languages, or approximately 8.7%. This is only about half the rate of [B].

3 In [A], /ȶ/ is mainly found in Southwest Asian languages, not Australian languages.

Table 5-1. Only two complex plosives are included in the top 10 and only seven within the top 20. Moreover, all high-frequency plosives that appear in more than 50% of languages are plain plosives.

Regarding the place of articulation, the frequency rankings are as follows: velar > bilabial > alveolar. There are five velar plosives in the top 20. Four bilabial and alveolar plosives each are included in [A] of Table 5-1. but the absolute frequency is higher among the bilabial than the alveolar plosives. If the alveolar and dental plosives are grouped together, they are more frequent than the bilabial plosives.

Next, I will consider the number of plosives in each language. In the previous chapter, I reviewed it according to the place of articulation, but the total number of plosives in the world's languages was not discussed. I will now examine the distribution of plosives in world languages.

In table 5-2, the number of plosives in each language varies considerably, ranging from a minimum of two to a maximum of forty.[4] Approximately three quarters of all languages have four to ten plosives. The proportion of languages with 14 or more plosives drops sharply.

The inventories of languages with two plosives illustrate several

Table 5-2. Number of plosives in languages

Number of plosives	Number of languages	Percentage	Number of plosives	Number of languages	Percentage
2	8	0.2%	11	160	3.7%
3	195	4.5%	12	201	4.6%
4	325	7.5%	13	126	2.9%
5	388	8.9%	14	43	1.0%
6	796	18.3%	15	62	1.4%
7	637	14.6%	16~20	179	4.1%
8	520	11.9%	21~25	18	0.4%
9	384	8.8%	26~30	13	0.3%
10	295	6.8%	31~40	6	0.1%

4 According to Maddieson (1984: 12), it varies from a minimum of three to a maximum of 36. Maddieson (1984: 12) included the affricate among the plosives, so the minimum number is higher than here. However, it is unclear why the maximum number is lower than that of this book. This is probably because the number and type of target languages are different.

characteristics. First, the two plosives in these languages are both plain and voiceless without exception. Voiced or complex plosives are not included. Second, all languages with two plosives share the velar plosive /k/ in common. Five of the eight languages have /t, k/, and the other three have /p, k/. Third, languages with two plosives have small-sized consonant inventories. The language with the most consonants is Lingao, which has 15, and there are three languages with as few as seven consonants. Considering that the average number of consonants across all languages is approximately 20, these languages have very small consonant inventories.

The language with the most plosives is Soga, which has 40, i.e. five times the average number of plosives. Since Soga has a total of 68 consonants, the proportion of plosives is also very high, at 58.8%.[5] In addition to Soga, other languages that have more than 31 plosives include Western Xiangxi Miao (31), Nyanja (32), Diriku (36), Diandongbei-Large Flowery Miao (37), and Maonan (37), which belong to the top class in Table 5-2.[6] Languages with a large number of plosives naturally have many consonants. Of those given above, the language with the fewest consonants has 63, whereas the average of these languages is 70.2, which is approximately 3.5 times that of all languages. Surprisingly, although these languages have numerous plosives, they only share /p, t, k/ in common of the more than 30 plosives, or slightly less than 10%. Generally, it is expected that if languages have numerous plosives, they will share many common plosives with other languages. However, this is not the case.

The presence of Western Xiangxi Miao, a member of Hmong-Mien language family, is responsible for this incomprehensible result. The remaining languages other than Western Xiangxi Miao have an opposition by [±voiced] and some voiced nasalized plosives in common. Therefore, there are more types of plosives to be shared. In contrast, Western Xiangxi Miao has neither voiced plain nor voiced nasalized plosives. For this reason, even in languages with a very large number of plosives, the types of common plosives are limited to /p, t, k/, which are

5 As will be presented later, the percentage of the plosive in the consonant inventory averages around 40%.

6 The numbers in parentheses indicate the number of plosives in the language.

all voiceless plain plosives.

Now, I will examine the average number of plosives and their proportions within the consonant inventory. The number of consonants has been calculated with certain parameters, as explained here. First, when counting the number of consonants, semivowels are excluded. In many typological discussions, semivowels are classified as consonants. However, since it is considered advantageous to distinguish between the semivowel and true consonant, the semivowels will be excluded from the discussion.

Second, the average number of consonants is calculated simply. In other words, after the number of consonants in the 4,356 languages to be discussed are added together, this sum is divided by the number of languages. When calculating the average number of consonants based on small language samples, some supplementary measures are necessary to avoid the problem of various biases. However, when using a large sample of more than 50% of the known languages, as in this book, there is no need to do so, and simple calculations do not cause problems.

The total number of consonants in the 4,356 languages examined here is 87,900, of which 35,017 are plosives. The average number of consonants and plosives are calculated as follows.

(1) Average number of consonants and plosives
 a. Average number of consonants: 87,900/4,356≒20.18
 b. Average number of plosives: 35,017/4,356≒8.04

The average number of consonants in (1a) is not significantly different from the values given in previous works. For example, in Maddieson (1984: 9), the number 22.8 was suggested, and since this figure includes the semivowel, it would be similar to the value of (1a) if the semivowels were excluded. In addition, Lee (2017b: 236) calculated the average number of consonants in six different ways depending on the nature of the sampling, with the results ranging from a minimum of 20.02 to a maximum of 22.25, which is not much different from (1a). The average number of plosives in (1b) is somewhat different from the 10.5 given in Maddieson (1984: 12). However, since the average number in Maddieson (1984: 12) is calculated by including both plosives and affricates, if only the number of plosives is targeted, there will be no substantial difference from (1b).

(2) Proportion of the plosives in the consonant inventory

35,017/87,900≒39.84%

(2) gives the proportion of plosives within the consonant inventory. Of all consonants, plosives account for an average of slightly less than 40%. Although this number does not exceed half of all consonants, no manner of articulation in the consonants is as frequent as the plosive.

If the results of (1) and (2) in addition to Table 5-2 are comprehensively considered, languages can be divided into several classes according to the number of plosives and their proportions within the consonant inventory. First, according to the number of plosives, languages can be divided into five classes as shown in Figure 5-1.

The average class is set as between seven and nine plosives in Figure 5-1 because the average number of plosives is approximately eight, and many languages in Table 5-2 are distributed in this category. The cutoff values for other categories are chosen to approximate a histogram with normal distribution. This setting is not considerably different from the method of division according to the number of consonants in the WALS (World Atlas of Language Structures). However, one problem with Figure 5-1 is that, although the number of languages with six plosives is the highest in Table 5-2, these languages are not located in the average

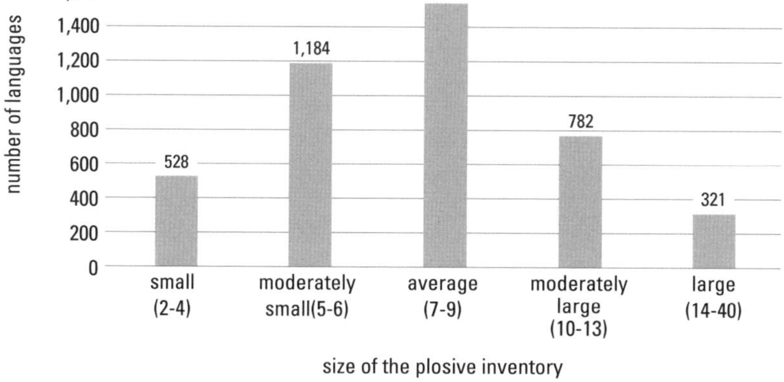

Figure 5-1. Classification of languages by number of plosives

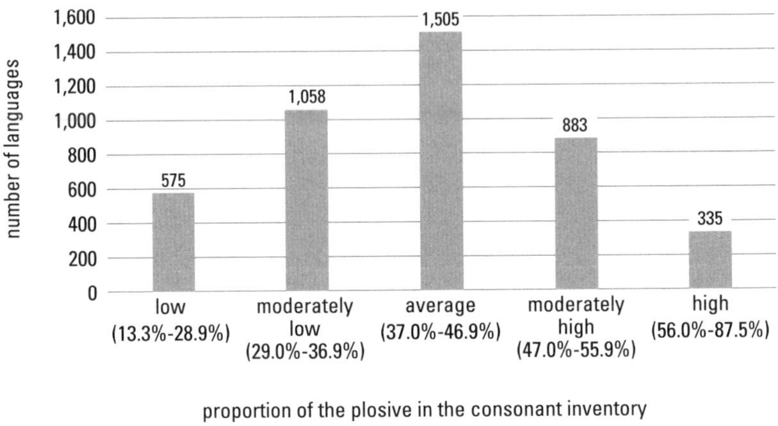

Figure 5-2. Classification of languages by proportion of plosives

class of Figure 5-1. Therefore, there is some room for adjustment of the classification.

Languages can be divided into five classes, depending on the proportion of plosives in the consonant inventory. Figure 5-2 is derived in the same way as Figure 5-1. The proportion of the plosive varies considerably, from a minimum of 13.3% to a maximum of 87.5%. Only two of the 15 consonants in Lingao are plosives (13.3%), whereas seven of the eight consonants in Desano are plosives (87.5%).[7] The average proportion of the plosive, 39.84%, is slightly skewed to the left of the average class band in Figure 5-2.

The number or proportion of plosives varies considerably depending on the size of the consonant inventory. Therefore, as in (1), statistics for all languages are important, but it is also necessary to see how these numbers vary depending on the size of the consonant inventory. In this book, as in Haspelmath et al. (2005), consonant inventory size is divided into five classes: small, moderately small, average, moderately large, and large. However, the results of this classification differ from Haspelmath et al. (2005). In Haspelmath et al. (2005), semivowels are included as consonants, which requires adjustment here. Moreover, it is difficult to

7 The plosives in Desano have a very wide range of phonetic realizations, so it is highly likely for them to include the fricatives, affricates, and nasals as allophones. Desano has the glottal plosive /ʔ/ as a marginal phoneme, which is excluded from discussion.

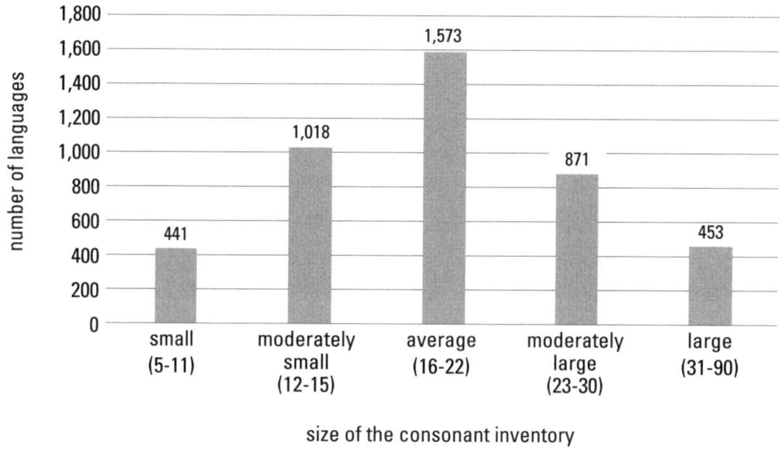

Figure 5-3. Classification of languages by consonant inventory size

follow the classification of Haspelmath et al. (2005) as it is because the number of languages discussed is very different. In this book, I will create five classes as above by referring to the category size in Figure 5-1 and 5-2.

Table 5-3 is a summary of how the average number and proportion of plosives vary according to the five classes in Figure 5-3. As shown in Table 5-3 and Figure 5-4 below, as the size of the consonant inventory increases, the average number of plosives naturally increases. However, the proportion of plosive in the consonant inventory is rather lower. For example, the proportion of plosives differs between the small and large classes by approximately 9.8%p. That is, there is an inverse relationship between the size of the consonant inventory and proportion of plosives. This relationship suggests that the plosive is the most essential within

Table 5-3. Average number and proportions of plosives according to five classes in Figure 5-3

Size of the consonant / Parameter	Small	Moderately small	Average	Moderately large	Large
Average number	4.2	5.8	7.7	10.2	14.0
Proportion	43.2%	42.7%	41.1%	39.1%	35.6%

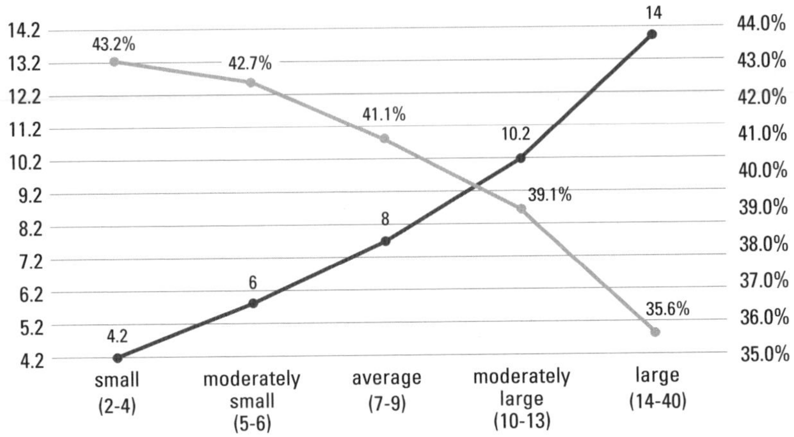

Figure 5-4. Correlation between average number and proportion of plosives

the consonant inventory. Regardless of the size of the consonant inventory, there are always a certain number of plosives because plosives are the foremost among the consonants. Therefore, the smaller the consonants inventory, the higher the proportion of plosives. However, the expansion of the consonant inventory is primarily performed by adding consonants other than plosives. In particular, languages with a large consonant inventory often have clicks. As a result, the larger the consonant inventory, the smaller the proportion of plosives. This is a clear conclusion from the analysis of many languages.

5.2. Some implicational relationships in the plosive

A frequent and longstanding topic of phonological typology is the implicational relationship between phonemes. The fact that the presence of one phoneme implies the presence of another has been pointed out in the past, which has attracted the interest of many linguists. For example, the presence of a voiced obstruent implies the presence of a voiceless obstruent. In the early days, a small number of languages were targeted, and the implicational relationships between phonemes were considered to be absolute. However, this perspective is no longer favored, as exceptions constantly appear. As seen in this discussion of the plosive, the voiced plosive does not absolutely imply the existence of its voiceless opposite. There are many cases in which only the voiced plosives exist. Moreover, as long as all languages, including those that have disappeared in the past or that may exist in the future, are not covered, discussing absolute implicational relationships has little meaning, and the results of such discussion are hard to trust.

These difficulties suggest that the approach to this implicational relationship should be changed. In other words, from a relative point of view, it is necessary to consider the rate at which one phoneme implies the existence of another. For example, instead of the statement that the existence of /g/ absolutely implies the existence of /k/, the statement that /g/ implies the existence of /k/ in 96.1% of languages should be made. This approach accords with the emphasis on the tendencies of linguistic phenomena in the study of language typology.

The problem is that, despite the recognition of the need to consider the implicational relationship from a relative perspective, interest in it has been on the wane. The process of determining the absolute implicational relationship has already captured the approximate trend, and thus, no further attention has been given to this issue. In addition, finding new implicational relationships based on large-scale language data is not easy and has generally not been performed properly. Nonetheless, it is still meaningful to examine whether implicational reationship between two units is high or low to grasp the degree of relative implication and to determine its origin. With this framework, I will examine some implicational relationships between the plosives in relative terms.

Prior to the detailed discussion, two issues related to the implicational relationship will be briefly addressed. First, it is necessary to examine the reasons for the appearance of the implicational relationship, which can be grouped into three categories: articulation, perception, and historical change. Phonemes that are simply articulated are more likely to appear frequently than phonemes that are complicatedly articulated. As a result, there is a greater likelihood that a phoneme with articulatory complexity implies the presence of a phoneme that is less complex in articulation. Next, phonemes that are perceptually confused with other phonemes are less likely to appear than phoneme that is not. Therefore, the presence of a phoneme that is easy to be confused with another is likely to imply the existence of a phoneme that is perceived clearly. Finally, when sound changes in one direction across languages, the input of change inevitably occurs less frequently than the output, so the phoneme corresponding to the input implies the existence of the phoneme corresponding to the output. Since the above three mechanisms are based on simple situations, it is difficult to be certain that all of the implicational relationships can be clearly explained. In particular, the establishment of an implicational relationship by sound change has not been proven but only imagined at the theoretical level.

Second, the implicational relationship should be more clearly described, i.e., it should not be stated as if a nonexistent structure could exist. One such example is the phonological description by Nartey (1979: 28), which pointed out that the following trend exists between glottal and oral stops.

(3) One example of an implicational relationship in Nartey (1979)
"No language has a glottal stop unless it also has a primary oral stop."

Although (3) is not a general statement form expressing an implicational relationship, it does refer to implicational content.[8] (3) indicates that there cannot be plosive inventores that consist only of glottal plosives, and if the glottal stop is present, there must be at least one plosive that is articulated in the oral cavity. The explanation in (3) has no exceptions among the languages known to date and is not, itself, incorrect.

However, upon closer examination, (3) only points out that if there is a glottal plosive, the primary oral plosive must also be present. It does not mention how many the primary oral plosive there should be. That is, (3) does not exclude the existence of plosive inventories consisting of one glottal plosive and one primary oral stop. The problem is that no such inventory currently exists in any language. As confirmed in Table 2-5, glottal plosives appear only in languages with three or more places of articulation for the plosive. (3) is insufficient to express this fact clearly and must be corrected as follows in (4).

8 If (3) is converted to the statement form of an implicational relationship, it would be as follows: A glottal stop implies the presence of a primary oral stop.

(4) Revision of statement in (3)
- a. No language has a glottal stop unless it also has at least two primary oral stops that are articulated in different places.
- b. A glottal stop implies two primary oral stops that are articulated in different places.

(4a) and (4b) express the same effect differently. (4a) modifies the statement in (3) while maintaining its form, and (4b) modifies (3) into the form in which the implicational relationship is stated. With (4), the inventory consisting of one glottal plosive and one primary oral plosive can be excluded. In addition, it can also be shown that for the glottal plosive to exist, there must be at least three places of articulation for the plosive. Therefore, the description of the implicational relationship needs to be as precise as possible.

Now, I will take a closer look at the implicational relationships that are found among plosives.[9] Three implicational relationships will be examined here. The first is between voiced and voiceless plosives, the second is between plosives accompanied by secondary articulation and plain plosives, and the third is between double- and single-articulated plosives. Plosives that are voiced, accompanied by secondary articulation, and double-articulated are 'implying members', whereas plosives which are voiceless, plain, and single-articulated are 'implied members'. Each implicational relationship will be presented by specifying the ratio at which it is valid. Such quantification is essential to examine the implicational relationship from a relative rather than an absolute perspective.

First is the implicational relationship between the voiced and voiceless plosives, which has received the most attention over time. It is well known that voiced plosives tend to imply the presence of voiceless plosives. However, few discussions have precisely reviewed the ratio of implication. As noted earlier, little attention has been paid to this issue since the concept of absolute implications was abandoned.

Among obstruent consonants, including plosives, the phonological opposition between voiced and voiceless consonants is the most common

9 For a detailed discussion on the implicational relationships between plosives, refer to Lee (2022).

and fundamental.[10] In most places of articulation, both voiced and voiceless plosives exist, except for plosives that are articulated at or near the larynx, such as the pharyngeal and epiglottal plosives. In addition, as seen in Table 3-3, over 70% of all languages have a phonological opposition by [±voiced].

Both voiced and voiceless plosives appear at nine places of articulation in single-articulated plosives and at two in double-articulated plosives. Limiting the target to plain plosives, I will examine to what extent the voiced plosive implies the presence of voiceless plosive at the 11 places of articulation above. The contrast between voiced and voiceless plosives is also seen in complex plosives with secondary articulation or liquid-colored release, but here, the subject is narrowed to plain plosives and briefly reviewed. The ratio at which voiced plain plosives imply the presence of their voiceless opposites according to the place of articulation is given in Table 5-4.

The ratio of implications in Table 5-4 was calculated with the number of languages that have voiced plosive as the denominator and the number of languages that have both voiced and voiceless plosives

Table 5-4. Implicational relationship between voiced and voiceless plosives

Place of articulation	Direction of implication	Ratio of implication
BI	b ⇒ p	86.1% (2,672/3,105)
LL	b̼ ⇒ p̼	50.0% (1/2)
DE	d̪ ⇒ t̪	94.2% (639/678)
AL	d ⇒ t	94.5% (2,323/2,458)
RE	ɖ ⇒ ʈ	75.9% (245/323)
AP	ȡ ⇒ ȶ	37.5% (3/8)
PA	ɟ ⇒ c	77.7% (404/520)
VE	g ⇒ k	96.1% (2,644/2,750)
UV	ɢ ⇒ q	73.8% (31/42)
LV	gb ⇒ kp	92.9% (404/435)
LA	bd ⇒ pt	100% (1/1)
Total	voiced ⇒ voiceless	90.7% (9,367/10,322)

10 The opposition by [±voiced] within the plosive was examined in 3.3.

as the numerator. In Table 5-4, the ratio of voiced plosives implying the presence of voiceless plosives ranges widely, from a minimum of 37.5% to a maximum of 100%, depending on the place of articulation. Excluding the linguolabial, alveopalatal, and labial alveolar plosives, which are extremely infrequent, the ratio of implication is at minimum 73.7% and at maximum 96.1%, greatly reducing the discrepancy. The overall average is 90.7%, which means that nine of ten languages with the voiced plosive have a voiceless opposite. There is no absolute criterion as to what proportion is needed to establish the implicational relationship, but approximately 90% seems sufficient.

In Table 5-4, there are three voiced plosives that have similarly low frequency: retroflex /ɖ/, palatal /ɟ/, and uvular /ɢ/. Their ratios of implication remain in the 70% range. These voiced plosives are not articulated at major places of articulation, such as the bilabial, alveolar, and velar. However, the connection between this commonality and their low ratios of implication is unclear.

Among the major places of articulation, the ratio of /b/ is low. As shown in Table 5-1, /b/ is the most frequent of the voiced plosives. In contrast, the rate at which /b/ implies the presence of /p/ is quite low compared to that of /d/ implying /t/ or /g/ implying /k/. This difference reflects that relatively numerous languages have only /b/ and no /p/. The absence of major plosives including /p/ will be discussed in 5.4.

Depending on the discussion, the results may be slightly different from those presented here, but the general trends derived from the large-scale data of 4,356 languages will remain valid in the future. Therefore, the correlation between the place of articulation and the ratio of implication in Table 5-4 can be acknowledged. The difference in the ratio of implication by place of articulation identified in Table 5-4 must be analyzed from various angles. It should be possible to explain the reason for this correlation in terms of articulation, perception, language change or other aspects. As such attempts bear fruit, our understanding of the implicational relationship will become increasingly wider.

Before finalizing the implicational relationship between voiced and voiceless plosives, it is worth mentioning two special cases, both of which are related to the complex, but not to the plain plosives. The first case is plosives accompanied by prenasalization. In the nasalized plosives, the direction of implication between voiced and voiceless plosives is opposite to that of other plosives. In other words, whether the voiceless nasalized

Table 5-5. Implicational relationship in the nasalized plosives

Place of articulation	[A]		[B]	
	Direction of implication	Ratio of implication	Direction of implication	Ratio of implication
BI	^{m}b ⇒ ^{m}p	13.7% (83/608)	^{m}p ⇒ ^{m}b	70.9% (83/117)
DE	^{n}d̪ ⇒ ^{n}t̪	8.6% (7/80)	^{n}t̪ ⇒ ^{n}d̪	43.8% (7/16)
AL	^{n}d ⇒ ^{n}t	15.3% (84/550)	^{n}t ⇒ ^{n}d	73.7% (84/114)
RE	^{ɳ}ɖ ⇒ ^{ɳ}ʈ	5.9% (1/17)	^{ɳ}ʈ ⇒ ^{ɳ}ɖ	10.0% (1/10)
PA	^{ɲ}ɟ ⇒ ^{ɲ}c	13.1% (11/84)	^{ɲ}c ⇒ ^{ɲ}ɟ	57.9% (11/19)
VE	^{ŋ}g ⇒ ^{ŋ}k	14.5% (86/592)	^{ŋ}k ⇒ ^{ŋ}g	70.5% (86/122)
UV	^{ɴ}ɢ ⇒ ^{ɴ}q	10.0% (1/10)	^{ɴ}q ⇒ ^{ɴ}ɢ	9.1% (1/11)
LV	^{ŋm}gb ⇒ ^{ŋm}kp	2.9% (3/102)	^{ŋm}kp ⇒ ^{ŋm}gb	75.0% (3/4)
Total	voiced ⇒ voiceless	13.5% (276/2,043)	voiceless ⇒ voiced	67.5% (276/409)

plosive implies the presence of its voiced opposite should be considered.

Table 5-5 shows how the ratio of implication varies according to the direction of implication. In [A], where the voiced plosive implies the presence of voiceless plosive, the ratio of implication is only 13.5%, whereas in [B], with the opposite direction of implication, the ratio of implication is 67.5%, five times higher than that of [A]. This overwhelming difference suggests that in the case of a nasalized plosive, the direction of implication between the voiced and voiceless plosives must be the opposite of the other plosives.[11] As reviewed in Chapter 4, the fact that the frequency of the voiced nasalized plosive is much higher than that of the voiceless nasalized plosive reflects this particularity. The ratio of 67.5% in [B] means that the implicational relationship is only valid for two-thirds of such plosives, with a full third constituting an exception. I do not know whether the implicational relationship can be considered as established based on this result because, as pointed out above, there is no criterion for judging whether an implication relationship exists. Nevertheless, no one can deny that the direction of implication in the nasalized plosives is clearly distinct from other

11 The very low rate of implication in [A] indicates that the implication relationship itself does not hold.

plosives.

The second case is plosives accompanied by aspiration. The voiced aspirated plosive not only implies the existence of its voiceless opposite, but also of a specific four-way opposition. In other words, a voiced aspirated plosive can imply both segment and multiple phonological opposition. Specifically, the voiced aspirated plosive has a very high rate to imply the four-way opposition consisting of voiceless plain (p, t, k, ...), voiced plain (b, d, g, ...), voiceless aspirated (p^h, t^h, k^h, ...), and voiced aspirated plosives (b^h, d^h, g^h, ...). Two distinctive features, [±voiced] and [±aspirated], are involved in this four-way opposition. Since the voiceless aspirated plosive is included in the four-way opposition implied by the voiced aspirated plosive, the implicational relationship between the voiced and voiceless aspirated plosives is automatically established, which can be confirmed in Table 5-6 below.

Table 5-6 shows two ratios of implication. [A] is the rate at which the voiced aspirated plosive implies the presence of four-way opposition, and [B] is the rate at which the voiced aspirated plosive implies the presence of voiceless opposite. The ratio of implication is evenly high at all places of articulation, which is different from that shown in Table 5-4, and the average percentage of implication exceeds 97%. With this high rate of implication, it is safe to assume that the implicational relationship is credibly established.

Table 5-6. Implicational relationship in the voiced aspirated plosives

Place of articulation	[A]		[B]	
	Direction of implication	Ratio of implication	Direction of implication	Ratio of implication
BI	b^h ⇒ four-way	91.1% (102/112)	b^h ⇒ p^h	92.0% (103/112)
DE	d̪^{h} ⇒ four-way	98.5% (66/67)	d̪^{h} ⇒ t̪^{h}	100% (67/67)
AL	d^h ⇒ four-way	100% (49/49)	d^h ⇒ t^h	100% (49/49)
RE	ɖ^h ⇒ four-way	98.7% (74/75)	ɖ^h ⇒ ʈ^h	98.7% (74/75)
PA	ɟ^h ⇒ four-way	100% (18/18)	ɟ^h ⇒ c^h	100% (18/18)
VE	g^h ⇒ four-way	100% (104/104)	g^h ⇒ k^h	100% (104/104)
UV	ɢ^h ⇒ four-way	100% (2/2)	ɢ^h ⇒ q^h	100% (2/2)
LV	gb^h ⇒ four-way	100% (6/6)	gb^h ⇒ kp^h	100% (6/6)
Total		97.2% (421/433)		97.7% (423/433)

This concludes the discussion of the implicational relationship between voiced and voiceless plosives. Next, I will examine the second type, that is, the implicational relationship between the plain and complex plosives accompanied by secondary articulation. Since secondary articulation is combined with the plain plosive, it is possible to speculate that the presence of a complex plosive accompanied by secondary articulation implies the existence of a plain plosive. The secondary articulations that will be reviewed here are aspiration, nasalization, labialization, and palatalization, which are very frequent. Since secondary articulation is combined with both voiced and voiceless plosives, I will differentiate between them and consider their ratios of implication separately.

The first implicational relationship to examine is that between the aspirated and plain plosives. Table 5-7 shows the rate at which the aspirated plosive implies the existence of the plain plosive. For both voiceless and voiced implying members, the ratio of implication is very high. There is no substantial difference depending on the place of articulation. Specifically, the rate at which the voiced aspirated plosive implies the voiced plain plosive is 99.3%, which is almost absolute. At the very least, the ratio of implication between the aspirated and plain plosives is higher than that between the voiced and voiceless plosives, which is directly related to the ratio of implication identified in Table 5-6. The voiced aspirated plosive very frequently implies the existence

Table 5-7. Implicational relationship between aspirated and plain plosives

Place of articulation	Direction of implication	Ratio of implication	Direction of implication	Ratio of implication
BI	pʰ ⇒ p	96.2% (754/784)	bʰ ⇒ b	99.1% (111/112)
DE	t̪ʰ ⇒ t̪	95.8% (230/240)	d̪ʰ ⇒ d̪	98.5% (66/67)
AL	tʰ ⇒ t	95.7% (616/644)	dʰ ⇒ d	100% (49/49)
RE	ʈʰ ⇒ ʈ	99.4% (172/173)	ɖʰ ⇒ ɖ	98.7% (74/75)
AP	ȶʰ ⇒ ȶ	100% (9/9)	ȡʰ ⇒ ȡ	None (0/0)
PA	cʰ ⇒ c	97.1% (101/104)	ɟʰ ⇒ ɟ	100% (18/18)
VE	kʰ ⇒ k	95.9% (797/831)	gʰ ⇒ g	100% (104/104)
UV	qʰ ⇒ q	92.5% (98/106)	ɢʰ ⇒ ɢ	100% (2/2)
LV	kpʰ ⇒ kp	88.9% (8/9)	gbʰ ⇒ gb	100% (6/6)
Total		96.0% (2,785/2,900)		99.3% (430/433)

of four-way opposition including the voiced plain plosive, so the rate at which the voiced aspirated plosive implies the presence of the voiced plain plosive in Table 5-7 must be the same or higher than that in Table 5-6.

Next, the ratio of implication between the nasalized and plain plosives is given in Table 5-8. There is a significant difference in the ratio of implication depending on whether the nasalized plosive is voiced or voiceless. The rate at which voiceless nasalized plosives imply the presence of plain plosives is 98.0%. In most places of articulation, the rate of implication is 100%, and the percentage for the bilabial plosive is only slightly lower. Therefore, a very strong implicational relationship can be established. By contrast, the rate at which the voiced nasalized plosive implies the presence of the voiced plain plosive is considerably lower (64.4%), although it is sufficient to establish the implicational relationship. However, its tendency is not strong. The ratio of implication among voiced nasalized plosives is in the 60% range at most places of articulation, with the labiovelar posing an exception with a ratio of more than 90%. It is necessary to clarify why the ratio of implication between the nasalized and plain plosives differs widely depending on whether the vocal folds vibrate and why the voiced labiovelar plosive is an exception.

Third, the ratio of implication between the labialized and plain plosives is given in Table 5-9. As shown in Table 5-9, the rate at which

Table 5-8. Implicational relationship between nasalized and plain plosives

Place of articulation	Direction of implication	Ratio of implication	Direction of implication	Ratio of implication
BI	ᵐp ⇒ p	94.0% (110/117)	ᵐb ⇒ b	66.0% (401/608)
DE	ⁿt̪ ⇒ t̪	100% (16/16)	ⁿd̪ ⇒ d̪	62.5% (50/80)
AL	ⁿt ⇒ t	100% (114/114)	ⁿd ⇒ d	62.2% (342/550)
RE	ᶯʈ ⇒ ʈ	100% (10/10)	ᶯɖ ⇒ ɖ	64.7% (11/17)
AP	ⁿȶ does not exist		ⁿȡ ⇒ ȡ	0% (0/2)
PA	ᶮc ⇒ c	100% (19/19)	ᶮɟ ⇒ ɟ	73.8% (62/84)
VE	ᵑk ⇒ k	99.2% (121/122)	ᵑg ⇒ g	60.0% (355/592)
UV	ᶰq ⇒ q	100% (11/11)	ᶰɢ ⇒ ɢ	20.0% (2/10)
LV	ŋᵐkp ⇒ kp	100% (4/4)	ŋᵐgb ⇒ gb	91.2% (93/102)
Total		98.0% (401/409)		64.4% (1,316/2,045)

Table 5-9. Implicational relationship between labialized and plain plosives

Place of articulation	Direction of implication	Ratio of implication	Direction of implication	Ratio of implication
BI	pʷ ⇒ p	99.2% (120/121)	bʷ ⇒ b	90.4% (85/94)
DE	t̪ʷ ⇒ t̪	100% (11/11)	d̪ʷ ⇒ d̪	100% (8/8)
AL	tʷ ⇒ t	100% (37/37)	dʷ ⇒ d	100% (18/18)
RE	ʈʷ ⇒ ʈ	100% (1/1)	ɖʷ does not exist	
AP	ȶʷ ⇒ ȶ	100% (2/2)	ȡʷ does not exist	
PA	cʷ ⇒ c	100% (3/3)	ɟʷ ⇒ ɟ	100% (3/3)
VE	kʷ ⇒ k	96.6% (543/562)	gʷ ⇒ g	94.1% (241/256)
UV	qʷ ⇒ q	98.5% (66/67)	ɢʷ ⇒ ɢ	100% (5/5)
GL	ʔʷ ⇒ ʔ	95.8%(23/24)	There is no voiced plosive	
LV	kpʷ ⇒ kp	20.0% (1/5)	gbʷ ⇒ gb	100% (2/2)
Total		96.9% (807/833)		93.8% (362/386)

the labialized plosive implies the presence of plain plosive is also very high, exceeding 93%. The voiceless labialized plosive shows a slightly higher rate of implication than the voiced labialized plosive, but the difference is only 3.1%p. Exceptionally, the rate at which /kpʷ/ implies /kp/ is very low, but this pair is so infrequent that this relationship does not require attention.

The final implicational relationship to be examined is that between the palatalized and plain plosives. The frequency of palatalized plosives is lower than that of other complex plosives that have been previously examined. However, the ratio of implication between palatalized and plain plosives is never inferior to those for other complex plosives, as shown in Table 5-10. In addition, there is no substantial difference according to the voicedness or place of articulation.

So far, I have examined the extent to which the complex plosive accompanied by secondary articulation implies the existence of plain plosive. Overall, the ratios of implication are very high and exceed the rate at which the voiced plain plosive implies the presence of voiceless plain plosive. In other words, the implicational relationship between the plosive accompanied by secondary articulation and the plain plosive is stronger than that between the voiced and voiceless plosives.

I will now examine the third implicational relationship, which so far has not been given much attention. It is related to the double-articulated

Table 5-10. Implicational relationship between palatalized and plain plosives

Place of articulation	Direction of implication	Ratio of implication	Direction of implication	Ratio of implication
BI	p^j ⇒ p	98.9% (91/92)	b^j ⇒ b	100% (68/68)
DE	t̪^{j} ⇒ t̪	100% (35/35)	d̪^{j} ⇒ d̪	100% (30/30)
AL	t^j ⇒ t	95.0% (113/119)	d^j ⇒ d	96.5% (55/57)
RE	ʈ^j ⇒ ʈ	100% (2/2)	ɖ^j ⇒ ɖ	100% (2/2)
PA	c^j ⇒ c	100% (1/1)	ɟ^j ⇒ ɟ	100% (1/1)
VE	k^j ⇒ k	96.4% (107/111)	g^j ⇒ g	94.4% (68/72)
UV	q^j ⇒ q	100% (2/2)	ɢ^j does not exist	
GL	ʔ^j ⇒ ʔ	90.0% (9/10)	There is no voiced plosive	
LV	kp^j ⇒ kp	100% (1/1)	gb^j ⇒ gb	100% (1/1)
Total		96.8% (361/373)		97.4% (225/231)

plosive. Because the double-articulated plosives have two primary places of articulation, it may be assumed for them to imply the existence of single-articulated plosives. For example, it is expected that a language with the double-articulated plosive /kp/ has one of /p/ and /k/, or both. Among the double-articulated plosives, the labiovelar plosive is moderately frequent, and its two primary places of articulation (bilabial and velar) are major places of articulation. Therefore, the rate at which labiovelar plosives imply the existence of bilabial or velar plosives is likely to be high. However, there has been little specific discussions of this possibility. The rate for labiovelars such as /kp/ or /gb/ to imply the presence of /p, b/ or /k, g/ is given in Table 5-11.

In Table 5-11, the ratios of /kp/ and /gb/, which imply the presence of /p, b/ and /k, g/, are summarized. If the labiovelar plosive is present, either a bilabial or velar plosive is also usually present. For example, every language with /kp/ has /p/ or /k/.[12] The only exceptions are Bamun and Pomo, which have neither /b/ nor /g/ despite having /gb/.[13] However, there are only two exceptions among the 435 languages with

12 As shown in Table 5-11, there are also many languages with both 'p' and 'k'.

13 Bamun and Pomo are African languages belonging to the Atlantic-Congo language family. The common labiovelar plosives in two languages are /kp, gb, ^{ŋm}gb/. Interestingly, /kp/ and /^{ŋm}gb/ imply the presence of /p, k/ and /^{m}b, ^{m}g/, respectively, but /gb/ does not.

Table 5-11. Implicational relationship between double- and single-articulated plosives

Direction of implication	Ratio of implication	Direction of implication	Ratio of implication
kp ⇒ p	84.7%(389/459)	gb ⇒ b	97.9%(426/435)
kp ⇒ k	75.6%(347/459)	gb ⇒ g	93.6%(407/435)
kp ⇒ {p, k}	75.6%(347/459)	gb ⇒ {b, g}	92.0%(400/435)

/gb/, and thus, the rate of exceptions is so low that it can be ignored.

Three characteristics are shown in Table 5-11. First, there is a clear difference between the ratios of implication for voiced and voiceless plosives. The implicational ratio of /gb/ is noticeably higher than that of /kp/. A similar pattern was also found in Table 5-8, although the voiceless plosive, not the voiced plosive, has a higher ratio of implication. Second, the rate at which labiovelar plosives imply bilabial plosives is higher than that implying velar plosives. The difference between the two is approximately 9.1%p for /kp/ and approximately 4.3%p for /gb/. Although these differences are not large, the tendency is confirmed. Third, the rate at which labiovelar plosives imply both bilabial and velar plosives is similar to that of the velar plosive. For example, /kp/ implies the existence of /p, k/ and /k/ at the same rate (75.6%). In the case of /gb/, the difference between the rates at which it implies /g, b/ and /g/ is very small, approximately 1.6%p. This result tells us that if a language with /kp/ (or /gb/) has /k/ (or /g/), it is highly like to have /p/ (or /b/) as well.

5.3. Commonly preferred inventories of the plosive

In Chapter 4, the frequency, inventory, and phonological opposition of the plosive were examined individually by the place of articulation. In the course of discussion, it was confirmed that there exist some typologically preferred inventories and oppositions of the plosive according to the places of articulation. Now, on the basis of these findings, it is time to conduct a comprehensive review of the commonly preferred inventories and phonological oppositions of the plosive from a typological view.

Three main topics are covered in this section. The first topic is the inventories of the plosive that appear most often. As seen in Table 5-2, the number of plosives varies greatly across languages, and the preferred inventory varies accordingly. A total of seven groups, from languages with four plosives to those with ten plosives, have a high proportion, each accounting for more than 5% of all languages. I will review the inventories of the plosive found most frequently in each group and analyze their phonological characteristics. Next, after classifying each inventory of the plosive into several types by the number of places of articulation and opposed members, I will examine the preferred inventories of the plosive. This is a slightly different approach to the topic than provided earlier, since previously, the inventory of the plosive was analyzed according to the number of plosives, but this time, it is analyzed according to the type of phonological opposition. Finally, I will determine the distinctive features that are actively involved in the opposition of the plosive through the preferred inventories and will establish an activeness hierarchy of these distinctive features. A brief investigation of the activeness of the distinctive features for individual places of articulation has already been offered, but here, the discussion expands the range to all plosives for a more comprehensive approach.

I begin by examining the high-frequency inventories according to the number of plosives. The first group to consider is the 325 languages with four plosives. The inventories appearing in more than 10 languages are given below. In Table 5-12, [A] indicates the inventory label, [B] the plosive inventory, and [C] the number of languages in which the inventory is found, i.e. its frequency.[14] Among languages with four plosives, type-(a) appears in 125 languages, making it by far the most frequent. Type-(a) is an inventory in which /ʔ/ is added to /p, t, k/, which is the most common inventory in languages with three plosives. Type-(e) is similar to type-(a) in that /ʔ/ is added to /p, t̪, k/. Of the 195 languages with three plosives, 134 have /p, t, k/, and 25 have / p, t̪, k/, so these two types account for most of the languages under consideration.[15] Given this proportion, many of the languages with four plosives have an inventory consisting of three common plosives plus the

14 This is common to all tables presented later.
15 The inventories such as /p, t, k/ and /p, t̪, k/ rarely appear in African languages.

Table 5-12. Preferred inventories in languages with four plosives

[A]	Type-(a)	Type-(b)	Type-(c)	Type-(d)	Type-(e)	Type-(f)
[B]	p, t, k, ʔ	p, t, k, k^w	p, t, k, q	p, t, c, k	p, t̪, k, ʔ	p, p^w, t, k
[C]	125	16	15	13	12	11

glottal plosive /ʔ/.

Several trends can be derived from Table 5-12. First, the voiceless plain plosives in major places of articulation, that is /p, t (t̪), k/, are included in all types, without exception. They are the most frequent plosives, and thus, if a language has a small inventory of plosives, it consists of high-frequency plosives. Second, in most types, there are four places of articulation. The exceptions are type-(b) and (f), but their rates are not high. Both of these exceptions include a labialized plosive instead of the plosive at fourth place of articulation. Third, Table 5-12 does not show any contrast by [±voiced]. None of the inventories in table 5-12 include the voiced plosive itself. Fourth, distributional constraints or biases toward specific regions are prominent. For example, type-(a), which is the most frequent, rarely appears in African languages, whereas it frequently appears in languages of the Americas.[16] Types-(b), (c) and (e) also rarely appears in African languages. Type-(f) is found mainly in the Austronesian language family. In general, the proportion of African languages that have inventories in Table 5-12 is very low.[17]

There are 388 languages that have five plosives. The most common inventories in these languages and their frequency are given in Table 5-13. Unlike Table 5-12, there is no type demonstrating an overwhelming frequency in Table 5-13. The inventory in Table 5-13 seems to be largely divided into two categories, given in (5).

(5) Two categories in the inventories of Table 5-13
  a. Category-A: (a), (b), (e)
  b. Category-B: (c), (d), (f), (g)

16 The rare appearance of type-(a) in African languages is related to the fact that the inventory like /p, t, k/ does not appear very often in African languages, as noted in footnote immediately above.

17 Type-(d) appears in some African languages, such as East Nyala and Karon, but it is not mainstream.

Table 5-13. Preferred inventories in languages with five plosives

[A]	Type-(a)	Type-(b)	Type-(c)	Type-(d)	Type-(e)	Type-(f)	Type-(g)
[B]	b, t, d, k, g	p, b, t, d, k	p, t, k, kʷ, ʔ	p, t, k, q, ʔ	p, b, t, k, g	p, t, ʈ, c, k	b, d, ɖ, ɟ, g
[C]	45	44	33	24	14	13	13

Category-A shows the contrast by [±voiced]. It has the forms with one plosive missing from /p, b, t, d, k, g/, which is the most common inventory in languages with six plosives. Category-B does not show the contrast by [±voiced]. Except for type-(g), its types consist of only voiceless plosives. Most of the inventories in category-B have a form in which another voiceless plosive is added to one of the inventories in Table 5-12. The added plosive is characterized by a different place of articulation from those of the inventories in Table 5-12. For example, type-(c) in Table 5-13 is a form in which a glottal plosive is added to type-(b) in Table 5-12, and type-(d) in Table 5-13 is a form in which a voiceless uvular plosive is added to type-(a) in Table 5-12. Type-(g) is unique in that it is made up of only voiced plosives. This trend is found only in Australian languages.

The two categories in Table 5-13 are distinguished clearly not only by the nature of their phonological opposition, but also in other respects. Types with contrast by [±voiced] show no particular regional bias. Additionally, these types share the number of places of articulation for the plosive, that is, three. In contrast, types without contrast by [±voiced] have a regional bias. For example, types-(c) and (d) are often found in American languages, whereas types-(f) and (g) appear only in Australian languages. Moreover, this category has four or five places of articulation for the plosive.[18]

These differences are due to the inventories on which the two categories are based. Category-A in Table 5-13 is closely related to /p, b, t, d, k, g/, which is the most common inventory in languages with six plosives. This inventory (p, b, t, d, k, g) is widely found in various regions

18 The only difference between type-(f) and (g) lies in the voicedness of the plosive, as its place of articulation is the same. Inventories whose plosives are articulated at four or more places but have no contrast by [±voiced] are widely found in Australian languages.

without any distributional restrictions and has three places of articulation for the plosive. These features are parallel to those of category-A in Table 5-13.

In contrast, category-B in Table 5-13 is related to inventories that appear frequently in languages with four plosives. As shown earlier, the inventories in Table 5-12 have no contrast by [±voiced] and have more than three places of articulation for the plosive. In addition, they demonstrate a bias toward a specific region. These characteristics are similar to those of category-B in Table 5-13.

It is now time to review the commonly preferred inventories in languages with six plosives. This group is the largest, with 796 languages, which is more than twice as many as those languages with four or five plosives. In Table 5-14, type-(a) constitutes the overwhelmingly majority. Type-(a) appears in various regions. Type-(b), which is very similar to type-(a) due to its inclusion of the dental rather than the alveolar plosive, is also considerably frequent. More than half of the languages with six plosives have an inventory consisting of two plain plosives at the three major places of articulation: bilabial, alveolar (including dental), and velar. Several well-known languages, including English, German, and French, also have type-(a) or type-(b) inventories.

Except for type-(a), many types are limited or biased by language family and region. Type-(b) has a high proportion of languages belonging to the Indo-European language family. Type-(c), an inventory that include the nasalized plosives, appears in oceanic languages, that is, members of the Austronesian and Nuclear Trans New Guinea language families. Type-(e) inventory occurs mainly in languages of the Pama-Nyungan language family. Type-(f), whose phonological opposition is based on [±aspirated], appears only in Asian languages, especially within the Sino-Tibetan language family. Exceptionally, type-(d) shows no particular limitation or bias.

There are 637 languages with seven plosives, which is the second

Table 5-14. Preferred inventories in languages with six plosives

[A]	Type-(a)	Type-(b)	Type-(c)	Type-(d)	Type-(e)	Type-(f)	Type-(g)
[B]	p, b, t, d, k, g	p, b, t̪, d̪, k, g	p, ᵐb, t, ⁿd, k, ᵑg	b, t, d, k, g, ʔ	p, t̪, t, ʈ, c, k	p, b, t, d, k, ʔ	p, pʰ, t, tʰ, k, kʰ
[C]	340	70	56	41	27	24	16

most common group after languages with six. The common inventories in these languages and their frequency are given in Table 5-15. The inventory types in Table 5-15 are more diverse than those examined previously. Many of them are based on the contrast by [±voiced]. The exceptions to this are type-(c), whose opposition is formed by [±aspirated], and type-(g), which includes two labialized plosives. The main trend among the types in Table 5-15 is that there are four places of articulation for the plosive, and the same opposition appears proportionally at three places of articulation.

In Table 5-15, type-(a) constitutes the overwhelmingly majority. Type-(a) is distributed across various language families and regions, but 172 languages are in the Austronesian language family. By contrast, in the Atlantic-Congo language family, which is similar in size to the Austronesian, only seven languages have the type-(a) inventory. Type-(b), which is similar to type-(a), also appears mainly in Austronesian languages, whereas few African languages have this type.

The other types also have distributional restrictions on the language family or region. Type-(c) appears mainly in Asian languages centered on the Sino-Tibetan language family.[19] Type-(e) has many similarities with type-(a) except that it includes a uvular plosive instead of a glottal plosive. Type-(a) and (e) share six of their seven plosives, and the places of articulation for the seventh plosives are very close. However, the distribution of the two types is quite different, as type-(e), unlike type-(a), is common in the Indo-European language family. Type-(g) appears in North American languages centered on the Salishan language family,

Table 5-15. Preferred inventories in languages with seven plosives

[A]	Type-(a)	Type-(b)	Type-(c)	Type-(d)	Type-(e)	Type-(f)	Type-(g)	Type-(h)	Type-(i)
[B]	p, b, t, d, k, g, ʔ	p, b, t̪, d̪, k, g, ʔ	p, p^h, t, t^h, k, k^h, ʔ	p, b, t, d, ɟ, k, g	p, b, t, d, k, g, q	b, t, d, k, g, kp, gb	p, t, k, k^w, q, q^w, ʔ	b, t, d, c, ɟ, k, g	p, b, t̪, d, k, g, ʔ
[C]	294	43	34	17	15	15	13	11	11

19 Certainly, the Sino-Tibetan languages tend to favor the phonological opposition by [±aspirated].

and type-(i) is often found in the Austronesian language family.

The region in which each type of the inventories reviewed above primarily appears includes Asia, the Americas and Australia, but not Africa. Despite this distribution, Table 5-15 has some inventories that are common in African languages. Types-(d), (f) and (g) in Table 5-15 are found in several African languages, although less than in other regions.

Types-(d), (f), (g) and (h) share very similar phonological characteristics. These four types are based on the inventories, which consist of eight plain plosives at four places of articulation.[20] The results of subtracting one plain plosive from these inventories with eight plain plosives are the same forms as types-(d), (f), (g) and (h). For example, types-(d) and (h) are forms that omit /c/ and /p/, respectively, from /p, b, t, d, c, ɟ, k, g/, which are found mainly in African languages with eight plosives. The same is true for type-(f) which is a form that subtracts /p/ from /p, b, t, d, k, g, kp, gb/, which is also a very common inventory in African languages.

Generally, the types reviewed so far, presented in Tables 5-12 to 5-15, do not commonly appear in African languages. There is a phonological reason for this absence. The typical inventories of the plosive in African languages have systems with the proportional contrast by [±voiced] at four or more places of articulation. However, most of the previous inventories differ from this typical form. If the number of plosives in a language is less than eight, it is difficult to expect the presence of these African types of inventory.

Before concluding the discussion of Table 5-15, it is necessary to mention type-(i) separately. At first glance, type-(i) seems to be a mixture of type-(a) and (b). Compared with type-(a) and (b), type-(i) differs as it has only voiceless plosive for the dental and only the voiced plosive for the alveolar. That is, in the dental and alveolar, the distribution of voiceless and voiced plosives is mutually exclusive. Type-(i) is common in languages belonging to the Austronesian language family. Interestingly, in most cases, the dental plosive is voiceless, while the alveolar plosive is voiced. Few inventories exist in which the dental plosive is voiced and the alveolar plosive is voiceless, which is contrary to type-(i). The cause of this particularity must be elucidated in the future.

---

20 For this, see Table 5-16 below.

There are 520 languages with eight plosives. The common inventories in these languages and their frequencies are given in Table 5-16. 'Eight' is close to the average number (8.04) of plosives in all languages. Except for type-(g), all other types in Table 5-16 are based on the contrast by [±voiced]. As the number of plosives increases, the ratio of inventories with the contrast by [±voiced] also increases. In addition, five of the seven types in Table 5-16 have four places of articulation. In other words, most of the inventories in Table 5-16 have two-way opposition at four places of articulation. Considering these points as a whole, the most typical inventory in languages with eight plosives consists of four contrastive pairs by [±voiced] in different places of articulation, such as types-(a), (b), (c) and (d). The validity of this conclusion is also supported by the fact that these four types are the top four in Table 5-16.

Many types in Table 5-16 show distributional biases regarding language families or regions. Types-(a) and (b), which are the first and second most frequent, are very common in African languages. Type-(c) appears in many languages of the Dravidian language family. Type-(d) is not biased toward a specific language family, but it does not commonly appear in African languages. For example, among languages belonging to the Atlantic-Congo language family, which is the largest, only Anyim is known to have type-(d). Type-(e) is found in many oceanic languages, including the Austronesian language family.

Type-(f) is related to an inventory with a three-way opposition between voiceless plain, voiced plain, and voiceless aspirated plosives. Type-(f) omits /g/ from the inventory /p, b, p^h, t, d, t^h, k, g, k^h/, which is the most common in languages with nine plosives. The three-way opposition, including a voiceless aspirated plosive, appears mainly in Asian languages centered on the Sino-Tibetan language family, and the distribution of type-(f) is consistent with this trend. Type-(g), unlike the

Table 5-16. Preferred inventories in languages with eight plosives

[A]	Type-(a)	Type-(b)	Type-(c)	Type-(d)	Type-(e)	Type-(f)	Type-(g)
[B]	p, b, t, d, k, g, kp, gb	p, b, t, d, c, ɟ, k, g	p, b, t̪, d̪, ʈ, ɖ, k, g	p, b, t̪, d̪, c, ɟ, k, g	p, b, t, d, k, g, k^w, g^w	p, b, p^h, t, d, t^h, k, k^h	p, p^h, t, t^h, k, k^h, q, q^h
[C]	92	48	22	19	19	15	11

previous six types, does not have a contrast by [±voiced], but instead has contrastive pairs by [±aspirated] at four places of articulation. Type-(g) appears mainly in languages that can be grouped into the so-called Altaic language family, including the Mongolic language family.

There are 384 languages with nine plosives. The inventories that are common in these languages and their frequency are given in Table 5-17. All types are based on the contrast by [±voiced], and there are no types that constitute an overwhelmingly majority. The inventories in Table 5-17 are divided into two categories. The first includes types that three-way opposition appears at three places of articulation. Types-(a) and (b), which are the first and second most frequent, fall into this category. Types-(a) and (b) differs in the kind of plosive that is added to the two-way opposition by [±voiced] to form a three-way opposition. Type-(a), with the addition of a voiceless aspirated plosive, appears mainly in Asian languages centered on the Sino-Tibetan language family, while type-(b), with the addition of a voiced nasalized plosive, is often found in African languages.

The other category includes types-(c) and (d), in which the glottal plosive /ʔ/ is added to the two most frequent inventories in Table 5-16. These types are slightly less frequent than types-(a) and (b). Many members of the Austronesian and Austroasiatic language families have type-(c), but not in sufficient proportions to say that it is biased toward these language families. Type-(d) appears mainly in African languages centered on the Atlantic-Congo language family, and its distribution is consistent with that of type-(a) in Table 5-16.[21]

Finally, I will examine languages with ten plosives. A total of 295

Table 5-17. Preferred inventories in languages with nine plosives

[A]	Type-(a)	Type-(b)	Type-(c)	Type-(d)
[B]	p, b, pʰ, t, d, tʰ, k, g, kʰ	p, b, ᵐb, t, d, ⁿd, k, g, ᵑg	p, b, t, d, c, ɟ, k, g, ʔ	p, b, t, d, k, g, kp, gb, ʔ
[C]	48	37	31	25

21 Since type-(d) of Table 5-17 is a form in which glottal plosive is added to type-(a) of table 5-16, it is sufficiently predictable that the distributions of these two types are similar.

languages have ten plosives, and the inventories that are common in these languages and their frequency are given in Table 5-18. As the number of plosives increases, the types of inventories that are common in multiple languages are likely to decrease. In Table 5-18, all four types include a contrastive pair by [±voiced]. In other words, the contrast between voiced and voiceless plosives plays an important role.

As in Table 5-17, the four types in Table 5-18 can be divided into two categories. Types-(a) and (c), comprising one category, share in common that the glottal plosive /ʔ/ is added to the two main types in Table 5-17. That is, type-(a) in Table 5-18 is a form in which /ʔ/ is added to type-(a) in Table 5-17, and type-(c) in Table 5-18 is a form in which /ʔ/ is added to type-(b) in Table 5-17. Due to the relationship between these types, the distribution across language families is also parallel. Type-(a) in Table 5-18 appears frequently in Asian languages centered on the Sino-Tibetan language family, and type-(c) in Table 5-18 is often found in large-scale language families such as the Atlantic-Congo and Austronesian.

Types-(b) and (d) in Table 5-18 constitute another category. Type-(b) has a two-way opposition at five places of articulation, and type-(d) has similar opposition at four places of articulation. These types have the labiovelar plosives /kp, gb/, which are common in African languages.

So far, I have examined the high-frequency inventories of the plosive according to the number of plosives. Now, I will review the preferred inventories by phonological opposition. After establishing certain patterns through the number of opposed members and places of articulation, I will consider the types and characteristics of the high-frequency inventories within each pattern. This approach makes it possible to determine directly the various oppositional relations of the plosive.

The label of each pattern will be expressed in the format 'A-B'. Label

Table 5-18. Preferred inventories in languages with 10 plosives

[A]	Type-(a)	Type-(b)	Type-(c)	Type-(d)
[B]	p, b, pʰ, t, d, tʰ, k, g, kʰ, ʔ	p, b, t, d, c, ɟ, k, g, kp, gb	p, b, ᵐb, t, d, ⁿd, k, g, ᵑg, ʔ	p, b, t, d, k, g, kʷ, gʷ, kp, gb
[C]	51	28	16	10

'A' in Roman numerals indicates the number of places of articulation in which the plosives appear, and label 'B' in Arabic numerals indicates the number of opposed members, that is, the number of plosives that are opposed at one place of articulation. For example, 'III-2' refers to a pattern in which two opposed members appear in three places of articulation, and 'IV-3' refers to a pattern in which three opposed members appear in four places of articulation.

For the purpose of this discussion, it is necessary to limit the subject. It is difficult to grasp the overall characteristics of phonological opposition for the plosive if the plosive inventories that are unbalanced, unstructured or infrequent are included in the target. For meaningful conclusions, the subject of discussion needs to be limited to those inventories that satisfy two conditions. First, the inventory should have a proportional opposition. In other words, only inventories in which the opposed members have the same character and number in each place of articulation are subject to discussion. For example, 'III-2' refers only to an inventory in which two opposed members with the same phonological features appear in all three places of articulation. Without this condition, the overall tendency may be distorted due to the presence of unbalanced inventories with different numbers of opposed members for each place of articulation. Second, the number of places of articulation is limited to from three to five, and the number of opposed members is limited to from one to four. As shown in Table 2-2, 95% of all languages have three to five places of articulation for the plosive. In addition, as seen in Chapter 4, languages with more than four opposed members in one place of articulation are very rare. Since infrequent and unique inventories are unnecessary for an examination of the common types of phonological opposition, it is preferable to limit the subject of discussion to inventories with some degree of frequency.

Inventories of the plosive that satisfy the above two conditions can be classified into the following 12 patterns.

(6) 12 patterns of plosive inventory to be discussed
  a. III-1 (3), III-2 (6), III-3 (9), III-4 (12)
  b. IV-1 (4), IV-2 (8), IV-3 (12), IV-4 (16)
  c. V-1 (5), V-2 (10), V-3 (15), V-4 (20)

There are four patterns each, according to the number of places of articulation, for a combined total of 12 types in (6). The numbers in parentheses next to each pattern indicate the number of plosives. That is, 'IV-3 (12)' refers to inventories which comprise 12 plosives, with three-way opposition appearing at four places of articulation. After extracting the high-frequency inventories that appear in more than 10 languages for each pattern, I will examine the phonological characteristics of each inventory. In (6), I will focus on the inventories patterns with more than ten plosives because we have already reviewed the inventories with four to ten plosives. Therefore, overlapping inventories will be briefly treated, and a separate description will be added only for the new inventories.

First, I will consider (6a). As shown in Table 2-4, 81.6% of languages with three places of articulation for the plosive have a combination of 'bilabial + alveolar + velar', and 14.9% have a combination of 'bilabial + dental + velar'. Unsurprisingly, many inventories in (6a) also have one of these two combinations. The high-frequency inventories belonging to the III-1 pattern are as follows.

There are only two types that appear in more than 10 languages. The articulators involved in these two types are the same: labial, coronal, and dorsal. The high-frequency inventories generally include all of the plosives in which these three articulators are involved. Types-(a) and (b) in Table 5-19 do not show a bias toward a particular region or language family. However, they are rarely found in languages belonging to the Atlantic-Congo, which is the largest language family.

The high-frequency inventories of the plosive that belong to the III-2 pattern are presented in Table 5-20. The four types belonging to the III-2 pattern were already presented in Table 5-14. The two opposed members at each place of articulation are commonly contrasted by [±voiced]. Among the secondary articulations, generally, the frequency of aspiration

Table 5-19. Preferred inventories in III-1 pattern[22]

[A]	Type-(a)	Type-(b)
[B]	p, t, k	p, t̪, k,
[C]	134	25

22 [A] indicates the label for the pattern, [B] the inventory, and [C] the number of languages that have [B]. This is the same in the following tables.

Table 5-20. Preferred inventories in III-2 pattern

[A]	Type-(a)	Type-(b)	Type-(c)	Type-(d)
[B]	p, b, t, d, k, g	p, b, t̪, d̪, k, g	p, ^{m}b, t, ^{n}d, k, ^{ŋ}g	p, p^{h}, t, t^{h}, k, k^{h}
[C]	340	70	56	16

is higher than that of nasalization, but interestingly, in the III-2 pattern, the type including nasalized plosives is more frequent than the type including aspirated plosives.

The III-3 pattern consists of a total of nine plosives due to its three-way opposition in three places of articulation. The two types that fall into this pattern have already been presented in Table 5-17. The two types in Table 5-21 have the same three contrastive pairs by [±voiced] such as 'p : b', 't : d', and 'k : g'. They differ in the kind of plosive that is added to them. Type-(a), which include the aspirated plosives, is more frequent than type-(b), which include the nasalized plosives.

The III-4 pattern consists of a total of 12 plosives, which is 1.5 times the average number. The inventories that belong to this pattern have never been examined in this book. There are only 50 languages with 12 plosives in three places of articulation. Moreover, the proportional appearance of four-way opposition in three places of articulation is very rare in the inventories of these languages. As a result, there is only one high-frequency inventory, as shown in Table 5-22.

This type is a form in which the contrast by [±voiced] is established in both the plain and nasalized plosives. In other words, this type

Table 5-21. Preferred inventories in III-3 pattern

[A]	Type-(a)	Type-(b)
[B]	p, b, p^{h}, t, d, t^{h}, k, g, k^{h}	p, b, ^{m}b, t, d, ^{n}d, k, g, ^{ŋ}g
[C]	48	37

Table 5-22. Preferred inventory in III-4 pattern

Inventory	p, b, ^{m}p, ^{m}b, t, d, ^{n}t, ^{n}d, k, g, ^{ŋ}k, ^{ŋ}g
Number of languages	14

Table 5-23. Inventories of III-4 pattern appearing in five languages

Type	Type-(a)	Type-(b)	Type-(c)
Inventories	p, b, p^{h}, b^{h}, t, d, t^{h}, d^{h}, k, g, k^{h}, g^{h}	p, b, p^{j}, b^{j}, t, d, t^{j}, d^{j}, k, g, k^{j}, g^{j}	p, b, p^{h}, ^{m}b, t, d, t^{h}, ^{n}d, k, g, k^{h}, ^{ŋ}g

has four-way opposition by two distinctive features, [±voiced] and [±nasalized]. Many languages with this type belong to the Atlantic-Congo language family.

Among the inventories belonging to the III-4 pattern, some appear in five languages, so I will present them in Table 5-23 for reference. Type-(a) in Table 5-23 is an inventory with opposition by [±voiced] and [±aspirated], which is common in the four-way opposition of the plosive. Type-(b) is an inventory in which [±palatalized] instead of [±aspirated] functions as a distinctive feature. In types-(a) and (b), phonological opposition is optimized by two distinctive features, whereas it is not in type-(c). In type-(c), the voiceless plain, voiced plain, voiceless aspirated, and voiced nasalized plosives are opposed to one another. Since the inventories in Table 5-23 appear only in five languages, it is difficult to discuss their distribution by region or language family.

Now, I will consider the patterns in (6b). The inventories belonging to the IV-1 pattern include four of the six inventories in Table 5-12. These have already been described, so the inventories are presented briefly in Table 5-24.

The IV-2 pattern consists of a total of eight plosives. Five of the seven inventories in Table 5-16 belong to this pattern. They are given in Table 5-25. The inventories belonging to the IV-2 pattern necessarily include bilabial and velar plosives but the selection of the dental or alveolar plosives is mutually exclusive. That is, no type has both dental and alveolar plosives. Additionally, most of the inventories have two-way opposition by [±voiced].

Inventories of the IV-3 and IV-4 patterns have not been previously

Table 5-24. Preferred inventories in IV-1 pattern

[A]	Type-(a)	Type-(b)	Type-(c)	Type-(d)
[B]	p, t, k, ʔ	p, t, k, q	p, t, c, k	p, t̪, k, ʔ
[C]	125	15	13	12

Table 5-25. Preferred inventories in IV-2 pattern

[A]	Type-(a)	Type-(b)	Type-(c)	Type-(d)	Type-(e)
[B]	p, b, t, d, k, g, kp, gb	p, b, t, d, c, ɟ, k, g	p, b, t̪, d̪, ʈ, ɖ, k, g	p, b, t̪, d̪, c, ɟ, k, g	p, pʰ, t, tʰ, k, kʰ, q, qʰ
[C]	92	48	22	19	11

reviewed. Both of these patterns have large plosive inventories. However, since the inventories in this pattern are infrequent, it is difficult to expect a variety of types.

The three types in Table 5-26 can be divided into two categories. Type-(a) consists of plain and nasalized plosives, whereas types-(b) and (c) consist of plain and aspirated plosives. These two categories are also clearly distinguished in their distribution across language families and regions. The former category, namely type-(a), appears mainly in the Atlantic-Congo language family and is not found in non-African languages. By contrast, the latter category, namely types-(b) and (c), is mainly seen in Asian languages belonging to the Sino-Tibetan and Indo-European language families.

The IV-4 pattern consists of 16 plosives at four places of articulation. Not only are there very few languages with this many plosives, there are also few inventories with proportional four-way contrast at all four places of articulation. Therefore, the variety of types is very limited, as shown in Table 5-27.

The two types in Table 5-27 are very similar in phonological opposition. Both have a four-way opposition by two distinctive features, [±voiced] and [±aspirated]. They differ only in the inclusions of the dental or alveolar plosives. Therefore, their similarities are sufficient to group the two types together. For this reason, these two types are similar in their distribution in language families or regions. Both types are found mostly in the Indo-European language family and in some languages

Table 5-26. Preferred inventories in IV-3 pattern

[A]	Type-(a)	Type-(b)	Type-(c)
[B]	p, b, ᵐb, t, d, ⁿd, k, g, ᵑg, kp, gb, ᵑᵐgb	p, b, pʰ, t̪, d̪, t̪ʰ, ʈ, ɖ, ʈʰ, k, g, kʰ	p, b, pʰ, t, d, tʰ ʈ, ɖ, ʈʰ, k, g, kʰ
[C]	23	14	10

Table 5-27. Preferred inventories in IV-4 pattern

[A]	Type-(a)	Type-(b)
[B]	p, b, p^h, b^h, t̪, d̪, $t̪^h$, $d̪^h$, ʈ, ɖ, $ʈ^h$, $ɖ^h$, k, g, k^h, g^h	p, b, p^h, b^h, t, d, t^h, d^h, ʈ, ɖ, $ʈ^h$, $ɖ^h$, k, g, k^h, g^h
[C]	35	12

of the Sino-Tibetan and Dravidian language families. Regionally, these language families are spoken in Asia, centered on India.

Next, the patterns in (6c) will be reviewed. Considering that the average number of places of articulation for the plosive in all languages is approximately four and that the proportion of languages with three or four places of articulation is very high, the inventories with five places of articulation deviate from the standard form.

Inventories belonging to V-1, the simplest pattern in (6c), match three of the seven inventories in Table 5-13. They have been described above, so only the inventories are presented below.

The V-2 pattern consists of a total of 10 plosives. Of the four inventories presented in Table 5-18, only one belongs to the V-2 pattern. The inventory in Table 5-29 is found in only African languages. Two of 28 languages are members of the Mande language family and others are members of the Atlantic-Congo.

In addition to the inventory in Table 5-29, there are two others that appear in more than five languages. Of the two types in Table 5-30, type-(a) is found in the Nilotic language family and type-(b) in the Pama-Nyungan language family. These distributions in language families differ from those in Table 5-29. The high-frequency inventories in the V-2 pattern consist of only plain plosives. Additionally, all two-way oppositions are established by [±voiced].

The V-3 pattern contains a large inventory with 15 plosives. According to Table 5-2, there are 62 languages that have 15 plosives, 27 of which have five places of articulation for the plosive. Because of

Table 5-28. Preferred inventories in V-1 pattern

[A]	Type-(a)	Type-(b)	Type-(c)
[B]	p, t, k, q, ʔ	p, t, ʈ, c, k	b, d, ɖ, ɟ, g
[C]	24	13	13

Table 5-29. Preferred inventories in V-2 pattern

Inventory	p, b, t, d, c, ɟ, k, g, kp, gb
Number of languages	28

Table 5-30. Inventories of V-2 pattern appearing in more than five languages

[A]	Type-(a)	Type-(b)
[B]	p, b, t̪, d̪, t, d, c, ɟ, k, g	p, b, t, d, ʈ, ɖ, c, ɟ, k, g
[C]	9	7

this quantitative limitation, there is no inventory of the V-3 pattern that appears in more than 10 languages. The following inventory, which appears in six languages, has the highest frequency in the V-3 pattern.

(7) The most frequent inventory in V-3 pattern

p, b, pʰ, t̪, d̪, t̪ʰ, ʈ, ɖ, ʈʰ, c, ɟ, cʰ, k, g, kʰ

In the inventory shown in (7), the three-way opposition between voiceless plain, voiced plain, and voiceless aspirated plosives appears in all five places of articulation. According to Table 2-7, among the combinations of the five places of articulation, the most preferred combination is 'bilabial + alveolar + velar + uvular + glottal' or 'bilabial + alveolar + palatal + velar + glottal'. However, the inventory in (7) does not match either of these combinations. The V-3 pattern is likely to be dissimilar to the general trend because a three-way opposition must appear at five places of articulation. For example, it is almost impossible for the glottal plosive, which is included in two preferred combinations in Table 2-7, to have the same three-way opposition as other oral plosives. The inventory in (7) is found only in languages of the Sino-Tibetan language family.

Finally, I will examine the V-4 pattern, which consists of as many as 20 plosives. This type has a four-way opposition in five places of articulation. The inventories that appear in several languages are given in Table 5-31.

The two types in Table 5-31 are very similar in phonological opposition. The relationship between the two types in Table 5-31

Table 5-31. Preferred inventories in V-4 pattern

[A]	Type-(a)	Type-(b)
[B]	p, b, p^h, b^h, t̪, d̪, t̪^{h}, d̪^{h}, ʈ, ɖ, ʈ^h, ɖ^h, c, ɟ, c^h, ɟ^h, k, g, k^h, g^h	p, b, p^h, b^h, t, d, t^h, d^h, ʈ, ɖ, ʈ^h, ɖ^h, c, ɟ, c^h, ɟ^h, k, g, k^h, g^h
[C]	13	7

precisely parallels to that in Table 5-27. The distribution by language family and region is also the same in Tables 5-27 and 5-31. Therefore, a detailed description will be omitted here.

So far, I have examined the high-frequency inventories that often appear in several languages, depending on the number of plosives and the type of opposition. These inventories share common properties, which means that there are common distinctive features involved in the opposition of the plosive across languages. In the following, I will comprehensively review the types of distinctive features actively involved in the plosive and their activeness hierarchy to provide further clarity.[23] A number of distinctive features are required to distinguish the plosives because the plosive itself is highly diverse, with 293 types, and several opposed members can appear at one place of articulation.

By targeting the plosives that appear in the high-frequency inventories, the following distinctive features can be extracted.[24]

(8) Distinctive features for the opposition of plosives
[±voiced], [±aspirated], [±nasalized], [±labialized], [±palatalized]

The distinctive features in (8) can, by themselves, distinguish the plosive. In other words, there are many contrastive pairs by only different values of the distinctive features in (8). For example, /p/ and /b/ are distinguished only by [±voiced], /p/ and /p^h/ only by [±aspirate],

23 The subject of discussion here is the distinctive feature related to the manner of articulation.

24 As mentioned in Chapter 4, for convenience, the distinctive features indicating the secondary articulations such as aspiration, nasalization, labialization, and palatalization are established as [±aspirated], [±nasalized], [±labialized], and [±palatalized].

/b/ and /^{m}b/ only by [±nasalized]. Through these contrastive pairs, it is possible to clarify and confirm the distinctive function of the features in (8).

The way each of the distinctive features in (8) is involved in the opposition of plosives is different. The distinctive feature [±voiced] is not limited to the plosive and is most actively used in consonant discrimination. Except for languages with four or less plosives, when there are two or more plosives in one place of articulation, they are overwhelmingly opposed by [±voiced]. Except for [±voiced], the other distinctive features in (8) are relatively limited in the range of the distinctive function.

The feature [±aspirated] is more likely to perform a distinctive function when three or more plosives are present in one place of articulation. The feature [±nasalized] has similar limitations to [±aspirated] but its frequency is lower than that of [±aspirated]. Moreover, in languages with five places of articulation for the plosive, the frequency at which [±nasalized] functions as a distinctive feature decreases sharply. This trend suggests that the distinctive function of [±nasalized] is less active than that of [±aspirated].

The range in which [±labialized] and [±palatalized] perform a distinctive function is much more limited than the above-mentioned distinctive features. This limitation can be fully predicted by the lower frequency of labialization or palatalization than that of aspiration or nasalization. It is difficult to find a case in which [±labialized] acts as a distinctive feature in the inventories that show proportional oppositions like the various patterns in (6). This trend suggests that there are few languages that have contrastive pairs by [±labialized] in all places of articulation. The inventory in which the plosives are distinguished only by [±labialized] is found sporadically in Table 5-12, 5-13, 5-15, 5-16. The feature [±labialized] has a distinctive function mainly in the velar because labialization most often accompanies the velar plosive.[25] An inventory in which [±palatalized] has a distinctive function appears in type-(b) of table 5-23. This type is found only in five languages, so its frequency is low. However, unlike [±labialized], [±palatalized]

25 In Table 5-12, the inventory in which [±labialized] distinguishes the bilabial plosives is included.

plays a distinctive function in the inventory showing proportional opposition.

The above results confirm that the distinctive features in (8) do not have the same degree of involvement in the opposition of the plosive. Therefore, it is possible to establish an activeness hierarchy of distinctive feature, targeting plosives as a whole. As briefly mentioned in Chapter 4, the activeness of distinctive feature refers to the degree to which a distinctive feature distinguishes phonemes. High activeness means that there are many contrastive pairs by the distinctive feature, whereas low activeness means that there are few contrastive pairs by the distinctive feature. The activeness hierarchy of distinctive feature can be established for one or many languages. The degree of activeness in one language is directly related to the functional load of distinctive feature proposed in 3.3. Here, I will consider the activeness hierarchy of the distinctive features in (8) for languages worldwide. Based on the phonological oppositions in the inventories examined so far, the following activeness hierarchy can be established for the distinctive features.

(9) Activeness hierarchy of the distinctive features in (8)
[±voiced] > [±aspirated] > [±nasalized] > [±labialized] > [±palatalized]

(9) is the hierarchy for the high-frequency plosive inventories. Even if the subject of discussion is expanded to all inventories rather than the high-frequency ones, the main trend is not expected to change. The hierarchy in (9) is exactly the same as the frequency order of the plosive. Plain plosives are much more frequent than complex plosives, and the frequency of secondary articulation accompanied by complex plosives is high in the following order: aspiration > nasalization > labialization > palatalization. Therefore, [±voiced], which is involved mainly in the discrimination of the two plain plosives, is placed at the top of the hierarchy, followed by the distinctive features related to the high-frequency secondary articulations.[26]

26 The two plain plosives in one place of articulation are opposed only by [±voiced]. Moreover, [±voiced] is also involved in the opposition of complex

This hierarchy is also closely related to which plosives are included when the inventory of the plosive is expanded. That is, plosives that contain more highly ranked distinctive features within the hierarchy are preferred. For example, if the number of opposed members is expanded from two to three, the possibility of including the voiceless aspirated plosive related to [±aspirated] is higher than that of the voiceless labialized plosive related to [±labialized]. This trend is clearly demonstrated in the inventories belonging to the III-3, IV-3 and V-3 patterns in (6). However, it should be remembered that this hierarchy is not absolute. Most inventories accord well with the above activeness hierarchy, but local exceptions can be made depending on the place of articulation or the type of plosive.

5.4. Absence of the major plosives

Among the plosives, /p, b, t, d, k, g/, which are the plain plosives in the three main places of articulation, can be grouped as major members. Because these consonants are very frequent, there are far more languages with them than those without them. However, not all of these consonants appear without exception in languages that have a contrastive pair by [±voiced]. In other words, there is a gap in the inventory with at least one of the major plosives missing. Some prior discussions have pointed out that this gap demonstrates a certain tendency. For example, to explain the types of plosives included in the gap, Gamkrelidze (1975: 236) proposed hierarchies such as ‘p<t<k’ for voiceless plosives and ‘g<d<b’ for voiced plosives. The lower a plosive is in the hierarchy, the more likely it is to be absent. As a result, it is highly likely that /p/ among the voiceless plosives and /g/ among the voiced plosives will be missing.

The tendency of plosive inventories to create gaps by omitting the voiced velar and voiceless bilabial has been largely accepted in later works. In addition, Engstrand (1997) pointed out that the absent plosives show regional biases. According to Engstrand (1997: 189), in African

plosives. For these reasons, the rank of [±voiced] is bound to be the highest in the hierarchy.

languages, the probability of not having /g/ is much lower than average but that of not having /p/ is relatively high. By contrast, the opposite pattern exists in the languages of the Americas and Eurasia.

Against this background, I will consider the absence of major plosives, targeting a larger number of languages than has been included in the past studies. The subject of present discussion is the languages that have both voiced and voiceless plain plosives at one or more of the three major places of articulation. That is, the languages must have at least one contrastive pair by [±voiced] in the bilabial, alveolar, and velar plain plosives. For convenience, the dental and alveolar plosives are grouped together as alveolar, and languages with both dental and alveolar plosives are excluded to avoid double counting. Since there are few languages with both dental and alveolar plosives, their exclusion does not diminish the credibility of the results.

A total of 2,944 of the 4,356 languages have at least one contrastive pair by [±voiced], composed of plain plosives in the three major places of articulation. Additionally, 2,160 languages have all six major plosives. In other words, 784 languages, or 26.6% of the 2,944 languages in this group, do not have one or more major plosives. Before determining which major plosives are missing, I first consider the number of plain plosives in these 784 languages.

A language can theoretically have from a minimum of two to a maximum of five plain plosives, as long as it does not have all of the six major plain plosives. However, languages with two, which have only one contrastive pair, do not appear in Table 5-32. As confirmed earlier, since there are at least two places of articulation for the plosive in a language, it is impossible for plosive inventories in which only one contrastive pair appears in one place of articulation to exist. According to Table 5-32, the more major plain plosives a language has, the more languages have such an inventory. Considering that 2,160 of 2,944 languages have all six major plain plosives, a trend that the more major plain plosives, the more general the inventory, can be expected. And this prediction accords with the results in Table 5-32.

There are only 10 languages with three major plain plosives. In all of these languages, there are two places of articulation for the plosive, and a contrastive pair by [±voiced] appears in only one of two places of articulation. The inventories in these languages are given in Table 5-33.

The results in table 5-33 do not reveal a bias toward a specific type.

Table 5-32. Number of plain plosives in languages with gaps

Number of plain plosives	3	4	5
Number of languages	10	191	583

Table 5-33. Inventories in languages with three plain plosives

[A]	Type-(a)	Type-(b)	Type-(c)	Type-(d)	Type-(e)	Type-(f)	Type-(g)
[B]	p, b, t	b, t, d	t, d, k	b, k, g	t, d, k	t, d, g	t, k, g
[C]	2	2	2	1	1	1	1

Table 5-34. Absence of major plosives in languages with three plain plosives

Missing plosive	p	b	t	d	k	g
Number of languages	8	5	1	4	5	7

However, the types in which the contrastive pair by [±voiced] appears in the alveolar are relatively more frequent. That is, six of ten languages have /t, d/. In contrast, /p, b/ appears in only one language and /k, g/ in just two languages. The absence of the major plosives from languages in Table 5-33 is shown in Table 5-34.

The results in Table 5-34 do not agree exactly with the hierarchy of Gamkrelidze (1975: 236). According to Gamkrelidze (1975: 236), the absence of /k/ among the voiceless plosives and /b/ among the voiced plosives should be the least common, but in table 5-34, that of /t/ and /d/, the alveolar plosives, are the least common. This severe discrepancy seems to be due to the fact that Table 5-34 is limited to the languages with three plain plosives.

There are 191 languages with four major plain plosives. The inventories in these languages are given in Table 5-35. The inventories in Table 5-35 can be divided into two categories according to the number of places of articulation. One is composed of types-(e) and (f), whose plosives appear in two places of articulation. None of the types in this category lack the alveolar plosive, although only the combination of the bilabial and alveolar or of the alveolar and velar are present. The other category has three places of articulation, one of which has two plain plosives. The type-(a) that include two bilabial plosives is the

Table 5-35. Inventories in languages with four plain plosives

[A]	Type-(a)	Type-(b)	Type-(c)	Type-(d)	Type-(e)	Type-(f)	Type-(g)	Type-(h)	Type-(i)	Type-(j)
[B]	p, b, t, k	b, t, d, k	p, t, k, g	p, t, d, k	p, b, t, d	t, d, k, g	b, d, k, g	b, t, d, g	b, t, k, g	p, b, d, k
[C]	59	47	30	25	8	8	5	5	3	1

Table 5-36. Absence of major plosives in languages with four plain plosives

Missing plosive	p	b	t	d	k	g
Number of languages	68	63	6	92	13	140

most frequent. However, among all the types in Table 5-35, those with two alveolar plosives /t, d/ are the most common. Type-(b), which is the second most frequent, is characterized by its inclusion of /b/ instead of the unmarked /p/ as the bilabial plosive. Table 5-35 contains several inventories, but there is a considerable difference between the frequencies of the top four and those of the remaining inventories.

The absence of the major plosives from languages in Table 5-35 is shown in Table 5-36. The results in Table 5-36 also do not correspond well with the hierarchy established by Gamkrelidze (1975: 236). The absence of the voiced plosive follows the hierarchy of Gamkrelidze (1975: 236), but that of the voiceless plosive does not. According to Gamkrelidze's hierarchy, the list without /k/ should be the least common, but the list without /t/ is actually the least common.

There are 583 languages with five major plain plosives. In these languages, both voiced and voiceless plain plosives appear in two places of articulation, and one plain plosive appears in the other place of articulation. The inventories of these languages are given in Table 5-37.

There are distinct differences among the frequencies of the six types presented here. Two types, in which /g/ or /p/ is missing from the six plain plosives, are the most frequent. The absence of the major plosives from languages in Table 5-37 is shown in Table 5-38.

In Table 5-38, the rates of omission for /p/ and /g/ are very similar. These two consonants constitute gaps in the inventories of many languages. In contrast, /t/ is included in almost every inventory. These results are similar to, but not entirely consistent with the hierarchy in

Table 5-37. Inventories in languages with five plain plosives

[A]	Type-(a)	Type-(b)	Type-(c)	Type-(d)	Type-(e)	Type-(f)
[B]	p, b, t, d k	b, t, d, k, g	p, b, t, k, g	p, t, d, k, g	p, b t, d, k	p, b, d, k, g
[C]	251	245	48	24	14	1

Table 5-38. Absence of major plosives in languages with five plain plosives

Missing plosive	p	b	t	d	k	g
Number of languages	245	24	1	48	14	251

Gamkrelidze (1975: 236).

I will now comprehensively examine the absence of the major plain plosives from languages in Tables 5-34, 5-36, 5-38. For Table 5-39, an overall hierarchy such as 'g<p<d<b<k<t' can be established. In addition, when distinguishing between voiceless and voiced plosives, hierarchies such as 'p<k<t' and 'g<d<b' can be set. These hierarchies are largely similar to those of Gamkrelidze (1975: 236) but differ in the rankings of /k/ and /t/. It is difficult to determine the precise cause of these differences. However, it is possible that the frequency of missing /t/ is lowered in these hierarchies due to the combination of the dental and alveolar plosives into one group.

Finally, I will briefly examine the correlation between the absence of major plosives and the regional bias addressed in Engstrand (1997: 189). According to the data of Engstrand (1997: 189), the absence of the major plosives in the four macroareas can be summarized as shown in Table 5-40.[27]

Table 5-40 provides two pieces of information for each macroarea.

Table 5-39. Absence of major plosives in languages

Missing plosive	p	b	t	d	k	g
Number of languages	321	92	8	144	32	398

27 Table 5-40 is not quoted from Engstrand (1997: 189) as it is, but has been reprocessed for discussion. No change have been made to the statistics from the original source.

Table 5-40. Absence of major plosives in four macroareas based on Engstrand (1997)

Missing plosive	Africa		America		Australasia		Eurasia		Total	
	[A]	[B]	[A]	[B]	[A]	[B]	[A]	[B]	[A]	[B]
p	5.1	23	0.9	4	1.1	5	0.9	3	7.8	35
t	0	0	0	0	0	0	0	0	0	0
k	0.2	1	0.2	1	0.7	3	0.2	1	1.3	6
b	0	0	0.9	4	0.9	4	0.4	2	2.2	10
d	0.2	1	2.4	11	0.7	3	0.9	4	4.2	19
g	0.7	3	5.3	24	1.3	6	2.7	12	10.0	45

[A] represents the proportion (%) of languages that do not have a major plain plosive among the 451 languages listed in the UPSID, and [B] represents the number of languages that do not have a major plain plosive. The last column presents the sum of the percentage and frequency.

Table 5-40 shows differences in the absence of major plosives depending on the region. Languages without /p/ commonly appear in Africa, and languages without /g/ appear to some extent in the Americas. A few languages without /b/ are found in the Americas and Australia, and some languages in the Americas do not have /d/. Now, separate from the analysis by Engstrand (1997: 189), I will approach this topic based on the data in Table 5-39.

Table 5-41 classifies the 784 languages that are the subject of analysis in Table 5-39 by macroarea, and summarizes the absence of major plain plosives. [A] and [B] represent the same contents as in Table 5-40. However, unlike in Table 5-40, Table 5-41 divided the macroareas into five regions by placing Papunesia in its own category.

There are both commonalities and differences between Table 5-40 and 5-41. They share the presence of languages in Africa that do not have /p/ and of languages that are frequent in the Americas without /d/ or /g/. However, there are also striking differences. In Table 5-41, many languages without /g/ appear in Africa as well, which is quite different from Table 5-40.

In addition, a few more features are found in Table 5-41. First, languages that do not have a major plain plosive are found more often in Africa than in other areas. In contrast, the languages of Australia

Table 5-41. Absence of major plosives in five macroareas based on Table 5-39

Missing plosive	Africa		America		Australia		Eurasia		Papunesia	
	[A]	[B]	[A]	[B]	[A]	[B]	[A]	[B]	[A]	[B]
p	24.5	192	2.3	18	0	0	2.3	18	11.9	93
t	0.3	2	0	0	0	0	0	0	0.8	6
k	0.8	6	0.4	3	0	0	0.8	6	2.2	17
b	3.8	30	3.8	30	0.6	5	1.1	9	2.3	18
d	4.5	35	6.9	54	0.5	4	2.4	19	4.1	32
g	12.8	100	11.6	91	2.7	21	13.9	109	9.8	77

generally have numerous major plain plosives. Certainly, the languages of Africa and Australia demonstrate an opposing pattern regarding the absence of major plain plosives. Second, in America and Eurasia, there are relatively numerous languages that do not have /g/. Fewer languages are spoken in these two macroareas than in Africa or Papunesia, but the number of languages in these regions that do not have /g/ is equal to or greater than that of Africa or Papunesia. Additionally, some languages without /p/ are found in Papunesia as well as Africa.

5.5. Unique inventories of the plosive in the world's languages

I will now discuss the final topic related to the phonological typology of the plosive. Unexpected and unique plosive inventories are often found in many languages. I will consider several types of these examples. The first subject is languages with an unusually high number of plosives. To determine whether there is a certain tendency in languages with numerous plosives, I will consider four inventories of the languages with the most plosives.

(10) Languages with an unusually high number of plosives

a. Soga: 40 plosives

Bilabial	Dental	Alveolar	Palatal	Velar
p, b, p^{w}, p^{j}, (b^{j}),[28] ^{m}p, ^{m}b, ^{m}p^{w}, (^{m}b^{w}), ^{m}p^{j}, (^{m}b^{j})	t̪, d̪, (t̪^{w}), d̪^{w}, d̪^{j}, ^{n}t̪, ^{n}d̪, ^{n}d̪^{w}, ^{n}d̪^{j}	t, d, t^{w}, d^{w}, t^{j}, d^{j}, ^{n}t, ^{n}d, ^{n}t^{w}, ^{n}d^{w}, ^{n}t^{j}, ^{n}d^{j}	c, ɟ, ^{ɲ}c, ^{ɲ}ɟ	k, g, k^{w}, g^{w}, ^{ŋ}k, ^{ŋ}g, ^{ŋ}k^{w}, ^{ŋ}g^{w}

b. Diandongbei-Large Flowery Miao: 37 plosives

Bilabial	Alveolar	Retroflex	Velar	Uvular	Glottal
p, b, p^{h}, ^{m}p, ^{m}b, ^{m}p^{h}	t, d, t^{h}, ^{n}t, ^{n}d, ^{n}t^{h}, t^{l}, d^{l}, t^{hl}, ^{n}t^{l}, ^{n}d^{l}, ^{n}t^{hl}	ʈ, ɖ, ʈ^{h}, ^{n}ʈ, ^{n}ɖ, ^{n}ʈ^{h}	k, g, k^{h}, ^{ŋ}k, ^{ŋ}g, ^{ŋ}k^{h}	q, ɢ, q^{h}, ^{N}q, ^{N}ɢ, ^{N}q^{h}	ʔ

c. Maonan: 37 plosives

Bilabial	Alveolar	Alveo-palatal	Velar	Glottal
p, b, p^{h}, p^{j}, b^{j}, p^{hj}, ^{m}b, ^{m}b^{j}, ^{ʔ}b, ^{ʔ}b^{j}	t, d, t^{h}, t^{w}, t^{j}, d^{j}, t^{hj}, ^{n}d, ^{n}d^{j}, ^{ʔ}d, ^{ʔ}d^{w}, ^{ʔ}d^{j}	^{n}ɖ	k, g, k^{h}, k^{w}, g^{w}, k^{j}, g^{j}, k^{hw}, k^{hj}, k^{wj}, k^{hwj}, ^{ŋ}g, ^{ŋ}g^{w}	ʔ

d. Diriku: 36 plosives

Bilabial	Dental	Alveolar	Velar
p, b, p^{w}, b^{w}, p^{j}, b^{j}, ^{m}p, ^{m}b, ^{m}p^{w}, ^{m}b^{w}, ^{m}p^{j}, ^{m}b^{j}	t̪, t̪^{w}, ^{n}t̪	t, d, t^{w}, d^{w}, t^{j}, d^{j}, ^{n}t, ^{n}d, ^{n}t^{w}, ^{n}d^{w}, ^{n}t^{j}, ^{n}d^{j}	k, g, k^{w}, g^{w}, k^{j}, ^{ŋ}k, ^{ŋ}g, ^{ŋ}k^{w}, ^{ŋ}g^{w}

Of the four languages in (10), Soga and Diriku are spoken in Africa, and the other two are spoken in West China. These languages have a high number of plosives, with 36 or more. It is obvious that when a language has a large number of consonants, it also has many plosives. These four languages each have more than 68 consonants, placing them in the top 0.3% of all languages. As so many plosives are present, there are also various complex plosives with secondary articulations, but the common plosives in (10a~d) are only the six plain plosives (p, b, t, d, k, g) and three nasalized plosives (^{m}b, ^{n}d, ^{ŋ}g). In addition, labialized and palatalized plosives appear in three languages. In contrast, the aspirated plosive, which is the most frequent among the complex plosive with

28 Consonants in parentheses are marginal phonemes. As mentioned earlier, the marginal phoneme is not recognized as a normal phoneme and is excluded from statistics related to the plosive.

secondary articulations, is seen only in two languages. It is difficult to find a common trend among (10a~d) in the place of articulation. Overall, the characteristics shared by languages with a large number of plosives are not well observed.

The second group of languages to review have inventories with numerous places of articulation for the plosive. As examined in Chapter 2, the number of places of articulation for the plosives in each language is at least two and can be up to seven. (11) below lists the inventories of languages with seven places of articulation.

(11) Languages with seven places of articulation for the plosive

a. Anguthimri: 13 plosives

Bilabial	Dental	Alveolar	Retroflex	Palatal	Velar	Glottal
p, b	t̪, d̪	t, d	ʈ, ɖ	c, ɟ	k, g	ʔ

b. Djambarrpuyngu: 13 plosives

Bilabial	Dental	Alveolar	Retroflex	Palatal	Velar	Glottal
p, b	t̪, d̪	t, d	ʈ, ɖ	c, ɟ	k, g	ʔ

c. Hmong Daw: 29 plosives

Bilabial	Dental	Retroflex	Palatal	Velar	Uvular	Glottal
p, p^{h}, ^{m}b, ^{m}b^{h}, p^{l}, ^{m}b^{l}	t̪, d̪, t̪^{h}, d̪^{h}, ^{n}d̪, ^{n}d̪^{h}	ʈ, ʈ^{h}, ^{ɳ}ɖ, ^{ɳ}ɖ^{h}	c, c^{h}, ^{ɲ}ɟ, ^{ɲ}ɟ^{h}	k, k^{h}, ^{ŋ}g, ^{ŋ}g^{h}	q, q^{h}, ^{N}ɢ, ^{N}ɢ^{h}	ʔ

d. Hmong Njua: 25 plosives

Bilabial	Dental	Retroflex	Palatal	Velar	Uvular	Glottal
p, p^{h}, ^{m}p, ^{m}p^{h}	t̪, t̪^{h}, ^{n}t̪, ^{n}t̪^{h}	ʈ, ʈ^{h}, ^{ɳ}ʈ, ^{ɳ}ʈ^{h}	c, c^{h}, ^{ɲ}c, ^{ɲ}c^{h}	k, k^{h}, ^{ŋ}k, ^{ŋ}k^{h}	q, q^{h}, ^{N}q, ^{N}q^{h}	ʔ

e. Kara (Central African Republic): 16 plosives

Bilabial	Dental	Alveolar	Retroflex	Palatal	Velar	Labiovelar
p, b, ^{m}b	t̪, d̪, ^{n}d̪	d	ʈ	c, ɟ, ^{ɲ}ɟ	k, g, ^{ŋ}g	kp, gb

f. Ngadjunmaya: 7 plosives

Bilabial	Dental	Alveolar	Retroflex	Palatal	Velar	Uvular
p	t̪	t	ʈ	c	k	q

g. Paiwan: 11 plosives

Bilabial	Alveolar	Retroflex	Palatal	Velar	Uvular	Glottal
p, b	t, d	ɖ	c, ɟ	k, g	q	ʔ

h. Southern Pashto: 11 plosives

Bilabial	Dental	Retroflex	Velar	Uvular	Pharyngeal	Glottal
p, b	t̪, d̪	ʈ, ɖ	k, g	q	ʕ	ʔ

Among the languages in (11), three (Anguthimri, Djambarrpuyngu, Ngadjunmaya) belong to the Pama-Nyungan language family and two (Hmong Daw, Hmong Njua) to the Hmong-Mien language family. The rest belong to different language families. The places of articulation in these languages have already been covered in 2.3 and are not discussed further here.

The number of plosives is expected to increase proportionally as the number of places of articulation increase. However, the results of (11) show that this is not necessarily the case. If the languages in (11) are divided into the classes in Figure 5-1, four languages are in the moderately large class, three languages in the large class, and one language in the average class. Contrary to expectations, the majority of languages do not belong to the large class. In addition, languages with two or fewer opposed members in one place of articulation constitute a majority in (11). Therefore, a large number of places of articulation does not necessarily guarantee a large number of plosives. The size of the inventories in (11) vary according to the language family. For example, Hmong-Mien languages have large inventories due to the large number of opposed members in each place of articulation, whereas Pama-Nyungan languages have a relatively small inventories.

The third group of languages to examine is unique in its phonological opposition of the phonation type. The phonation type can be classified according to voicedness, aspiration, breathiness, creakiness, etc. There are some languages with peculiar phonation types for the plosive.

(12) Languages with unique phonation types for the plosive

a. Chantyal: 17 plosives

Bilabial	Alveolar	Velar
p, b, p^h, p̈, b̤	t, d, t^h, t̤, d̤, t̤^{h}	k, g, k^h, k̤, g̈, k̤^{h}

b. Achumawi: 13 plosives

Bilabial	Alveolar	Velar	Uvular	Glottal
p, p^h, p^ʔ	t, t^h, t^ʔ	k, k^h, k^ʔ	q, q^h, q^ʔ	ʔ

c. Zhongu: 20 plosives

Bilabial	Alveolar	Velar	Uvular
p, b, p^h, ^{h}p, ^{m}b, ^{m}p^h	t, d, t^h, ^{h}t, ^{n}d, ^{n}t^h	k, g, k^h, ^{h}k, ^{ŋ}g, ^{ŋ}k^h	q, q^h

According to Noonan (2005: 3), Chantyal in (12a) has five or six members of the plosive in three places of articulation. These plosives are opposed by three phonation types: voicedness, aspiration, and breathiness. Moreover, there are voiceless aspirated breathy-voice plosives in the alveolar and velar. This means that up to six types of phonation are distinguished in Chantyal. It is difficult to find another inventory in which such complicated phonation types are involved in the phonological opposition of plosives.

Achumawi in (12b) has three series of plosives: voiceless plain plosive, voiceless aspirated plosive, and voiceless laryngealized plosive. Many languages with three-way opposition have a contrast between voiced and voiceless plosives, but Achumawi does not. Table 5-42 shows how many languages with a three-way opposition have the contrastive pair by [±voiced] in three major places of articulation.

In Table 5-42, [A] refers to the number of languages with three-way opposition, [B] to the number of languages without contrast by [±voiced] among [A], and [C] to the number of languages in [B] that have only voiceless plosives. The distinction between [B] and [C] is necessary because voiced plosives can exist in languages without contrast by [±voiced]. The fact that [B] is very small compared to [A] means that most languages with three-way opposition have a contrastive pair by [±voiced]. Additionally, [C] is a more extreme type than [B] in that it has no voiced plosive.

Achumawi in (12b) belongs to [C] in Table 5-42. Moreover,

Table 5-42. Contrast by [±voiced] in languages with three-way opposition

	Bilabial	Alveolar	Velar
[A]	693	631	625
[B]	41	39	59
[C]	8	9	19

languages with the voiceless laryngealized plosive as one of three opposed members are very rare. There are only three such languages: Achumawi, Eastern Tamang, and Korean.[29] Korean has three way-opposition at the three places of articulation in Table 5-42, but Achumawi and Eastern Tamang have the same three way-opposition at four places of articulation, which include those in Table 5-42 plus an additional place.[30]

Zhongu in (12c) is unique in that both preaspirated and postaspirated plosives exist as separate phonemes. The same opposition also appears in Bonan and Osage. However, in Zhongu, some of the voiceless nasalized plosives are accompanied by aspiration. Thus, the voiceless plosives in Zhongu show a four-way opposition. Moreover, two types of voiced plosives are also present, so the phonation type of Zhongu is very rare and unique.

The fourth language to review has a very high number of voiceless plosives. Western Xiangxi Miao, a language of the Hmong-Mien language family, has a large inventory of 31 plosives, which is presented in Table 5-43. This inventory is peculiar as it consists exclusively of voiceless plosives.

Table 5-43. Plosives in Western Xiangxi Miao

Bilabial	Alveolar	Velar	Uvular
p, p^h, p^j, p^{hj}, ${}^{m}p$, ${}^{m}p^h$, ${}^{m}p^{hj}$	t, t^h, t^j, t^{hj}, ${}^{n}t$, ${}^{n}t^h$, ${}^{n}t^j$, ${}^{n}t^{hj}$	k, k^h, k^j, k^{hj}, ${}^{\text{ŋ}}k$, ${}^{\text{ŋ}}k^h$, ${}^{\text{ŋ}}k^j$, ${}^{\text{ŋ}}k^{hj}$	q, q^h, q^w, q^{hw}, ${}^{\text{N}}q$, ${}^{\text{N}}q^h$, ${}^{\text{N}}q^w$, ${}^{\text{N}}q^{hw}$

29 Without the requirement of three-way opposition, laryngealized plosives appear in more languages.

30 Achumawi has three-way opposition in the uvular and Eastern Tamang in the palatal.

According to Sposato (2015: 59), Western Xiangxi Miao has seven or eight plosives in each of the four places of articulation. All of these plosives are voiceless. Of the 31 plosives, except for four voiceless plain plosives, the rest are complex plosives accompanied by various secondary articulations. Western Xiangxi Miao has the highest number of plosives among languages that do not have a contrast by [±voiced]. Of the 63 languages with 20 or more plosives, seven do not have a contrast by [±voiced], of which six belong to the Hmong-Mien language family and the other to the Tai-Kadai language family. Both language families are distributed in Asia. As a result, the inventories consisting only of large-scale voiceless plosives show severe distributional bias.

Unlike Western Xiangxi Miao, there are also languages whose inventories consist only of voiced plosives. Fifty-four languages have only voiced plosives, representing over 1% of the 4,356 languages considered in this book. The majority of these languages are distributed in Australia, centered on the Pama-Nyungan language family.[31] The number of plosives and places of articulation in these languages are given in Table 5-44.

As shown in Table 5-44, languages with only voiced plosives have from a minimum of three to a maximum of six for the number of plosives and places of articulation. The number of plosives is very small compared to the average (8.04) of plosives for all languages. The average value in Table 5-44 is only 4.7. In contrast, the number of places of articulation averages 4.6, which is higher than the average value (3.93) of all languages. In particular, the fact that the number of plosives and of places of articulation do not differ significantly suggests that languages with only voiced plosives tend to have only one plosive per place of articulation. Nine of the languages in Table 5-44 have six plosives that appear at six places of articulation. Eight of these languages excluding Wubuy share the inventory /b, d̪, d, ɖ, ɟ, g/.[32]

Diandongbei-Large Flowery Miao, the fifth language to examine,

---

31 According to Hyman (2008: 89-90), of the 451 languages included in the UPSID, four languages have only voiced plosives, all of which are spoken in Australia.

32 Wubuy has 'b, d̪, d, ɖ, ȡ, g'. Compared to the other languages, Wubuy has 'ȡ' instead of 'ɟ'. The places of articulation for these two plosives are very close, so Wubuy can be grouped into same type with other eight languages.

Table 5-44. Number of plosives and places of articulation in languages with only voiced plosives

Number of plosive	Number of places of articulation	Number of languages
3	3	8
4	4	12
5	4	2
	5	20
6	5	3
	6	9

notably maintain the six-way opposition proportionally in many places of articulation. As pointed out in 5.3, the multi-way opposition in a language may or may not be proportional to all places of articulation. In general, it is not easy to maintain a proportional opposition when the number of opposed members increases. However, Diandongbei-Large Flowery Miao is an exception, as shown in Table 5-45.

In Diandongbei-Large Flowery Miao, except for the glottal plosive, six-way opposition is proportionally maintained at five places of articulation. The six-way opposition in this language is formed by three distinctive features: [±voiced], [±aspirated], and [±nasalized]. Furthermore, in the alveolar, the six-way opposition is maintained in the lateral-released plosive as well as the plosive with normal release. Therefore, in reality, the six-way opposition appears in the seven types of plosives. No language in which many opposed members appear proportionally, such as in Diandongbei-Large Flowery Miao, has been reported to date.

In contrast, there are languages that show the opposite pattern of Diandongbei-Large Flowery Miao. In other words, they show different types of opposition for each place of articulation. Kalanga and Luopohe Hmong, for example, have extremely asymmetric inventories.

Table 5-45. Plosives in Diandongbei-Large Flowery Miao

Bilabial	Alveolar	Retroflex	Velar	Uvular	Glottal
p, b, p^{h}, ^{m}p, ^{m}b, $^{m}p^{h}$	t, d, t^{h}, ^{n}t, ^{n}d, $^{n}t^{h}$, t^{l}, d^{l}, t^{hl}, $^{n}t^{l}$, $^{n}d^{l}$, $^{n}t^{hl}$	ʈ, ɖ, $ʈ^{h}$, $^{ɳ}ʈ$, $^{ɳ}ɖ$, $^{ɳ}ʈ^{h}$	k, g, k^{h}, ^{ŋ}k, ^{ŋ}g, $^{ŋ}k^{h}$	q, ɢ, q^{h}, ^{N}q, $^{N}ɢ$, $^{N}q^{h}$	ʔ

(13) Plosives in Kalanga and Luopohe Hmong

a. Kalanga: 26 plosives

Bilabial	Dental	Alveolar	Velar	Labiovelar
p, b, p^h, b̤, ^mb	t̪, d̪, $t̪^h$	d, t^h, d^w, (t^{hw}), nd, d̤	k, g, k^h, k^w, g^w, k^{hw}, $g̈^w$, ^ŋg, $^ŋg^w$	gb, kp^h

b. Luopohe Hmong: 23 plosives

Bilabial	Alveolar	Retroflex	Velar	Uvular	Glottal
p, p^h, ^mp, ^{mʔ}p, $^{mʔ}p^h$, p^l, $^mp^l$	t, t^h, ^nt, ^{nʔ}t, $^{nʔ}t^h$	$^{ɳʔ}ʈ^h$	k, k^h, ^ŋk, ^{ŋʔ}k	q, q^h, q^w, q^{hw}, q^l	ʔ

Kalanga and Luopohe Hmong have various plosives at five or six places of articulation, and the opposition between plosives is not proportional in any place of articulation. That is, the number of opposed members differs for each place of articulation. Additionally, even if the number of opposed members is the same, the nature of the opposition is different. The two inventories in (13) even seem to combine parts of disparate inventories. The opposition between the plosives is so asymmetric that the efficiency of phonemic description through distinctive features is inevitably reduced. This aspect is the opposite of Diandongbei-Large Flowery Miao with its symmetric and balanced system.

Chapter 6

CONCLUSION

The purpose of this book is to study phonological typology of the plosive based on large-scale language data. I have attempted to examine how various phonological features related to the plosive appear in languages worldwide and to derive the main trends illustrated in this data. A total of 4,356 languages, a considerable sample size for typological research, formed the basis of discussion in this book. Therefore, it was able to consider many topics in detail that have not been covered in previous textbooks of phonology or phonetics.

The plosive is the most basic type among consonants. However, it is difficult to say that much of the typological research on this topic has already been conducted. For example, Gordon (2016), the first introductory book to phonological typology, devoted half a page to the plosive briefly, and it clearly explains the current situation. The discussion in this book is sufficient to contribute to diversifying the perspectives on the plosive. However, although various topics related to the plosive have been covered, and many trends have been identified in this book, the explanation of the causes underlying them is insufficient. There is a need for work to supplement this book through precise phonetic analysis.

I conclude all discussion with a brief summary of the overall contents. In Chapter 2, I dealt with the place of articulation for the plosive. The place of articulation was examined by dividing the plosive into single- and double-articulated plosives according to the number of primary articulations. There are 12 places of articulation in the former and four in the latter, resulting in a total of 16 for the plosive. However, the number of places of articulation in one language is limited to a minimum of two and a maximum of seven. Languages with four places of articulation are the most frequent, and many languages have three or four places of articulation. Depending on the number of places of articulation, there are more preferred combination types. A general trend is that the place of articulation is composed of three major articulators evenly: labial, coronal, and dorsal.

In Chapter 3, I considered the manner of articulation for the plosive. Various plosives at the same place of articulation are distinguished by the manner of articulation. Plosives are largely divided into plain and complex plosives. The former is a plosive that undergoes a simple articulatory process, while the latter is accompanied by additional articulations such as secondary articulation or special glottal action. The main reason why there are 293 types of plosive is because there are so many complex plosives with secondary articulation. Aspiration, nasalization, labialization, and palatalization are frequently found among these secondary articulations. The representative distinctive feature involved in the opposition of the plosive is [±voiced], which is related to the presence or absence of vocal fold vibration. Approximately 71% of all languages have at least one contrastive pair by [±voiced]. The contrast by [±voiced] in one language may or may not be proportional at every place of articulation.

In Chapter 4, I described individual plosives for each place of articulation. The most frequent plosive is the velar plosive /k/, which appears in 4,205 languages, or 96.5% of all languages. In contrast, there are also several plosives that appear in only one language. The overall tendency for each place of articulation was examined in detail, and then the phonological characteristics, frequency, and distribution of each plosive were discussed.

In Chapter 5, quantitative and qualitative features of the plosive were reviewed. The quantitative features include the average number, the proportion in the consonant inventory, and the classification of languages according to the number of plosives. The qualitative characteristics encompass the implicational relationship between the plosives, the absence of major plosives, and the unique plosive inventories.

One of the main purposes of the phonological typology is to find the tendencies that appear in numerous languages and to provide a phonetic or phonological explanation for them. In a small language sample, it is easy to detect trends, but there are many exceptions in larger samples, and it becomes difficult to find a mainstream. However, the discussion in this book has revealed several universal tendencies, some of which have been known to some extent and others that have not. Moreover, even those tendencies that were already known have been further confirmed and verified through much more language data. Those tendencies that have been unknown to date will need to be dealt with in more depth.

One regret at the end is that, as mentioned earlier, the causes of various tendencies have not been sufficiently elucidated. I lack the knowledge of phonetics and recent phonetic theory, so it is beyond my ability to accomplish this. Instead, I have provided the results of various typological analyses based on much more language data than any other typological research to date. In that sense, this book comes close to being a starting point for the typological study of the plosive.

References

Anderson, S. R. (1985), *Phonology in the Twentieth Century: Theories of Rules and Theories of Representations*, Chicago: The University of Chicago Press.

Andersen, T. (1986), The phonemic system of Madi, *Afrika und Übersee* 69, pp. 193~207.

Árnason, K. (2011), *The Phonology of Icelandic and Faroese*, Oxford: Oxford University Press.

Battistella, E. L. (1990), *Markedness-The Evaluative Superstructure of Language-*, New York: State University of New York Press.

Bickel, B. (2007), Typology in the 21st century: Major current development, *Linguistic Typology* 11, pp. 239~251.

______ (2011), Absolute and statistical universals, in P. C. Hogan ed., *The Cambridge Encyclopedia of the Languages Sciences*, Cambridge: Cambridge University Press, pp. 77~79.

Blevins, J. (2004), *Evolutionary phonology*, Cambridge: Cambridge University Press.

Bolaños, K. (2016), A Grammar of Kakua, Doctoral Dissertation of Amsterdam University.

Bommelyn, L. (1997), The prolegomena to the Tolowa Athabaskan grammar, Master's Thesis of Oregon University.

Browman, C. P. & L. Goldstein (1992), Articulatory phonology: An overview, *Haskins Laboratories Status Report on Speech Research* 111/112, pp. 23~42.

Brown, K. & S. Ogilvie eds. (2009), *Concise Encyclopedia of the Languages of the World*, Oxford: Elsevier.

Butcher, A. (2004), 'Fortis/lenis' revisited one more time: the aerodynamics of some oral stop contrasts in three continents, *Clinical Linguistics & Phonetics* 18, pp. 547~557.

Bybee, J. (2001), *Phonology and Language Use*, Cambridge: Cambridge University Press.

Campbell, L. (1973), On glottalic consonants, *International Journal of American Linguistics* 39-1, pp. 44~46.

Carr, P. (2008), *A Glossary of Phonology*, Edinburgh: Edinburgh University Press.

Catford, J. C. (1977), *Fundamental Problems in Phonetics*, Bloomington: Indiana University Press.

______ (1988), *A Practical Introduction to Phonetics*, Oxford: Clarendon Press.

Chasaide, A. N. (1985), Preaspiration in phonological stop contrasts: an instrumental phonetic study, Doctoral Dissertation of University of Wales.

Chebanne, A. (2000), The Sebirwa Language-A Synchronic and Diachronic Account-, *Botswana Journal of African Studies* 14-2, pp. 186~195.

Chinebuah, I. (1973), Grammatical categories of the verbal piece in Nzema, Doctoral Dissertation of London University.

Cho, T. & P. Ladefoged (1999), Variation and universals in VOT: evidence from 18 languages, *Journal of Phonetics* 27, pp. 207~229.

Chomsky, N. & M. Halle (1968), *The sound pattern of English*, New York: Harper & Row.

Constenla, A. (1981), Comparative Chibchan Phonology, Doctoral Dissertation of Pennsylvania University.

Croft, W. (2003), *Typology and Universals* (2nd edition), Cambridge: Cambridge University Press.

Daniel, G. & R. Blench (2008), Phonology of the Rigwe language, Unpublished Manuscript.

Dart, S. (1987), An Aerodynamic Study of Korean Stop Consonants: Measurements and Modeling, *Journal of Acoustic Society of America* 81, pp. 138~147.

Dawod, T. (1952), The Phonetics and Phonology of an Aden Dialect of Arabic, Doctoral Dissertation of London University.

Dodd, R. (2014), V'ënen Taut: grammatical topics in the Big Nambas language of Malekula, Master's Thesis of Waikato University.

Dresher, B. (2009), *The contrastive hierarchy in phonology*, Cambridge: Cambridge University Press.

______ et al. (2018), Contrastive feature hierarchies as a new lens on typology, in L. Hyman & F. Plank eds., *Phonological Typology*, Berlin: De Gruyter Mouton, pp. 273~311.

Englund, P. (1963), Ngbaka: Phonology and Verb Morphology, Doctoral Dissertation of Northwestern University.

Engstrand, O. (1997), Areal biases in stop paradigms, *Phonum* 4, pp. 187~191.

Fallon, P. (1998), The Synchronic and Diachronic Phonology of Ejectives, Doctoral Dissertation of Ohio State University.

Fleischer, J. & S. Schmidt (2006), Zurich German, *Journal of the International Phonetic Association* 36-2, pp. 243~253.

François, A. (2002), *Araki-A disappearing language of Vanuatu-*, Canberra: Research School of Pacific and Asian Studies in Australian National University.

Gamkrelidze, T. V. (1975), On the correlation of stops and fricatives in a phonological system, *Lingua* 35-3, pp. 231~261.

Gandour, J. T. (1975), The features of the larynx: N-ary or Binary?, *Phonetica* 32-4, pp. 241~253.

Gerlach, L. (2016), *N!aqriaxe: the phonology of an endangered language of Botswana*, Wiesbaden: Harrassowitz.

González, H. (2003), A Typology of Stops in South American Indian languages, in *Proceedings of the Conference on Indigenous Languages of Latin America(I)*.

Gordon, M. (2016), *Phonological typology*, Oxford: Oxford University Press.

______ & P. Ladefoged (2001), Phonation types: a cross-linguistic overview, *Journal of Phonetics* 29, pp. 383~406.

Greenberg, J. (1966), Synchronic and diachronic universals in phonology, *Language* 42-2, pp. 508~517.

Hall, D. (2007), The role and representation of contrast in phonological theory, Doctoral Dissertation of Toronto University.

Halle, M. & K. N. Stevens (1971), A note on laryngeal features, *MIT Quarterly Progress Report* 101, pp. 198~213.

Hammond, M. (2006), Phonological typology/Phonological Universals, in K. Brown et al. eds., *Encyclopedia of Language & Linguistics* (2nd edition) vol. 9, Oxford: Elsevier, pp. 523~531.

Han, J. (1996), The phonetics and phonology of "tense" and "plain" consonants in Korean, Doctoral Dissertation of Cornell University.

Haspelmath, M. (1993), *A Grammar of Lezgian*, New York: De Gruyter Mouton.

______ et al. eds. (2005), *The world atlas of language structures*, Oxford: Oxford University Press.

Henderson, J. (1995), *Phonology and Grammar of Yele, Papua New Guinea*, Canberra: Australian National University.

Henton, C., P. Ladefoged & I. Maddeison (1992), Stops in the World's Languages, *Phonetica* 49-2, pp. 65~101.

Hyman, L. (2007), Where's phonology in typology?, *Linguistic Typology* 11, pp. 265~271.

______ (2008), Universals in phonology, *The Linguistic Review* 25, pp. 81~135.

______ (2018), What is phonological typology?, in L. Hyman & F. Plank eds., *Phonological Typology*, Berlin: De Gruyter Mouton, pp. 1~20.

______ & F. Plank eds. (2018), *Phonological Typology*, Berlin: De Gruyter Mouton.

Ismailee, M. (1976), A Phonological Study of the Verbal System in Urdu, Doctoral Dissertation of London University.

Keating, P. (1984), Phonetic and phonological representation of stop consonant voicing, *Language* 60-2, pp. 286~319.

Khalilova, Z. (2009), A Grammar of Khwarshi, Doctoral Dissertation of Leiden University.

Killian, D. (2015), Topics in Uduk Phonology and Morphosyntax, Doctoral Dissertation of Helsinki University.

Kim, C. (1965), On the Autonomy of the Tensity Feature in Stop Classification (with Special Reference to Korean Stop), *Word* 21-3, pp. 339~359.

______ (1970), A theory of aspiration, *Phonetica* 21-2, pp. 107~116.

Kirk, P. et al. (1984), Linguistic use of different phonation types, *UCLA Working Papers in Phonetics* 59, pp. 102~113.

Komen, E. (2007), A Proposal for a Chechen Orthography, Unpublished Manuscript.

Ladefoged, P. (1964), *A Phonetic Study of West African Languages*, Cambridge: Cambridge University Press.

______ (1973), The features of the larynx, *Journal of Phonetics* 1, pp. 73~83.

______ & I. Maddieson (1996), *The Sounds of the World's Languages*, Oxford: Blackwell.

Laver, J. (1994), *Principles of phonetics*, Cambridge: Cambridge University Press.

Lee, J. (2017a), *Gukeo Eumunron Yongeo sajeon* [A glossary of Korean phonology], Seoul: Youkrack Publishing Co.

______ (2017b), Eoneo Yuhyeongron Yeongueseoui Pyeonggyungaps Dochul Bangan [A Method for Making Mean Value in Linguistic typology], *Genji Inmunhak* 19, pp. 221~240.

______ (2020), *Inventories of the Plosive in the World's Languages*, Seoul: Jipmoondang.

______ (2022), Payeoleumui Hamui Gwangyenuin Eolmana Yuhyohanga? [How valid are the implicational relationships between plosives?], *Inmunnonchong* 79-1, pp. 497~524.

Lindblom, B. & I. Maddieson (1988), Phonetic Universals in Consonant Systems, in L. Hyman & C. Li eds., *Language, speech, and mind*, London: Routledge, pp. 62~78.

Lisker, L. & A. S. Abramson (1964), A Cross-Language Study of Voicing in Initial Stops-Acoustical Measurements, *Word* 20-3, pp. 384~422.

Lu, T. (2008), *A Grammar of Maonan*, Boca Raton: Universal Publishers.

Maddieson, I. (1984), *Patterns of sounds*, Cambridge: Cambridge University Press.

______ (1987), Revision of the IPA: linguo-labial as a test case, *Journal of the International Phonetic Association* 17-1, pp. 26~30.

______ (1997), Phonetic universals, in W. Hardcastle & J. Laver eds., *The Handbook of Phonetic Science*, Oxford: Blackwell, pp. 619~639.

Möhlig, W. (1997), A Dialectometrical Analysis of the Main Kavango Languages: Kwangali, Gciriku and Mbukushu, in W. H. G. Haacke & E. E. Elderkin eds., *Namibian Languages: Reports and Papers*, Köln: Rüdiger Köppe Verlag, pp. 211~234.

______ (2005), *A grammatical sketch of Rugciriku (Rumanyo)*, Köln: Rüdiger Köppe Verlag.

Moran, S. P. (2012), Phonetics Information Base and Lexicon, Doctoral Dissertation of Washington University.

Moravcsik, E. A. (2013), *Introducing Language Typology*, Cambridge: Cambridge University Press.

Nabirye, M. et al. (2016), Illustrations of the IPA: Lusoga (Lutenga), *Journal of the International Phonetic Association* 46-2, pp. 219~228.

Naito, M. (2006), Tutuba Apicolabials: Factors Influencing the Phonetic Transition from Apicolabials to Labials, *Oceanic Linguistics* 45-1, pp. 217~228.

Nakagawa, H. (2006), Aspects of the Phonetic and Phonological Structure of the G|ui Language, Doctoral Dissertation of Witwatersrand University.

Namkung, J. ed. (1996), *Phonological Inventories of Tibeto-Burman Languages*, Berkeley: The Regents of the University of California.

Nartey, J. (1979), A Study in Phonemic Universals-especially Concerning Fricatives and Stops-, *UCLA Working Papers in Phonetics* 46, pp. 1~89.

Nevin, B. (1998), Aspects of Pit River phonology, Doctoral Dissertation of Pennsylvania University.

Niederer, B. (1998), *Les langues Hmong-Mjen (Miáo-Yáo)-Phonologie historique-*, München: Lincom Europa.

Noonan, M. (2005), Chantyal Discourses, *Himalayan Linguistics* 2, Retrieved from https://escholarship.org/uc/item/4221169b.

Nurse, D. & G. Philippson (2003), *The Bantu Languages*, New York: Routledge.

Park, H. (2002), Temporal and Spectral Characteristics of Korean Phonation Types, Doctoral Dissertation of the University of Texas at Austin.

Pericliev, V. (2008), Implicational phonological universals, *Folia Linguistica* 42-1, pp. 195~225.

Pinkerton, S. (1986), Quichean (Mayan) Glottalized and Nonglottalized Stops: a Phonetic Study with Implications for Phonological Universals, in J. J. Ohala & J. J. Jaeger eds., *Experimental phonology*, Orlando: Academic Press, pp. 125~139.

Plank, F. (2018), An implicational universal to defy: typology⊃¬phonology≡ phonology⊃¬typology≡¬(typology∧phonology)≡¬typology∨¬phonology, in L. Hyman & F. Plank eds., *Phonological Typology*, Berlin: De Gruyter Mouton, pp. 21~53.

Rogers, H. (2000), *The Sounds of Language: An Introduction to Phonetics*, New York: Routledge.

Sampson, D. (1997), Update on Baka Phonology and Orthography, as of 1996, *Occasional Papers in the Study of Sudanese Languages* 7, pp. 114~120.

Scaraffiotti, Z. (2011), *Parlons Xhosa: Afrique du Sud*, Paris: L'Harmattan.

Sherman, D. (1975), Stop and Fricative Systems-A Discussion of Paradigmatic Gaps and the Question of Language Sampling-, *Working Papers of Language Universals* 17, pp. 1~31.

Shimizu, K. (1979), *A Comparative Study of the Mumuye Dialects (Nigeria)*, Berlin: Verlag von Dietrich Reimer.

______ (1990), A Cross-Language Study of Voicing Contrasts of Stop Consonants in Asian Languages, Doctoral Dissertation of University of Edinburgh.

Smith, D. (1969), The Kapsiki Language, Doctoral Dissertation of Michigan State University.

Sposato, A. (2015), A grammar of Xong, Doctoral Dissertation of State University of New York at Buffalo.

Steever, S. ed. (1998), *The Dravidian Languages*, London: Routledge.

Stewart, Jr., T. W. (2004), Mutation as morphology: Bases, Stems, and Shapes in Scottish Gaelic, Doctoral Dissertation of Ohio State University.

Tent, J. (1993), Phonetic Symmetry in Sound Systems, *Symmetry: Culture and Science* 4-4, pp. 345~368.

Trask, R. (1996), *A Dictionary of Phonetics and Phonology*, New York: Routledge.

Westbury, J. R. & P. A. Keating (1986), On the naturalness of stop consonant voicing, *Journal of Linguistics* 22-1, pp. 145~166.

Wurm, S. A. ed. (1977), *New Guinea Area Languages and Language Study (I)-Papuan Languages and the New Guinea Linguistic Scene-*, Canberra: Research School of

Pacific and Asian Studies in Australian National University.

Zue, V. W. (1976), *Acoustic characteristics of stop consonants*, Bloomington: Indiana University Linguistics Club.

Subject index

Language index